19. Centory the Hearbes and Flowers chopped in the end of June.
20. Violet Flowers in Aprill.
21. Wood bynd the Flowers in the beginning of June.

To know the right Bezar Stone.

Take a peece of cleane Paper and rubb some Chalke on it: then rub your Bezar Stone; if it be good it will make the paper yellow. You may try it thus to take a wire, and make it red hott in the Fire; then touch the Stone: if it be good it will not stirr, if it be bad it will hisse & enter into it

A pound physicall consisteth of 12 ounces, a pound common consisteth of 16; An ounce consisteth of 8 drames, A drame consisteth of 3 scruples, A scruples consisteth of 20 graines.

Lady Fanshawe's Receipt Book

BY THE SAME AUTHOR

Nijinsky: A Life

Anything Goes: A Biography of the Roaring Twenties

Liberty: The Lives and Times of Six Women in Revolutionary France

Maharanis: The Lives and Times of Three Generations of Indian Princesses

Amphibious Thing: The Life of a Georgian Rake

The Thieves Opera: The Remarkable Lives and Deaths of Jonathan Wild, Thief-Taker, and Jack Sheppard, House-Breaker

Con Men and Cutpurses: Scenes from the Hogarthian Underworld

Lady Fanshawe's Receipt Book

The Life & Times of a Civil War Heroine

LUCY MOORE

Atlantic Books
London

First published in hardback in Great Britain in 2017 by Atlantic Books,
an imprint of Atlantic Books Ltd.

10 9 8 7 6 5 4 3 2 1

A CIP catalogue record for this book is available
from the British Library.

Hardback ISBN: 978 1 78239 810 3
E-book ISBN: 978 1 78239 811 0
Paperback ISBN: 978 1 78239 812 7

Text design and typesetting by Lindsay Nash

Endpaper image: Ann's instructions for preparing and
distilling herbs (*MS7113*, *Wellcome Library*)

Printed in Great Britain by Bell and Bain Ltd

Atlantic Books
An imprint of Atlantic Books Ltd
Ormond House
26–27 Boswell Street
London
WC1N 3JZ

www.atlantic-books.co.uk

For my sisters

Contents

Illustrations

→→•←←

Colour section

Black and white illustrations

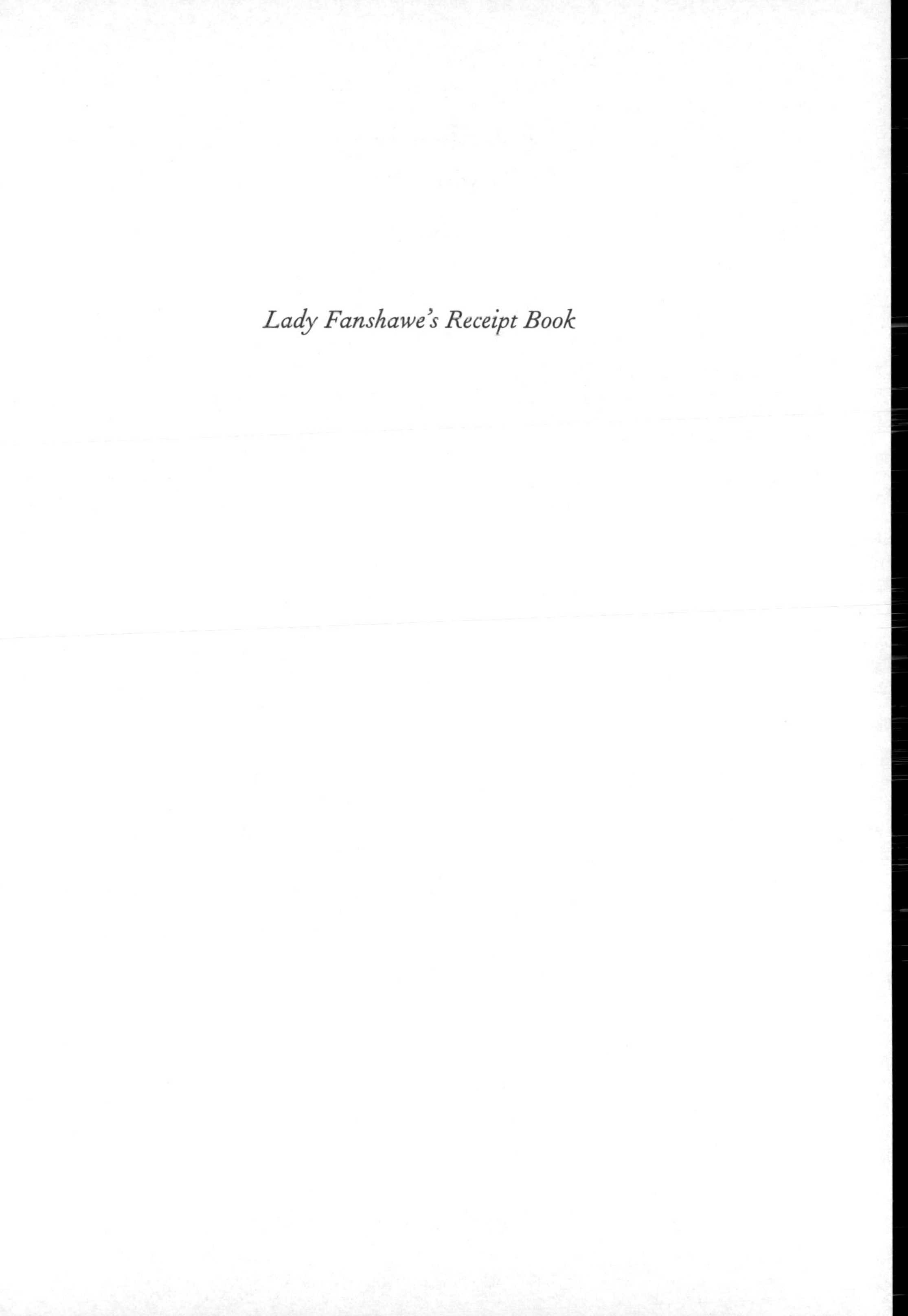

Lady Fanshawe's Receipt Book

Lady Fanshawe's Family Tree

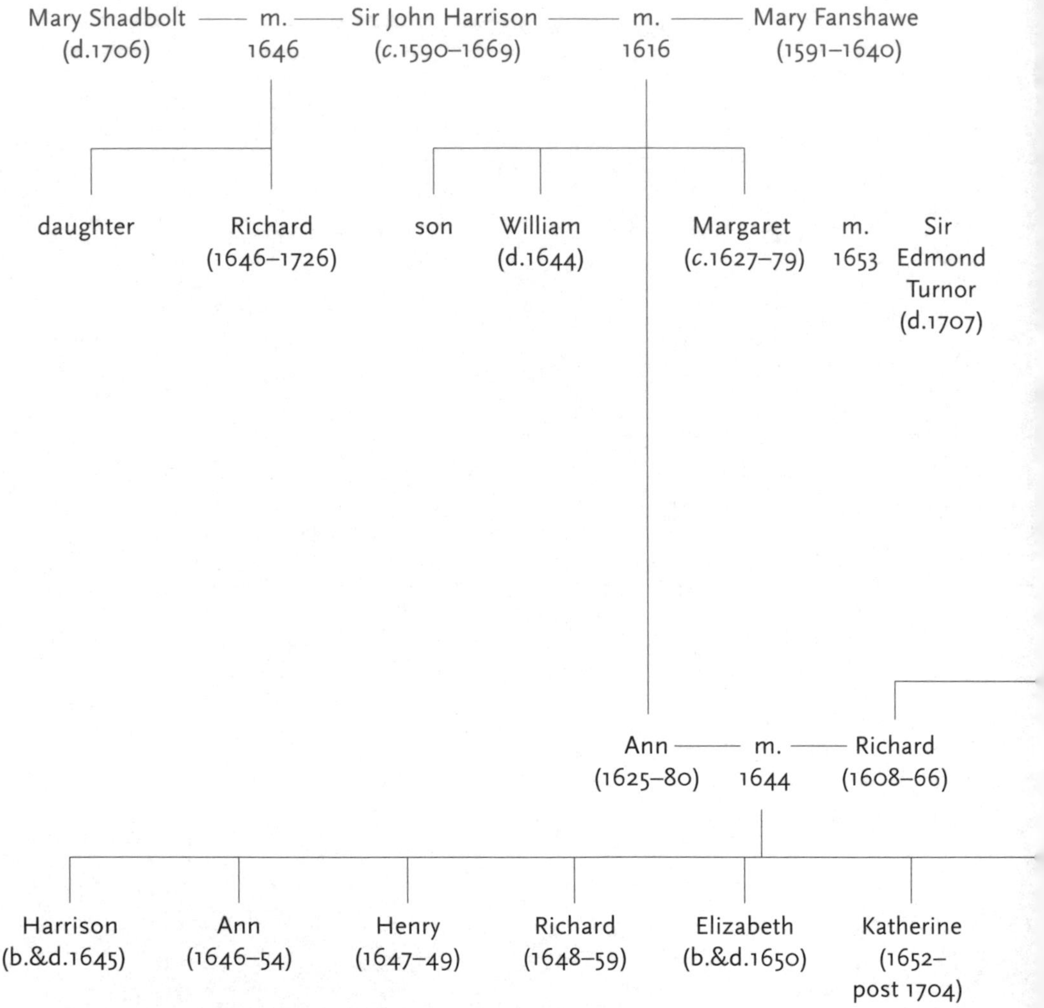

Mary Shadbolt (d.1706) — m. 1646 — Sir John Harrison (*c.*1590–1669) — m. 1616 — Mary Fanshawe (1591–1640)

daughter

Richard (1646–1726)

son

William (d.1644)

Margaret (*c.*1627–79) m. 1653 Sir Edmond Turnor (d.1707)

Ann (1625–80) — m. 1644 — Richard (1608–66)

Harrison (b.&d.1645)

Ann (1646–54)

Henry (1647–49)

Richard (1648–59)

Elizabeth (b.&d.1650)

Katherine (1652–post 1704)

(*Where date of death not given it is unknown*)

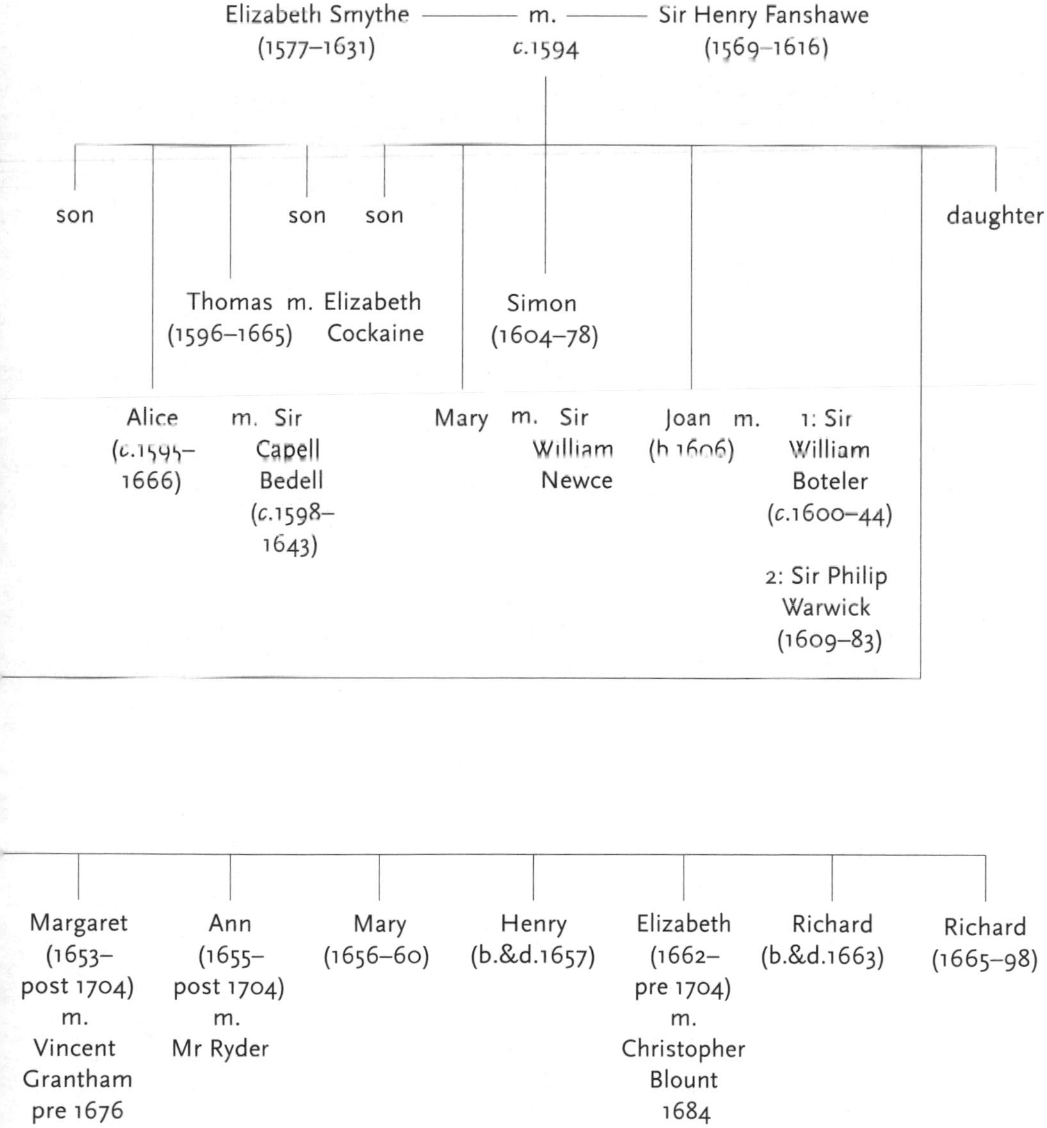
Elizabeth Smythe (1577–1631)
m. c.1594
Sir Henry Fanshawe (1569–1616)
son
son
son
daughter
Thomas m. Elizabeth Cockaine
(1596–1665)
Simon (1604–78)
Alice (c.1595–1666)
m. Sir Capell Bedell (c.1598–1643)
Mary m. Sir William Newce
Joan (b.1606) m.
1: Sir William Boteler (c.1600–44)
2: Sir Philip Warwick (1609–83)
Margaret (1653–post 1704) m. Vincent Grantham pre 1676
Ann (1655–post 1704) m. Mr Ryder
Mary (1656–60)
Henry (b.&d.1657)
Elizabeth (1662–pre 1704) m. Christopher Blount 1684
Richard (b.&d.1663)
Richard (1665–98)

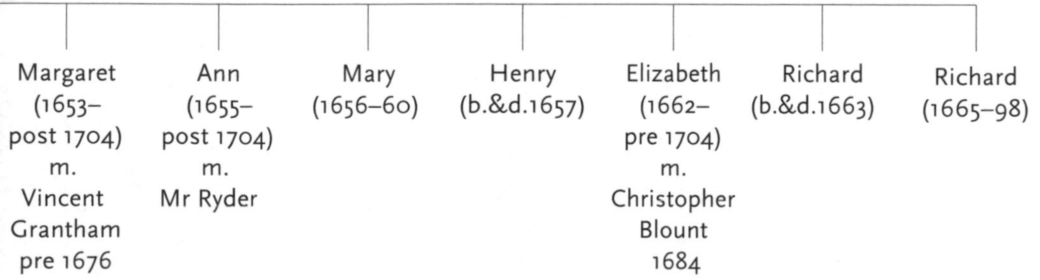

Introduction

In the seventeenth century a receipt book was not, as you might imagine, an aid to accountancy – according to the OED, it didn't acquire that meaning for another century. Four hundred years ago, a receipt book was what today we would call a recipe book but containing medicinal remedies as well as culinary recipes, both referred to as receipts. It was the indispensable handbook for every woman who commanded a household, compiled by her from receipts given to her by friends and relations, her guide and manual as she travelled through life, wherever it might take her.

Ann Fanshawe, whose receipt book will serve as our guide to her life, was born in 1625, the daughter of a prosperous servant of the crown. Her father, Sir John Harrison, had arrived in London as a young man with £13 in his pocket and made a great fortune as a customs officer. He owed everything to the king. When they began, the civil wars spun the Harrisons' world on its axis. A decade of dissatisfaction with Charles I's autocratic rule had turned much of the country – and, significantly, a great proportion of his MPs – against him. In January 1642, after the king ignominiously failed to force Parliament to charge its five leading critics of his rule with high treason, he fled London and began to gather his forces together, preparing for war.

At seventeen, taking flight from her home to join Sir John with Charles at his court-in-exile in Oxford the following winter, Ann brought with her only what she could carry on horseback: some clothes, quilted or fur-lined against the cold, and a sheaf of her mother's receipts that she had copied out as a childhood hand-writing exercise, thrust into a cloak bag. Today, refugees carry their world in their mobile phone – contacts, memories, plans and dreams. For Ann, the world she hoped to remember and recreate was in that slim bundle of papers.

These remedies and recipes were the core of what would become Ann's large (20 by 32 cm) book, thick cream pages handsomely bound in gold-tooled brown leather and written out in sepia ink probably mixed by Ann herself from copper sulphate, oak-galls and gum. (Her book does not contain instructions for making ink, but many did.) There are remedies from society doctors and one from a London apothecary; one medical recipe comes from an advertisement, torn out of a news-sheet and stitched into the pages. Although most entries are undated, the earliest is marked 1650, when Ann was a young wife and mother aged twenty-five, and the last was added long after her death, indicating that her daughter, to whom she left the book, continued using it for many years. (What happened to it next we don't know: Ann's daughter was unmarried and didn't have a daughter of her own to hand it on to.) Other surviving receipt books, like commonplace books, contain evocative extraneous material: lines of poetry, snippets from the Bible, shopping lists, pressed flowers and leaves, shaky letters of the alphabet in a child's hand, rough copies of correspondence, scrawled accounts, sketches, prayers. They are maps of their owners' worlds, records of their hopes, demonstrations of wealth or poverty, culture and social ties, witnesses to joy, failure and despair.

The recipes for food are wonderfully redolent of seventeenth century England: syllabubs, 'makeroons',* possets, roast meats, 'sallets' or salads, a myriad of methods of preserving fruit and vegetables so they could be enjoyed all year round. Ann's book contains eleven cherry recipes – preserved, dried, pickled, put into jelly and made into wine – testament to her lifelong weakness for them. Foreign recipes, including French bread and beef *à la mode*, Spanish eggs, bacon and *limonado*, and an Italian dish of hogs' heads, reveal her cosmopolitan lifestyle. She was at the cutting edge of culinary fashion: her book contains the first recipe in English for 'icy cream' – though it doesn't work, according to various experts in seventeenth century food technology – and the first in English for hot chocolate, mixed with a *molinillo*, a wooden whisk still used in Central America, and accompanied by a drawing of 'the same chocelaty pottes that are mayd in the Indis'.[1] Except for chocolate from the Indies, she noted with characteristic attention to detail, the best was made in Seville.

I have concentrated on the medicinal receipts, using one to introduce each chapter. Usually placed at the front of receipt books, the remedies were at the heart of this type of book, vital for the basic survival of every family. At a time when there was only one licensed doctor at work in the entire county of Shropshire, for example, a woman of status, as Ann was, would be depended upon

* Spelling was not standardized in the seventeenth century so where possible I have kept to the original, often idiosyncratic spelling (sometimes it's been modernized in printed sources). It can look strange but it's always legible phonetically, if you say it out loud: two of my favourites are 'postibelly' for possibly and 'liques' for likewise.

Ann's sketch of a chocolate pot, used for making the fashionable new drink of chocolate, and its molinillo, or whisk.

to dispense medicine and nursing advice not just to her own family but to the families of her dependents and neighbours of all classes. In the absence of hospitals as we know them today women attended each other in childbirth and nursed even the mortally sick in their own homes. Whatever medical knowledge they had gleaned from their mothers, friends or doctors over the years might well turn out to be the difference between life and death for themselves or their loved ones.

Ann's receipts are notable for being useful and surprisingly modern in outlook. She included many of the popular remedies of the day under one name or another – Lucatella's Balsam, Gascoigne Powder (also known as the Countess of Kent's Powder), Aqua Vitae, the Flower of Oyntments (or the yellow salve), the King of France's Balsome (or the green salve to be made in May) – but was evidently unpersuaded by the excessive use of snails and worms, and there are no receipts that call for things like skinning puppies or roasting live pigeons, featured in other books of this era. There are receipts to induce vomiting and methods of taking blood, both remedies in vogue in the seventeenth century, and one for laudanum, a risky but effective new painkiller.

But there was another, more subtle significance to these carefully guarded morocco-bound books or scraps of ink-stained paper wrapped up in fraying ribbon. Life in the mid-seventeenth century was terrifyingly insecure, whichever side of the political divide you found yourself on. Ann Fanshawe had been forced to leave her comfortable childhood home before her childhood was over and spent the next seventeen years living (as she put it) 'in tents, like Abraham'[2] as she and her family gave not just their life savings but literally their life blood to restore the Stuart monarchy and with it their place in English society.

During Ann's adulthood, roughly the years of the civil wars, Commonwealth and Protectorate, the English body politic was on its sickbed. Divided by war and bloodshed, torn apart by dissenting ideologies, father opposed son and brother met brother on the battlefield. But while war raged on the cobbled streets and green fields of England, for their mothers, wives, sisters and daughters, inside the home, domestic life continued as it always had done, marked by births and deaths, illness and good health, hunger and feasting. The rituals of daily life were by necessity unaltered: even if men were fighting there were still children to be taught, clothes to be mended, sick relatives to be nursed, marriages to be arranged. Across the country, all through this turmoil, women struggled to maintain their households, families and social networks. Their silent efforts contributed powerfully to the restoration of peace once the fires of conflict had burned themselves out.

In this world, a receipt book was at once a jewel of knowledge to be treasured from generation to generation (like Ann's, these books were often itemized in wills) and an amulet you could carry with you which would offer you real protection from the perils you were facing. It was a memento of absent friends and family, whose love for you was demonstrated by their contributions to your receipts and thus to your well-being: a peculiarly feminine response to the upheavals of war at a time when politics infused every aspect of society, a 'rich and important intersection between domestic practices and national identity, of private and public, of everyday and state affairs'.[3] For Royalists in particular, receipt books were endowed with special significance as reminders of happier times past and images of what they believed they were working so hard to restore: civility, hospitality, security, generosity – a healed and whole country. As Ann would write of her husband, 'he loved hospitality, and would often say, it was wholly essential for the constitution of England'.[4]

Receipt books were seen at once as practical manuals and, because there was so little understanding of why certain remedies worked, repositories of arcane, almost miraculous knowledge. Another seventeenth century manuscript book held by the Wellcome Collection, by Mary Doggett, includes a water to relieve 'ye passion of the heart' alongside the usual receipts for jaundice, ringworm, pickling cucumber and washing 'partie-coloured stockings'.[5] The heroines of a 1644 play, *The Conceal'd Fancies*, bored with their French lessons, steal the keys to their father's cabinet and discover 'rare cordials for the restoration of health, and making one young'.[6] The claims of remedies like these were satirized in the late 1630s in the final masque performed at Charles I's court, with a quack doctor called Wolfgangus Vandergoose whose receipts included a spirit of Bacchus to make one dance well, an opiate to make one forget one's creditors, various love potions, a drink 'to make a sufficient Linguist without travelling' and 'Treakle of the gale [*sic*; I think it should read 'tail'] of Serpents, and the liver of Doves to initiate a Neophite courtier'.[7]

Ann does not seem to have used published receipt books (a new feature of this period) as sources, relying instead on friends and especially family for remedies and recipes they had found successful. What emerges, when you look at the list of names in her manuscript, is a network of Royalists, often émigrés like her and her husband and often connected to the Fanshawe family into which she would marry or with shared roots in Hertfordshire. Her mother Margaret is the most cited; her godmother is there as well alongside several of her children's godparents and frequent, repeated references to siblings, in-laws and cousins.

This deep immersion in family and place is evident in her memoirs, too, written in the 1670s, more than twenty years after the receipt book was begun, and left to her only surviving son in her will. An extended, established family and wide-spreading networks of kin were a source of pride for Ann and her contemporaries as well as being invaluable practical supports. Particularly during the troubled 1640s and 1650s it was family who provided Ann and her husband, Richard, with places to stay and live, whether as guests or tenants, and income in the form of cash, bequests and loans; they acted as godparents, advised about marriages, doctors and servants, and gave and received news, favours, presents – and receipts.

In causing her receipts and her memoirs to be written down, Ann was very much part of her generation, 'this scribbling age'.[8]

The sixteenth and seventeenth centuries saw an explosion of literacy, writing and investigations into selfhood that can only be compared to our own internet revolution. In the words of Thomas Browne, another seventeenth century writer, Ann and her contemporaries wanted to communicate their powerful sense 'that [the] masse of flesh that circumscribes me, limits not my mind'.[9]

Women as well as men were active participants in these arenas. The first autobiography published in English was the mystic Margery Kempe's in 1501 (long after her death); the first secular text translated by a woman was published in 1578; *Hamlet* came out in 1603, the year of the first English translation of Montaigne's essays; ten years later, for the first time, a play written by a woman was published under her own name – significantly, a nascent Royalist, Elizabeth Cary, Lady Falkland, whose son would die at the Battle of Newbury fighting for the king. Sarah Jinner, compiler of ladies' almanacs (annotated calendars which included astrological information and useful miscellanea, including medicinal receipts) published in the late 1650s, is a candidate for the first English woman to make a living with her pen.

Ann's writing, both family memoir and receipt book, was purely domestic and wholly conventional. She never dreamed of publishing her work. Even so, taking up a pen was a feminist statement, whether she would have regarded it as such or not: a declaration of identity and independence. Although she never challenged her role as wife and mother, simply by writing she was subverting contemporary ideas about proper female conduct.

Women were expected to be silent and submissive and men could be scathing about them trespassing on their intellectual territory. The Cavalier poet Richard Lovelace attacked female poets who snatched the quill from their husbands' hands, deriding their attempts to adorn their minds just as they painted their faces:

> Now as her self a Poem she doth dresses,
> And curls a Line as she would so a tresse,
> Powders a Sonnet as she does her hair,
> Then prostitutes them both to publick Aire.

Speaking publicly was explicitly associated with sexual promiscuity, publication with prostitution. Lovelace reserved his praise for only 'one Sapho',[10] probably the famously retiring Royalist poet Katherine Philips.

Sarah Jinner disputed this. Citing Semiramis, Pope Joan, Elizabeth I, Margaret Cavendish and the countess of Kent as well as Katherine Philips, she introduced her first almanac in 1658 with a passionate justification of a woman's right to express herself:

> Why [should] not women write, I pray? Have they not souls as well as men, though some witty coxcombs strive to put us out of conceit of ourselves, as if we were but imperfect pieces?... Why should we suffer our parts to rust? Let us scowre the rust off, by ingenious endeavouring the attaining higher accomplishments: this I say, not to animate our Sex, to assume or usurp the breeches: No, but perhaps if we should shine in the splendour of vertue, it would animate our husbands to excell us: So by this means we should have an excellent world.[11]

Jinner's message evidently chimed with her female readers: her books were bestsellers.

Margaret Cavendish, held up as an example by Jinner but largely ridiculed by her peers, attached a rambling explanatory note to her autobiography, published in 1656:

> I hope my Readers, will not think me vain for writing my life, since there have been many that have done the like… and I know no reason I may not do it as well as they; but I verily believe some censuring Readers will scornfully say, why hath this Ladie writ her own Life? Since none cares to know whose daughter she was, or whose wife she is, or how she was bred, or what fortunes she had, or how she lived, or what humour or disposition she was of? [But] I write it for my own sake, not theirs.[12]

Ann guarded against such 'censuring Readers' by not publishing her work and also by ostensibly prioritizing her husband's life over her own, much as Katherine Philips constructed an image as a blushing poetess shying away from any public recognition of her work in order to reconcile her literary ambitions with contemporary views of ideal womanhood (perhaps one reason Lovelace approved of her).[13] Her receipt book and memoirs can be seen at once as the manifestation of Ann's maternal and wifely devotion and as the creation of an independent identity outside these roles.

Self-effacement came into conflict with self-assertion as women navigated the boundaries between the ways they were expected to conduct themselves and the ways they actually behaved.[14] Their writing shows how inventive seventeenth century women could be in exploiting the limited space available to them, managing at once to conform to cultural expectations and to express themselves as creative, autonomous individuals. The historian Cissie Fairchilds dedicated her book, *Women in Early Modern Europe*, to her mother, a housewife in 1950s America: 'Like them [Fairchilds's subjects], she lived in a time when society's expectations for women were very restrictive, yet like them she made for herself within those parameters a full and meaningful life.'[15]

Although women were often cautioned against writing, still – just like their men – they kept diaries and memoirs, composed letters, religious prayers and meditations, collated receipt books and commonplace books, and wrote conduct books (manuals on behaviour, very useful in a changing world), poetry, plays and translations. Despite or perhaps because of its perceived moral dangers, writing was fashionable. While it carried a risk to a woman's reputation, equally it could bestow on her social prominence, respect and a kind of glamour she could gain in no other way: it was not an accident that the few women mentioned by John Aubrey in his *Brief Lives*, an idiosyncratic guide to the great and good of the seventeenth century, were either learned or 'fallen' – or both.

Throughout this book, taking advantage of the upsurge of literacy that inspired Ann Fanshawe, I've also turned to the correspondence, diaries, poetry and devotional writings of people of similar age, background and preoccupations to cast light on the corners of her life not revealed in her receipt book and memoirs, my main sources. The names of these people and others, separated from Ann by only a degree or two, appear throughout the book and will become almost as familar as hers: Dorothy Osborne, the star-crossed lover; Ralph and Mary Verney, like Ann and her husband a young couple tossed by the storms of rebellion and exile; John Evelyn, a cousin through marriage and a keen recorder of his own life; the passionate, pious Elizabeth Mordaunt; and, towards the end, the irrepressible young diarist, Samuel Pepys.

Ann's memoirs were written in 1671 for her only surviving son and her receipt book was collated over decades and given to one of her daughters in 1678, two years before she died. While the memoirs, first published in the nineteenth century, are familiar to scholars of the civil wars and Ann is a frequent subject of early life-writing and gender studies, her receipt book, which exists only in manuscript and was in private hands until 1997, when the Wellcome Collection bought it, is less well known. (It is now digitized and available to everyone.) The two sources have never been written about together and although there are modern editions of Ann's memoirs there has never been a biography of her.

Part of the reason Ann Fanshawe is not better known, I think, is that her writings are so personal. They were intended to be read by members of her family; in different ways they were her bequests to them when she had little else to give. Just as the trinkets at the bottom of a jewellery box hold little glitter for anyone except the person who has collected them, so Ann's detailed account of her own and her husband's families and their conduct during the civil wars is tailored to her son and no one else. She wanted him to embark on his adult life with a pride in what his parents and ancestors had achieved. In both her books she was passing on to her children practical lessons for life and her concerns reflect those of her time and class as well as the devastating effect the wars had on that class.

Looking a little deeper, we can see in Ann's memoirs and receipts the tight-gripped effort to hold her family together in the most challenging of circumstances, and her attempts, through the creation of a network of friends and relatives – often but by no means exclusively female – to create a bulwark against the destructive impact of the war, a reality she lived alongside from her earliest adulthood and which claimed her brother and numerous other friends. Receipt books, as one historian observes, were 'a powerful expression of cultural belief in human transformation and of women as authors of such transformation'[16] and Ann's is no exception.

Blood – in the sense both of bloodlines and of healthy blood – preoccupied Ann. Her memoirs counsel her son to be proud of his family, his blood; her receipts teach her daughter how to run a good household, which meant keeping her family well. Extending these ideas to the seventeenth century concept of the body politic, in which the nation was metaphorically viewed as a body, with the monarch as its head, we can think of the sick body that was England being healed by books like Ann's, in which friendship and social harmony, webs of social networks as constructed by women, become as crucial an element of their families' and their nation's survival as their husbands' service and loyalty to the king or to Parliament.

On one hand this book is the portrait of an individual, detailed and intimate, while on the other it conjures up the world in which she lives: her place in society, as the wife of a Royalist diplomat and servant of the crown, as a woman, as a Protestant but not a Puritan. I want to challenge two preconceptions about this period. One is that the women of the period who mattered were either made prominent by their birth, like the queen, Henrietta Maria, or were exceptions – women who defied convention to preach, to act, even to publish. I hope to show that ordinary women* like Ann Fanshawe shaped their world in quieter but no less fundamental ways.

The other is that the civil wars were all about masculinity, a brutal, hard-edged era dominated by Roundheads in their metal helmets marching off to battle and tense debates in Parliament between stern-faced men in monochrome. They were also about women and femininity: soft power, friendship, family and loyalty; bloodlines and blood ties, rather than bloodshed. Ann may not have fought in the wars that defined her century but she was a heroine of them as surely as any bloodstained soldier.

Always, in times of war and crisis, the roles men and women play in society change. The civil wars and their aftermath were no exception. Ann had to become a different person than the one she would have been to cope with the tests with which her times confronted her. Not for her a serene, constrained existence as a housewife and matriarch, rooted in the home; instead she had to become a woman of business, of action, of decision, a woman on the move. To survive she had to be independent, quick-thinking and brave at frightening moments. Her marriage had to be a

* The historian David Cressy estimates from surviving signatures on legal documents that nine-tenths of English women were illiterate at the time of the civil wars as compared to two-thirds of men, so in this one important way Ann had to be extraordinary: by necessity, for my purposes, she had to be literate and was thus part of a very small, prosperous elite.

partnership of equals rather than a relationship between superior and inferior. In a patriarchal world women are used to working outside the rules, negotiating boundaries; that skill becomes even more valuable when no one knows the rules. Ann never questioned the way her society worked, but she had to function outside its conventions to thrive in the new order thrown up by war and rebellion and she relished those challenges.

I often wondered, as I wrote this book, whether she would have chosen peace and a less interesting life, if she could have. For Ann the civil wars must have been much as the twentieth century's world wars were to the generations who lived through them – moments of such drama and intensity, personal as well as political, that they coloured and shaped everything they touched. Just as my grandmother never forgot the horror of being in London during the Blitz – and equally the snatched bliss of dancing at a basement nightclub beneath the blown out streets with the man she'd just met, who would become my grandfather – I am sure that part of Ann was always the windswept, exhilarated girl dressed up in a sailor's clothes on a Dutch ship in the Mediterranean, or the bereaved mother weeping over the frail body of a dead newborn in unfamiliar lodgings, afraid she would never visit his or her resting place again.

In her memoirs and receipt book Ann left us part of her story and I have tried to fill in the gaps, to get and give some idea of the fullness of her life, what it felt like to be a woman in her extraordinary times. Her devoted marriage combined with her sense of adventure make her a wonderfully modern heroine. I want to show how it felt to inhabit her skin, to love and support a man fighting what must have seemed to be a losing war, to live because of that war not in a home but in a series of lodgings she could never call her own, to bear children almost annually and for them to die almost as quickly, and then to have to leave them in graveyards she knew she might never see again. Her struggles and her joys give us a fresh perspective on the troubled but thrilling times she lived through.

Three gypsies stood at the castle gate,
They sang so high, they sang so low.
The lady sat in her chamber late
Her heart it melted away like snow.

They sang so sweet, they sang so shrill
That fast her tears began to flow.
And she laid down her silken gown,
Her golden rings and all her show.

Then she took off her high-heeled shoes
All made of Spanish leather-O!
She would in the street in her bare, bare feet
All out in the wind and the weather-O...

'What care I for a goose-feather bed?
With the sheets turned down so bravely-O!
For tonight I'll sleep in a cold open field
Along with the wraggle taggle gypsies-O!'

SEVENTEENTH CENTURY BALLAD,
ANONYMOUS

SPRING

The Spring like to a Virgin fully growne
Stands heere or like an Early Rose new blowne

Shee's Natures Darling, and doth make the Earth
Giue to the smiling flowers a happy birth,

…ted & sold by Peter Stent at the Crowne in Giltspurre-street Betweene Newgate & Pye Corner A° 1644.

CHAPTER ONE

1643
For the Greene Sicknes

Take of the dust of the purest Spanish Steele a Spoonfull up heapt, a Nutmeg made into fine Powder, as much weight of Anyseeds in powder finely searsed [sifted] and halfe so much Liquorish, and a quarter of a pound and two ounces of Sugar finely beaten and searst. Take as much as will lye upon a shilling in a morning fasting in Warme Beer or warme Sack [fortified wine] in three spoonfulls of either. You must not eate in two hours after, but rub, or saw, or Swing, or walke very fast. For diet refrain all Milke Meats whatsoever, and use Broths with opening herbes espetially Penny Royall, Veale and Mutton chiefly.

Early in 1643, Ann Harrison's father summoned her and her younger sister, Margaret, from their handsome new house in Hertfordshire to join him in Oxford, which had over the past winter become the wartime capital of the beleaguered king, Charles I. Dutifully they rode into the unknown, seventy miles or so through the unsettled country north-west of London, over the chalky hills and through the beech woods of the Chilterns, to his side, taking only what 'a man or two' could carry on horseback in their cloak bags.

Ann and Margaret did not question their father's order. 'We knew not at all how to act any part but obedience,' Ann wrote later of her seventeen-year-old self, using a dramatic idiom well suited to her theatre-obsessed age and narrating events that could have graced a Jacobean melodrama. Later, it is implied, she would learn to be less biddable. 'From as good a house as any gentleman of England had, we came to lie in a very bad bed in a garret, to one dish of meat, and that not the best ordered, no money, for we were as poor as Job, [and had] no clothes'.[1] I love that single dish of 'meat...not the best ordered'; artlessly it speaks of such privilege.

'The scene was so changed,' said Ann: not just the scenery and their costumes but the parts they were playing. From the role of cosseted and protected daughters at the pinnacle of Stuart society they had been recast as refugees, exiles in their own land. The only analogies that could help her describe their situation were Biblical. 'I began to think we should all, like Abraham, live in tents all the days of our lives.'[2] She was right. This strange existence would become her reality.

If, a year earlier, Ann Harrison had imagined her future, it would almost certainly have looked very much like her mother's: marriage to a man not unlike her father, from a family which had grown prosperous in the service of the crown; comfortable houses both in London and set in knot-gardens, orchards and green fields outside the city, their warm-panelled, candlelit rooms the backdrop for celebrations of future christenings and marriages as well as the grief of unavoidable funerals, man's lot on earth being to suffer as well as to be joyful.

Apart from her mother's death two years earlier, fate had been kind to Ann. 'We lived in great plenty and hospitality,'[3] she remembered of her childhood, and no expense was spared by her doting father to equip her for life as a woman with all the responsibilities as well as privileges of gentle status. At their newly built rose-coloured brick mansion in Hertfordshire, Balls Park (see plate section), in the summer, and during the autumn and winter in London at Montague House, Bishopsgate, Ann was taught the bearing and accomplishments considered essential in the world she inhabited: to dance gracefully, to play the lute and the virginals, to sing and to speak French and to sew and embroider.

But though she 'learned as well as most did' she was, she said, 'a hoyting girl'[4] – that is to say, a hoyden, wild and carefree. She delighted in running, skipping and riding. Although her mother's death, when she was fifteen, made her grow up, her sense of adventure would never leave her.

It was the example of her mother, Margaret Harrison, that made the young Ann 'as an offering to her memory… [fling] away those childnesses that had formerly possessed me'. As the elder of his two daughters, she took charge of her widowed father's household. Despite her independent streak, all through her adult life, as her memoirs and receipt book demonstrate, Ann would strive to be, like Margaret, 'a loving wife, and most tender mother'[5] and, implicitly, the final element in the triad that made up the sole acceptable vocation of a seventeenth century woman, mistress of a well-run house.

As the daughter of a rich man and future wife of another, Ann would need to do no more than expertly oversee most domestic chores, such as butter-making, everyday cookery and laundry. Perhaps the most important practical skill she would learn from her mother was household medicine. Her mother's remedies form the core of the medical section of Ann's receipt book and she must have stood at Margaret Harrison's shoulder in the still-room of her childhood home watching her make up many of them. A still-room (short for distillation-room) or still-house was the desirable household adornment of the day, where the mistress of the house would dry herbs, extract essences and concoct ointments and cordials. As the repository of these complex skills, a still-room demonstrated the mistress of the house's compassion, learning, status and femininity.

Only one such still-house survives, almost intact, at Ham House, just south of Richmond on the River Thames, built in the 1670s – significantly, for its female owner, who would have told her architect exactly what she wanted. Bright and well lit, with its own entrance by a side door (leading out towards the herb garden) and the original crisp, black and white chequerboard floor, it is dominated by an oven with compartments for cooking at different temperatures, a large work-table and tall, shelved, heated cupboards lining one wall. Still-room inventories list pestles and mortars of wood and stone, braziers, scales and weights, small refrigerators for cooling heated liquids, presses, bain-maries, glass funnels and bottles, containers of earthenware, brass and silver, gallypots (small glazed pots for storage), graters, strainers and sieves, chopping boards and a collection of 'queer tin vessels of many shapes with spouts at all angles'[6] alongside a bewildering variety of potent ingredients ranging from the humble (locally gathered wild herbs and fresh eggs) to the expensive and exotic (nutmeg from the Banda Islands in Indonesia, ground pearls or olive oil from the Mediterranean) to the dangerous (opium, mercury and arsenic).

Ann would also have been given instruction in financial matters, for as a good wife she would need to administer her household with discretion and frugality. As with healthcare, this skill was too important to delegate. A rare account book survives from c.1610–13, detailing the personal expenses of Margaret Spencer (another Margaret, not Ann's mother; it was a popular name, redolent of feminine strength, harking back to that legendary fifteenth century matriarch, Margaret Beaufort) between the ages of thirteen and sixteen and kept as an educational exercise. The concern with pin-money demonstrated by this book was far from trivial. Margaret's father, reckoned one of the richest men in England and the source of her generous allowance, examined her accounts regularly, because a woman who could take responsibility for appropriate expenditure would be a valuable wife and thus a successful daughter.

Most of Margaret's spending was on clothes, a necessary expression of her status as much as frivolity or luxury – fine lawn to be made into smocks, spangled lace sewn onto ribbon, kid gloves stitched with silk flowers, velvet masks, a tall, fashionable hat of albino beaver fur from the Americas – or on looking after her wardrobe, having clothes made or expensively laundered and starched. But she also paid for lessons in dancing and playing the virginals and for small gambling debts as well as buying a 'silver thimbell' for her embroidery, a 'picktooth cass and picktooth' and, somewhat surprisingly, 'a payer of pistolls'.[7]

It is a measure of how independent young women of gentle birth were expected to be that, in her early teens and unmarried, Margaret commissioned friends and relations with errands, requesting feathers for a hat to be sent to her from London, for example, and then tipping the servant who delivered them, or buying presents for friends and family. Gift-giving was an important social function of seventeenth century society, encompassing valuable concepts of favour and obligation: it was a skill even girls could not be too young to learn. Far from being sheltered, Margaret's account book reveals a young woman immersed in society and serving her apprenticeship to it, learning to supervise servants, sewing and reading, visiting and entertaining, attending sermons and performing private devotions, a young woman much as Ann Harrison must have been at the same age some thirty years later. Its particular poignancy today lies in the knowledge that the lessons in adulthood Margaret was learning were acquired in vain, for she would die unmarried at sixteen.

Existence was precarious in the seventeenth century. Ann was just two years older than Margaret Spencer when her world and expectations changed forever. The comfortable security of her early life was shattered in 1642 when her father, Sir John, was arrested and his house and its contents were confiscated by the Parliamentary forces hostile to his master, Charles I.

In 1642, unable to persuade Parliament to grant him the taxes he wants and control over the army, King Charles I rides out of London and raises his banner against the men opposing him,

whom he calls rebels. The Parliamentarians believe royal power should be subject to Parliament; the king's men, Royalists or Cavaliers, believe royal dignity is divinely ordained and must not be challenged. Support for Parliament against the king, warns an ominous royal proclamation that July, would 'end in a dark equal chaos of confusion'.[8] *The first inconclusive battle of the civil wars that will define the next eighteen years of British history, Edgehill, takes place that October. With neither side able to claim victory, the scene is set for a long struggle ahead.*

Ann's father, Sir John Harrison, had made a great fortune serving the king. A man of humble background and great talent from Lancashire, arriving in London with nothing but his education, he had risen through the Treasury (and an advantageous marriage) to become a loyal MP as well as the first Commissioner of Customs, a position he created. Throughout Ann's childhood, the family's main home was near the parish church of St Olave's, Hart Street (also Samuel Pepys's church, where he and his wife are buried, and indicating a similar government and businesslike milieu for John Harrison). This area of Thames-side London was within sight of the White Tower built by William the Conqueror nearly six hundred years earlier and at the heart of the city's burgeoning trading centres, excise offices and customs houses, warehouses, exchanges and sales rooms.

Sir John, whose impressive wealth and influence derived from this area, was a familiar figure in these bustling, narrow streets as one of the crown's senior officials. When sides had to be chosen – and as the diplomat Sir Thomas Roe wrote to the Elector Palatine the month after Edgehill, 'No neutrality is admitted... Both parties resolve that those who are not with them are against them... and all who will not are as corn between two millstones'[9] – Harrison didn't really have a choice. He owed his fortune and his hopes for the future to his association with the crown and, unlike more established gentry or aristocratic families whose loyalties were sometimes divided, his allegiance was never in doubt. Like Lord Goring, he could truly say, 'I had all from his Majesty, and he hath all again.'[10]

That summer of 1642, Parliamentarian forces ransacked the houses of prominent Hertfordshire Royalist families, including the Fanshawes, kinsmen of Ann's mother who lived at Ware Park just a few miles from Balls, and their relations, the Capels of Hamerton, and sent the weaponry they found stored there to their leaders in London. Ann's older brother, William Harrison, then in his early twenties, rode to join the king's army at Nottingham. Soon afterwards Parliamentary forces plundered the Harrison house in Bishopsgate and took Sir John prisoner. Pretending he needed to fetch some papers they were demanding from him 'concerning the public revenue',[11] astute Sir John managed to evade their grasp and, summoning his daughters, left London for Oxford in early 1643, to the king's court-in-exile.

This is the historical account. From the almost prosaic tone in which Ann related it, years later, it seems likely that when her father was arrested she and her sister were safely out of the way, presumably at Balls; there is little immediacy in her version of events. No other account records Balls being searched or plundered, the word in common use at the time. Contemporary letters, however, reveal how frightening it was to watch your country splinter into civil wars even from the sidelines and how divided individuals were about how to cope with the coming conflict. Twenty-two-year-old Lord Henry Spencer (who would have been the nephew of the diligent young accountant Margaret Spencer) wrote to his wife of three years from the king's camp at Shrewsbury, where William Harrison was among his fellow officers: 'If there could be an expediency found to salve the punctilio of honour, I would not continue here an hour.' (He added with half a smile, and just a drop of puritanical distaste, that though the king was 'very cheerful... by the bawdy discourse [of camp], I thought I had been in the drawing room [at court].')[12]

Sir Edmund Verney, of Sir John's rather than William Harrison's generation, was equally torn. Before joining the king's army as his hereditary standard bearer he told Sir Edward Hyde, 'I do not like the quarrel and do heartily wish that the king would yield and consent to what they [the Parliamentarians] desire'. Like Sir John, though, he saw no options available to him. 'I have eaten his bread and served him near thirty years, and will do no so base thing as to forsake him; and choose rather to lose my life (which I am sure I shall do) to preserve and defend those things that are against my conscience.'[13] His words were prophetic: he would die at Edgehill with Charles's banner in his clenched fist, still unconvinced by the cause for which he gave his life and knowing that his beloved eldest son and heir, Ralph, had chosen Parliament over the king.

Before he left his estate in Buckinghamshire, Sir Edmund had written to his steward anticipating worse times to come and instructing him to do all he could to safeguard their precious corner of England. 'I praye have a care of my howse, that roages break not into it, have stoare of bullett and powder, and gett some boddy to lodg in the howse that may defend it if need bee. Have my wagon in readiness, if I should att any time send for it; gett in all such monys as are owing you with all speede for wee shall certainly have a great warr.'[14]

Women were by no means excluded from these agonizing debates. A family friend and neighbour from London, Lady Sydenham, wrote from the king's camp to Sir Edmund's daughter-in-law, Mary, wife of the young rebel Ralph Verney, in part to assure her that whatever choice her husband made politically their friendship would remain unaltered, in part to reassure her because 'you ded exspres a trobell in yours [letter] to me about your hosband's reselushons' and in part to question those resolutions.

> i kno he has chossen the strongest part, but i cannot thinke the best, but i am confedent he dus believe tis the best, and for that he chos it. But truly my hart it stagers me that he shold not se clearly all thar [Parliament's] ways, being it tis so aparrant, for how tis for the lebberty of the subget to tacke all from thim which are not of thar mind... Nor do i find that it is in god's lay [law], to tacke arms aganst thar lawful king.[15]

Sir Edmund's daughter Cary Verney, newly married at fifteen and staying with her husband's family in Bedfordshire, wrote to her brother Ralph with more practical worries later in the year. 'The parlement has frittened ous [us] from Hill [house], and sinc has frittened our carreg that was comin to ous back agane, and ther it is in danger of plondarin'.[16] Her brother-in-law's servant had been arrested by Parliamentary soldiers and £52 that he was carrying for his master taken from him; Cary begged Ralph to ask a family friend, a prominent fellow Parliamentarian, to do what he could to help, notwithstanding that her own husband of only a few months was in the king's army, on the other side. Another Verney correspondent wrote indignantly with the news that when she had sent some horses to collect her children from London they had been confiscated by Parliamentarians.

Plundering, however, was a mere inconvenience compared to the increasingly common reports Ann would certainly have heard of frightening violence, often against women as well as men, being committed by both sides. In February, perhaps while Ann and her sister were making their uneasy way across country to Oxford, more than three hundred people were killed on the streets of Cirencester in a battle between Royalists and Parliamentarians that took place amid the mellow stone houses, outbuildings and gardens of the town, with narrow streets barricaded with overturned wagons and musketeers firing from windows tucked into the thatched eaves of cottages. One woman, Lady Jordan, was said to have been sent mad by the bombardment, reverting to childhood. She was noteworthy at the time because of her status; many other people, whose names were not recorded, were surely similarly traumatized.

During the long, wet, muddy summer of 1643, women became actors in rather than witnesses to the war, their stories recounted with either scorn or admiration (depending on the affiliations of the story-teller) across the country in conversation, letters and news-sheets. The Puritan Brilliana, Lady Harley, stoutly defended her house, Brampton Bryan in rural Herefordshire, during a three-month siege by Royalist soldiers. (Her husband, Sir Robert, was busy elsewhere, heading the newly created Commons Committee for the Demolition of Monuments of Superstition and Idolatry; the Puritans had become a powerful political force, motivated by their distrust of the traditionalist Charles and his openly Catholic queen.) The Royalist Lady Mary Bankes kept Parliamentary forces at bay outside Corfe Castle in Dorset for three years from May 1643 before being betrayed by one of her officers.

Though he chose to follow the king rather than remain to defend his estate, Sir John Harrison was one of many royal servants whose houses, lands and furniture had been sequestered by Parliament, living in exile from their homes with scant access to income. (Despite his losses, Sir John was still able to form part of a group of seven customs farmers who, in October 1643, lent the king more than £250,000, though he refused to buy a baronetcy, titles money-strapped Charles was selling for £1095 apiece.) Eighteen years later Sir Edward Nicholas, Secretary of State to Charles I and Charles II, petitioned for compensation for what he had lost in 1642 from his houses in London and Surrey when they were overrun by Parliamentarians: five black trunks filled with linen, bedding and a brass warming pan, four kettles and his valuable still-room equipment, ironware, another hamper and two bundles, altogether 'at the value of £1500 at lease [least]'.[17]

Oxford in 1643 was full of men like Harrison and Nicholas, not thrusting youths on the make but established men trailing newly rag-tag families, squeezed into tiny lodgings, living on what they would have considered scraps a few months earlier. Even the royal family had become gypsies. After Edgehill, the previous October, which they had watched from a distance with their tutor, nine-year-old Prince James, duke of York, turned to his older brother and asked when they would go home. With all the authority of twelve years, Charles replied, 'We have no home.'[18]

The city of students was transformed into a city of soldiers, its wartime population swelling to 10,000. New College School became a storehouse for barrels of gunpowder; tailors stitched soon-to-be bloodstained coats of blue, red and yellow* in the Music and Astronomy Schools; and oxen and sheep to feed the men were kept in Christ Church College quad, hard by the royal quarters. Schoolboys intoxicated by the whiff of gunpowder in the air gathered to watch soldiers practising drills in Christ Church Meadow and artillery in Merton College Grove. Once the soldiers arrived 'they could never be brought to their books again'.[19]

Alongside this martial energy and glamour, so potent to young men, ran its realities: hunger, cramped conditions, filth and contagion. Corpses of animals and rotten herbage choked the Cherwell and the Isis rivers, rubbish filled the streets and regular outbreaks of disease – 'the sickness' in 1643 and plague in 1644 – swept through the city and its muddy camps. 'We had the perpetual discourse of losing and gaining towns and men,' remembered Ann, and 'at the windows the sad spectacle of war'.[20]

Reports of deaths and casualties flooded into Oxford after every skirmish and engagement. After the battle at nearby Newbury in September cart-loads of dead and wounded were carried into the town, among them 'that modest, courageous and loyall young Lord, the Earle of Sunderland',[21] the Henry Spencer who had

* There were no single colour uniforms at this stage, which lent battlefields a terrible confusion. Soldiers distinguished their friends from the enemy by devices chosen on the day: at Newbury, in September 1643, Royalists wore green boughs on their hats as identification.

written so regularly to his beloved wife Doll from the king's camp the previous summer. She was just twenty-six, heavily pregnant and with three young children, when she heard news of his death, which had been a dreadful one. He died in agony on the battlefield, wounded and conscious to the end, and his corpse was robbed and defiled by Parliamentary soldiers so that it was unfit for burial; only his heart was sent home to Althorp. Doll's father consoled her as best he could: 'I know you lived happily, and so as nobody but yourself could measure the contentment of it. I rejoiced at it, and did thank God for making me one of the means of procuring it for you [in arranging her marriage]. That now is past, and I will not flatter you so much as to say I think you can ever be so happy in this life again; but this comfort you owe me, that I may see you bear this change and this misfortune patiently.'[22] It was advice women all over the country were learning to heed.

Ann's own 'dear brother William'[23] died in June 1643 when his horse was shot out from under him during a skirmish, days after formally being expelled as a Royalist from the House of Commons, to which he had been elected in 1640 but from which he had quickly dissociated himself as the times shifted beneath his feet. 'He was a very good and gallant young man,' she wrote in her memoirs, remembering her lost brother from a distance of thirty-three years, 'and they are the very words the king said of him, when he was told of his death: he was much lamented by all who knew him'.[24]

But Ann was young and this was her first taste of adult life. Despite the horrors, the dangers, the tragedies of war, evident all around her, she knew nothing else. And although it was a military court-in-exile, lacking much of the formality and splendour of times gone by at Whitehall or Windsor, Oxford was still a royal court. Feasts and ceremonies continued; Charles was dressed by grooms and attended by trumpeters; he processed in ceremony from Christ Church to Merton to visit his queen, Henrietta Maria; he took the royal beagles hunting (an excellent form of military exercise); the royal portraitist William Dobson was at work in a studio at St John's College; even masquing may have taken place, though the evidence to support this is fragmentary. Parliamentary newspapers disdainfully reported the Royalists in Oxford dancing 'through the streets, openly with musick before them':[25] vibrant, hedonistic, living for pleasure in the shadow of death.

So persistently sumptuous was his court that in June 1643 Charles was forced to issue a proclamation outlawing lace, ribbons and gold buttons and clasps as much in an effort to change the public perception of his Cavaliers as idle fops as to reflect the straitened circumstances of wartime. The name Cavalier was originally a derogatory one, given to the king's followers by disapproving Parliamentarians, but Royalists soon began identifying themselves as Cavaliers, saying that the original meaning of the word was mounted soldier – which they proudly were.

In the normal course of things, Ann might barely have gone to court. Though rich, her father lacked the aristocratic connections to place her in Henrietta Maria's household. Marriage and a family to look after, in the most comfortable but retired of circumstances, would have been the future her parents desired for her. But at Oxford, where favoured soldiers ran up and down the back stairs at Christ Church in their buff coats (leather coats typically worn by soldiers, beneath a metal breastplate or cuirass for battle; the finest examples had strips of gold and silver lace on the sleeves), military informality extended to women too. Suddenly the sheltered eighteen-year-old had an entrée to an intriguing new world.

A court lady was a particular creature whose attributes, as popularly imagined, can best be seen in the negative, as in this defence of a Puritan wife from the Parliamentary press:

> She is not like your court madams, Aulicus [literally, princely. The *Mercurius Aulicus*, printed at Oriel from January 1643, was the most prominent Royalist newsletter]; uses no oil of talc, no false teeth, no wanton frisking gate [gait], no caterwauling in Spring Garden [a park near Whitehall, frequented by the fashionable elite]... She cannot measure out a whole morning with curling irons and spend the afternoon in courting and vanity and toying.[26]

The diarist Elizabeth Delaval remembered her misspent youth in the 1660s, before marriage and sobriety overtook her, as a time of 'maidenly indulgences':[27] flirting and running up debts at court, gorging on fruit and mounting an elaborate production at home of *Il Pastor Fido* (*The Loyal Shepherd*), one of the favourite plays of the period, almost certainly using the 1647 translation from the Italian by the poet, courtier and diplomat Richard Fanshawe, who would become Ann's husband. 'Many an houer have I robed my selfe of rest to waist them in dancing, in play [at cards], in reading unprofitable books, and such foleish devertions,'[28] she lamented afterwards. Other women remembered spending their youth 'in exquisite and curious dressing',[29] going to the theatre, reading romances, playing musical instruments, dining in barges on the Thames, wandering through pleasure gardens and, that archetypical seventeenth century extravagance, eating too much fruit. 'Hid Park and the cheries there is veri pleasant to me,'[30] wrote fifteen-year-old Betty Verney, fresh from Buckinghamshire. Girls were not alone in being seduced by the pleasures of the capital: the young diarist John Evelyn, a cousin, kinsman and friend of Richard Fanshawe's, was in London for two months in 1642, aged twenty-two, 'studying a little, but dancing and fooling more'.[31]

Sir Edward Hyde, one of Charles's advisors, deplored the mores of the early years of the war, when 'the young women conversed without any circumspection or modesty'.[32] This concern about women speaking out was associated, in the popular press, with sexual disarray. In 1642 and 1643, a flurry of satirical pamphlets appeared, ostensibly by women petitioning Parliament, mocking women in the most basic sexual imagery for daring to comment on the great events of the day (on one title page a woman was shown urging her husband, wearing the horns of a cuckold, to 'go to the wars') but containing within them a kind of recognition of the validity of their comments.

'The Mid-Wives' Just Petition' was published in January 1643, a plea for peace from a spurious London guild of midwives, an inversion of the Fishmongers' and Apothecaries' which held such power in the city. War, the imaginary midwives argued, was devouring England's youth and, by extension, their livelihood. 'Little gettings have we in this age barren of all naturall joyes, and onely fruitfull in bloudy calamities, we desire therefore that for the better propagating of our owne benefit, and the general good of all women, wives may no longer spare their husbands to be devoured by the sword, but may keep them fast locked within their own loving armes day and night.' Bawdy innuendoes apart, this was a difficult argument to counter. It was better, urged the authors, in terms everyone would have understood, for men to be 'at home with their wives, then for them to runne abroad to be a common souldier, and stand sentinel two or three hours in the cold for a little Suffolk cheese and a piece of browne bread, and at length kill one another for eight pence a day.'[33]

At a time when, as these pamphlets demonstrate, women were seen as possessing the legacy of Eve, a sexual appetite that could threaten themselves and society if left unchecked, young unmarried women posed a distinct danger. They even had their own disorder, green-sickness, also known as the Virgin's Disease. The name conjured up the green of fresh leaves, fresh life; the green of inexperience and adolescent love sung by classical poets (Sappho's fragment 31, translated by Anne Carson: 'and cold sweat holds me and shaking/grips me all, greener than grass/I am and dead – or almost/I seem to me'); and the pallid green tinge of the complexion of its sufferers. Wives and widows could succumb, noted the midwife Jane Sharp, 'yet it is more common to maids of ripe years when they are in love and desirous to keep company with a man'.[34]

Today green-sickness is called hypochromic anaemia, a condition in which the red blood cells are paler than usual due to iron deficiency and which can cause a greenish pallor. Its symptoms are headaches, passivity, lack of appetite and dyspepsia, a want of energy and irregular or no periods; Jane Sharp added the 'longing after hurtful things'.[35] In 1943, the medical historian Henry Sigerist described green-sickness, known as chlorosis in the nineteenth century, as 'the disease of the young girl of the upper classes who lived an indoor life without physical exercise, doing some needlework, playing some music and waiting for her husband to relieve her'.[36] Others have speculated that it might have been an early form of anorexia; some of the symptoms resemble Chronic Fatigue Syndrome, particularly prevalent among teenagers. I see it as a physical expression of powerlessness, as an unmarried girl waited for a husband to be produced for her, for her fate to be decided by others.

Almost every contemporary receipt book contained remedies for green-sickness, ranging from eating six bitter almonds, or alternatively six raisins, every morning, to drinking a glass of white wine infused with a powder made from earthworms – washed, of course – soaked in vinegar and then dried. (Earthworms are still a feature of Chinese medicine: they are used to unblock hot and painful obstructions, which might be applicable here.) Most recommended exercise – indeed, one medical advice book claimed that it could be cured by exercise alone – and it was well known that the best time of year to cure green-sickness was spring, when the warmth in the air would help thin blocked menstrual blood. The late seventeenth century doctor Thomas Sydenham is credited with recognizing iron as a remedy for anaemia, but steel filings and powders had long been a feature of popular and receipt book remedies for green-sickness.

There is no evidence that Ann Harrison suffered from green-sickness – perhaps her hoyting tendencies preserved her from it – but a remedy for it, attributed to a Mrs Ailiffe (probably her cousin Margaret Ayloffe), appears on the first page of her receipt book marked by the cross that she seems to have used where others used the letters 'prob.', short for *probatus*, or proved. The treatment contained powdered Spanish steel as well as aniseed, which the herbalist John Gerard noted stirred up 'bodily lusts' and was also used to relieve menstrual cramping. Costly nutmeg, from Indonesia, could be used – like aniseed – to bring on a miscarriage, and as such was specifically left out of most remedies for women, but here it was intended to stimulate menstruation. The active ingredient in liquorice, glycyrrhizin, is antiviral, antimicrobial, anti-inflammatory, increases blood pressure and is hepatoprotective, which means it protects a healthy liver – good for the blood – as well as helping the body absorb other medicines. Finally, the toxic herb pennyroyal was traditionally used to stimulate menses (and indeed as an abortifacient).

However effective the ingredients of Ann's remedy might have been, it was commonly accepted that the best way to cure green-sickness was vigorous sex. For a young, unmarried girl, regardless of how many raisins she ate for breakfast, green-sickness meant one thing: a husband.

CHAPTER 2

1644
The King of France his Balsome

Take Red Sage, and Rue of each one pound, of young Bay leaves and Wormwood of each ½ a pound, doe not wash them, but picke, wipe, and cutt them very small, and beate them well in a Stone Morter, take a pound of Sheepes Suett hot from the Sheepe, mince it small & breake it with those herbes till it be all of one coulour; then putt all into a faire boule with a pottle of the best oile Olive, worke all together till it become alike, then putt it into an Earthen pott well-stoppt with Parchment and waxe for 8 dayes. Then seethe all in a panne with a soft Fire. When it is sodden putt to it 4 Ounces of the oil of Spike [Lavandula Spika]. Then straine it thorow a Canvas Strainer into a pott, cover it with parchment, and with a Leather upon that; In the boyling of it take heed that it burne not, for the avoyding whereof putt 2 or 3 drops still in a Saucer, and when it is greene as the Emrod [emerald] it is enough.

This is excellent for all Aches, or paines of the Head that come of Cold, black wooll being dipt in it, and stopping the Eares, for shrinking of Sinewes, or Ague Cakes [a swollen spleen, often the result of malaria] being chaft in against the Fire, & a Cloth dipt hot in the same applied to the Place.

In May 1644, the chaplain to the Prince of Wales's Life Guards preached a sermon at Shrewsbury to the newly mustered troops of Prince Rupert, the dashing Cavalier commander and cousin of the king, encouraging them in their struggle against the Parliamentarian rebels they were marching to face. The first, and major, part of the sermon dealt with discovering 'out of God's Book the nature of Rebellion and rebellious men',[1] but tucked into the middle section was a description of the kind of man these soldiers should aspire to be. It serves as a useful model for the pin-up of the 1640s, the *beau idéal* the spirited Ann Harrison was hoping would choose her as his bride.

'The complete Cavalier', declared the Reverend Symmons, was 'a Child of Honour, a Gentleman well borne and bred... of a clearer countenance and bolder looke than other men, because of a more loyall heart'. Wreathed in noble qualities like a marble hero, the Cavalier was pious and conscientious, prudent but generous, honest and good; he was also amiable, gallant and discreet: 'the only Reserve of English Gentility and ancient valour'.[2]

This description might have been written for Richard Fanshawe, the king's trusty and beloved Dick, with whom Ann fell in love in late 1643 or early 1644. Richard was the tenth and youngest child of Hertfordshire neighbours of the Harrisons, the Fanshawe family who lived barely two miles across the Lea valley in a Tudor mansion, Ware Park, set in much-admired gardens and parkland. There was a family link – Margaret Harrison had been born a Fanshawe and was Richard's great-great-aunt – but the Fanshawes, although also in service to the crown, were slightly grander and more established than the self-made Harrisons, holding for several generations the lucrative Exchequer position of King's Remembrancer.

At thirty-six, Richard was seventeen years older than Ann. She doesn't mention whether they had encountered one another before meeting in Oxford at the king's court-in-exile, but it is unlikely the sheltered girl would have come across her sophisticated young neighbour except briefly, despite the closeness of their fathers' houses. Having given up his legal studies to concentrate on languages, Richard was away in Europe over much of the 1630s, travelling in France and Spain for a couple of years in the early 1630s and then as secretary to the Spanish Ambassador from 1635 to 1638, where one of his bosses described him warmly as 'likely to prove a proper man'.[3] He was an accomplished Latinist and spoke fluent Italian as well as French and Spanish; he had a taste for that most fashionable of pursuits, poetry. These, combined with his court connections, heralded a stellar career in crown and diplomatic service.

John Aubrey recalled Richard, in 1642, debating whether to join the king with his friend, the poet Thomas May, whose admiration for the Roman poet Lucan had made him a republican. But 'being the king's sworn servant',[4] as Ann put it, Richard had come to Oxford the following year, where, early in 1644, he had been made secretary to the Council of War, which advised the fourteen-year-old Prince of Wales, the future Charles II.

Dick Fanshawe was a tall man, 'strong, and of the best proportion', with dark, curling hair, pale skin, a 'high nose' and penetrating grey eyes. His countenance was 'gracious and wise, his motion good, his speech clear and distinct'. His royal masters loved him for his delightful, curious, cheerful conversation, as well as his parts, or virtues, and his straight-forwardness and loyalty to them. He spent his 'idle hours' in poetry, his wife continued fondly, 'but his most delight was, to go only with me in a coach some miles, and there discourse of those things which then most pleased him, of what nature soever'.[5]

'Glory be to God,' Ann went on, tears 'gushing' out of her eyes as she remembered him and their life together, 'we never had but one mind throughout our lives. Our souls were wrapped up in each other's; our aims and designs one, our loves one, and our resentments one. We so studied one the other, that we knew each other's minds by our looks. Whatever was real happiness, God gave it me in him.'[6] They would share twenty-three years of marital bliss, their personal happiness and delight in one another unshaken by the tremors that rocked their world.

Ann barely touched on their meeting in her memoirs, commenting instead on the strange turbulence of the times, in which joy sat so closely alongside tragedy. 'Having buried my dear brother, William Harrison, in Exeter College Chapel, I then married your dear father in 1644 in Wolvercot [*sic*] Church, two miles from Oxford, upon the 18th day of May.' (By coincidence, the day before Reverend Symmons spoke about Cavaliers at Shrewsbury.) She then briefly introduced Richard, concluding, 'Now we appear on the stage, to act what part God designed us.' This is the start of my story, she was saying; everything else has been background. Our marriage is where our lives begin.

But I want to consider courtship because it is something to

delight in, even – or perhaps especially – in times of conflict. Dorothy Osborne's charming letters to her beloved, William Temple, illuminate how these things worked in war-torn seventeenth century England. They met in 1647, both aged nineteen, and fell in love; but Dorothy's family forbad the match. Her parents disapproved of William less on political grounds – though the Osbornes were Royalists,* they were still pragmatic enough to try to negotiate a marriage with the up-and-coming Parliamentarian Oliver Cromwell's son Henry – than for financial reasons, not considering him rich or promising enough to offer Dorothy a secure future. Dorothy and William had to wait seven years, until both their fathers had died, to marry at last.

Dorothy's letters to William from the final two years of their secret engagement, 1653 and 1654, survive. They reveal not just her expectations of love and marriage but the unspoken assumptions of the society in which she lived. First, she displays a very competent grasp of the material considerations behind marriage, teasing William about another suitor with '£5000 besydes the reversion of an estate'.[7] She never dreamed of marrying without the consent of her father or brothers – she is not afraid of material want, she declares, but to be scorned by society, as a woman who flouted her family's wishes in marriage would be, is too much to contemplate. Off the page (his letters don't survive), William urges her to create her own fate. 'Alasse,' she replies, 'how can you talk of deffying fortune, noe body lives without it'.[8] It is hardly surprising that, delicately without specifying green-sickness, she mentions

* They were also friends and associates of the Fanshawe family, with significant Exchequer connections.

in her letters taking a cure of steel shavings for an unnamed malaise.

True love was what she longed for. Scathingly she describes her brother John loving his new wife, Eleanor, 'at the ordinary rate of husbands… that would kill mee were I as shee for I could bee infinitly better sattisfyed with a husband that had never Loved mee in hope hee might, then with one that began to Love mee lesse'.[9]

She writes to William in triumph to tell him she's persuaded her brother to admit that the celebrated beauty Lady Isabella Rich, her best friend's sister, 'had better married a begger, then that beast [Sir James Thynne; it was a notoriously unhappy marriage] with all his estate… what should she doe with beauty now'.[10] But forsaking convention for infatuation had its pitfalls, too. Unfortunate Lady Anne Blunt, who had run away with an undeserving suitor, has become 'the talk of all the footmen and Boy's in the street, and will bee company for them shortly, who is yet soe blinded by her passion as not at all to perceave the missery shee has brought her self to'.[11] A clear lesson was intended here for William.

In time-honoured fashion, the star-crossed lovers sent one another tokens of their faithfulness. Dorothy asks William for a lock of his hair; he sends it with a ring. 'I have bin thinking of sending you my Picture till I could come myself but a Picture is but dull company and that you need not,' she tells him, after Peter Lely makes her portrait. 'Besyd's I cannot tell whither it bee very like mee or not though tis the best I have ever had drawne for me and Mr Lilly will have it that hee never took more pain's to make a good one in his life. And that was it I think that spoiled it.'[12]

Richard and Ann had their portraits painted at this time, probably just before their wedding as the portraits are not companions by the same artist. Richard was painted by Charles I's official painter, William Dobson (see plate section), in the shimmering satin and lace of a courtier, with a large, gentle black and white hound, symbol of fidelity – both to future wife and royal master – at his knee. His pose is relaxed and assured, his gaze steady and quietly confident.

Cornelius Johnson, a fashionable Dutch portraitist who had recently made a large-scale family portrait of some Hertfordshire neighbours, the Capels, was chosen for Mistress Ann (see plate section). This is our first sight of her and, since appearances meant so much to Ann and her contemporaries, we must look closely at how she has presented herself. Clothes could bestow upon a person the character they wanted others to think they possessed, as Samuel Pepys's resolve to 'go a little handsomer than I have hitherto'[13] demonstrates. 'Weare your Clothes neat,' one mother urged her son in 1656, 'exceeding rather than comming short of others of like fortune; a charge borne out [an expenditure repaid] by Acceptance where ever you come'.[14] They invested the wearer not just with shape, in that era of starch, whalebone and billowing silks, but with function, status and identity. 'Mens apparel is commonly made according to their conditions,' wrote the poet Edmund Spenser, earlier in the century, 'and their conditions are oftentimes governed by their garments'.[15]

For her portrait Ann is wearing rich but relatively simple black satin with immaculately white, lace-trimmed linen (that essential and expensive mark of gentility) at the neckline. Her only adornment is two roses in her dark, pomaded curls, which are loose, as befitted a maiden. 'Done' hair was another signifier of status, indicating as it did the attentions of a lady's maid and heated hair tongs, and Ann's hair is down but very much done. Unusually, she wears no jewels – perhaps they had been left hidden at Balls, waiting for better times to be brought out on display again; maybe even sold to fund the king's struggle against his rebels – but she doesn't need them. Her skin is creamy, her dark brown eyes coolly level, her mouth a perfect rosebud to match the flowers in her hair. Richard, a Hispanophile who had spent his formative years at the court of Madrid, must have been captivated by her dark, Spanish looks.

Physical beauty, particularly in women, was an ambivalent attribute in the seventeenth century. On one hand, it was considered the reflection of inner goodness and spirituality. 'Loveliness… is impressed upon the body in varying degrees as a token by which the soul can be recognised for what it is, just as with trees the beauty of the blossom testifies to the goodness of the fruit'.[16] On the other, a beautiful woman was inherently a temptation into sin, inciting men to lust and the woman herself to vanity and, almost inevitably, to unchasteness. 'A faire woman is a paradise to the eie, a purgatorie to the purse, and a hell to the soule,'[17] ran one contemporary epigram.

Despite these caveats, toilet sets were a common wedding present for a young woman of status. Boxes of tortoiseshell or precious inlaid woods, they opened to reveal a mirror inside the lid – often there are integral candle holders for making up at night – and might contain a range of implements in silver or gold: scissors, tweezers, nail files, pincushions, pots for patches and glue, hair pomade and powder, and pots and glass bottles for the beautifying creams, lotions and scent bought at an apothecary's or made in the still-room.

Ann's receipt book is unusual in that it includes only one recipe for a cosmetic,* 'almond milk for the fase' containing a dangerous dash of whitening saltpetre, the active ingredient in gunpowder, and her portrait shows no trace of rouge – but then her husband, to judge by his translation of *Il Pastor Fido*, may not have approved of make-up:

> How much against my stomack doth it go
> To see you paint your cheeks, to cover so
> The faults of Time and nature! How ye make
> Pale Feulement a pure Vermilion take,
> Fill up the wrinkles, die black white, a spot
> With a spot hide, where 'tis, make't where 'tis not.[18]

Youth, as much as the lover's gaze, was the only truly reliable source of beauty. According to Dorothy Osborne's friend, Diana Rich, nineteen – Ann's age in this painting – was only just acceptable for a good portrait. After having her likeness made Dorothy Osborne had asked Lely to draw Diana but she had refused on the grounds that she was 'past the time of having Pictur's taken of her. After eighteen shee say's there is noe face but decays apparently'.[19]

There must have been advantages to falling in love with a poet. Although no verses written from Richard to Ann survive, several of Richard's poems appear in the commonplace book of Constance

* Popular cosmetics of the day might include pig or puppy blood, snails and their shells, lead or mercury. The known, potentially fatal, risks of mercury poisoning – it could permanently damage the teeth and cause consumption – were thought by many to be outweighed by the smooth, pale complexion it produced.

Aston, the daughter of the Spanish ambassador in the mid-1630s to whom Richard was secretary, some including plays on the words constance and constancie. In his translation of *Querer por solo querer* (*To Love for Love's Sake*, a courtly drama of the 1620s by Antonio de Mendoza) he describes a gallant haunting his mistress, 'Hat in the hand, her colours in the hat' and, later,

> Nor so alone in things of Love;
> But my Life over and above,
> Because on her it doth depend,
> I have no power to make it end.[20]

In 1644 two sisters of about Ann's age, Ladies Jane and Elizabeth Cavendish, wrote *The Concealed Fancyes*, a play in which their characters debate the ideal qualities of potential husbands. The mid-1640s were especially turbulent years for them, during which their mother died, their father William, marquess of Newcastle, fled England after disaster as losing commander at the Battle of Marston Moor in July 1644, and their home, Welbeck Abbey, was captured by Parliamentarians that August before being retaken briefly by Royalist forces in 1645 and returned to Parliamentary control later that year. This light-hearted drama was their escape from real life, even though the theme with which it deals – how to have a happy marriage – was acutely relevant to them both. When they wrote the play, Elizabeth had already been married three years, since she was fifteen, though she would not begin living with her husband's family until the following year, while Jane, unmarried at twenty-three, was arguably in a worse postion.

The plot centres on a pair of sisters and their suitors. Luceny, aware of the charms of her large dowry, worries that she won't know 'whether 'tis... wisdom or affection that makes choice of me'.[21] She fears the years of marriage to a man she does not respect in which she will be 'condemned to look upon my nose whenever I walk; and when I sit at meat [dinner], confined by his grave wink, to look upon the salt [cellar; meaning, not to raise her eyes]; and if it be but the paring of his nails, to admire him'.[22] How often, she asks her sister, 'have you read the Bible over, and have forgotten man and wife should draw equally in a yoke?'[23]

The suitors, too, are confused. Courtly wants a modern wife who 'in private know no matrimony law/In public all should think I did her awe',[24] but his friend, Presumption, believes he will have to control and humiliate a wife to tame her: 'She shall not stay with her own friends or family after she is married, not three days. Then, once a year, I'll bring her down a gown in fashion, which with continuing long in the country, she shall not know how to put on; then all my discourse shall be to praise the ladies in London.' He will make her bear children, keep the 'week books' (accounts) and respect his mother and sisters.

As Presumption shows, courtship and matrimony were just as often affairs of family and business as romance. If Ann and Richard had married in the 1630s, older relatives would have smiled on the union. Though Richard was the youngest of five sons, a brilliant career at court seemed assured due to his charm, literary and linguistic talents and family connections. Ann's promised dowry of £10,000 was generous, reflective of her position as the daughter of a vastly wealthy but not aristocratic father; by comparison, when Lady Mary Boyle married Charles Rich, later earl of Warwick, in 1641, her portion was £7000. The ties between the Harrisons and Fanshawes, of geography as well as blood, made it an entirely suitable match.

But times were uncertain and good marriages, by the mid-1640s, were no longer something upon which the gentry could depend. 'If these times hold up I think there will be no men left for women,'[25] wrote Ralph Verney's aunt in 1644. Because of the wars only one of Ralph's five sisters, all like Ann of marriageable age in the 1640s, got the dowry she expected. Betty Verney, the girl who loved the cherries in Hyde Park, wrote desperately at thirty, 'I think my marrying very unlikely in any place and impossible in this',[26] shortly before running away with an impoverished clergyman of whom her family disapproved. Each of the sisters did eventually marry, but older, to lesser men and after much more protracted negotiation than would have been the case five years earlier or ten years later. The witty young playwright Jane Cavendish would not marry until she was thirty-three – an unthinkable fate for a woman of her wealth and rank at any other time in the century.

A love match, when the couple's families approved, made everything easier. With his small inheritance and her dowry in 'expectation', Ann and Richard embarked on their life together with not '£20 betwixt us', enough to buy 'pen, ink and paper, which was your father's trade, and by it, I assure you, we lived better than those that were born to £2000 a year'. You can almost hear her remembered excitement, that feeling of the wind in her hair, when she says proudly that at their marriage they might truly have been 'called merchant adventurers'.[27]

She may not have had ropes of pearls or the expected portion from her father, but Ann did bring something valuable from her mother into her new life as a married woman: that sheaf of Margaret Harrison's receipts, copied out in her own impatient hand as a childhood writing exercise and slipped in a rush into the cloak bag of her most treasured possessions when she had ridden off to join her father the previous year. It was her dead mother's bequest to her, an amulet that could guard and protect her throughout her life, even when her mother was no longer by her side.

The King of France's Balsome is the first receipt in the ointments section of Ann's own receipt book, copied out years later, and (like so many of her recipes and remedies) it is attributed to her mother and marked with the X that signalled she had used it successfully. Its ingredients, mixed in a still-room over several days' preparation in an oily base of sheep's fat and olive oil, were all powerful medicinal herbs. Rue is used as a sedative and antispasmodic; like wormwood, or Artemisia, it is known for its bitter taste. Some Artemisia varieties are used to treat malaria – therefore active against Ague-Cheeks, or a swollen spleen, often malarial – while others are sedatives and painkillers. Bay is an astringent and can be used to treat rashes, earache, high blood pressure and arthritis and rheumatism; at high concentration its active ingredient is known to be an inhibitor of human melanoma, or skin cancer. Red sage – a variation of *Salvia officinalis* with purple leaves – is another potent herb, traditionally used for heating blood and easing joint stiffness. Apart from its soothing, sleep-bringing qualities, lavender is anti-inflammatory and antiseptic. As the receipt says, it would have been an excellent salve for all sorts of common ailments – deliciously bay- and lavender-scented, emerald green in colour, and as precious to a young bride embarking on married life as any jewel.

There's a very similar remedy in the redoubtable Brilliana Harley's receipt book (she who resisted Royalist forces in 1643) probably compiled in the 1630s. Rather than the King of France's Balsome, she calls it 'an excellent green ointment to be made in May'[28] when the herbs needed would be at their springlike best. It's pleasant to imagine Ann on her wedding day in May, trailing her skirts through fields full of the blossoming plants and shrubs she would have gathered to make her mother's healing balm.

Flowers were always a part of weddings: in church, on the feast-table, in garlands, wreaths and buttonholes. Roses, like those in Ann's hair in her portrait, were especially suitable for brides as the flower of love, along with violets (humility and faithfulness) and rosemary (remembrance), reminders of the virtues needed in married life. The happy couple would wear new clothes and shoes. Attendants tied coloured ribbons on their hats and garters, and favours, often of gloves, were handed out to guests (and sent to those who couldn't attend), who would throw wheat, representing fertility, on the couple as they left the church. Music and feasting, dancing and the drinking of toasts followed the ceremony, often including rowdy games laden with sexual innuendo like cutting the bridegroom's points (the lacings joining hose to doublet), throwing the bride's garter to the guests, 'sewing into the sheet, and twenty other petty sorceries'.[29]

But in 1644 things were different, for this was the year in which Parliament was writing its new Directory of Public Worship, a manual for churches of Puritan religious conduct sanctioned by government and severely restricting ritual and custom. From 1644

Christmas was decreed a fast-day; kneeling and singing in church were forbidden; the sign of the cross could not be given in baptism; godparents were no longer required to assert their faith. Fathers would no longer give brides away and the giving and receiving of rings was removed from the ceremony. Behind closed doors and in Royalist strongholds these customs persisted, of course, but they could no longer be taken for granted and in many places those who resisted the imposition of Parliament's new practices were actively prosecuted.

For all his loyalty to the crown, Richard Fanshawe had decidedly Puritan tendencies – proof, if any were needed, of the blurred ideological lines of the period. Ann held the Catholic-sympathizing Secretary of State, Sir Francis Windebank, a favourite of the Queen, responsible for Richard not being promoted at court in the early 1640s. Windebank, she wrote, had called 'him a Puritan'.[30] It's tempting to attribute the plain black dress Ann is wearing in her portrait to the desire to please her austere husband, though it's just as likely to be simply the best dress she owned at the time. They married at Wolvercote Church, a couple of miles outside Oxford, which was known for being simpler in its liturgy than the churches in Oxford, in thrall to the High Church ideas of Archbishop Laud. (Laud, who had been arrested in 1640, was unsuccessfully tried for treason in the spring of 1644 before being executed, under a bill of attainder, in January 1645 aged seventy-one.)

Their wedding was a small one, but from what Ann reveals, traditional: no one there, she said, 'but my dear father, who, at my mother's desire, gave me her wedding-ring, with which I was married, and my sister Margaret, and my brother and sister Boteler [Richard's sister Joan and her husband Sir William], Sir Edward

Hyde, afterwards Lord Chancellor [a friend of Richard's dating back to their student days in the Inner Temple in the late 1620s], and Sir Geoffrey Palmer, the King's Attorney'.[31] We will have to imagine Ann's sister and sister-in-law preparing her for the flower-heaped marriage bed, helping her into a new shift, bringing her the traditional bride's posset, curded cream enriched with wine and egg yolks and sweetened with sugar and spices, and leaving her to wait for Richard to draw back the bed curtains.

And so Mr and Mistress Fanshawe step onto the stage to begin their life together.

Marriage meant new rules and new roles for Ann to learn. Women, it was thought, were made whole by marriage, spiritually and physically as well as socially. A letter of 1610, from a bride's father to her new parents-in-law, declared, 'none… be properly in the world till they be married'.[32] But if marriage gave a woman status, 'embodied in sexual respectability, the maternal role, reproductive knowledge, and physical authority over other women… [at] the same time it put her body under the authority of her husband'.[33]

A wife's foremost duty was obedience, her husband's tender consideration. Although conduct books might condemn adultery on both sides, encourage love matches (presumably because compliance was easier for both parties when it was willingly offered) and even recommend that wives were consulted and listened to, ultimately good wives were meant to submit to their husbands unquestioningly, as subjects did to the king. 'Iff Ever our fortun's will allow us to marry you shall dispose of mee as you please,'[34] Dorothy Osborne promised William Temple, somewhat disingenuously.

Samuel Pepys – not exactly an ideal husband – described his wife Elizabeth, during an argument, reading out to him part of her diary. It was 'so picquant, and wrote in English and most of it true, of the retiredness of her life and how unpleasant it was, that being writ in English and so in danger of being met with and read by others, I was so vexed at it and desired her and then commanded her to teare it'.[35] Perhaps it's no wonder that his diary, rather than hers, survived.

Examples of bad wives abounded. Sir John Oglander included in his commonplace book this sarcastic account of a housewife's day: 'To go in fine clothes and silver-laced shoes that must not touch the ground, to lie a-bed till ten in the morning and have her breakfast a-bed; never to come down until meat is on the table and, in the afternoon, to ride abroad a-hawking and stay forth till night. Fare high and well, and do nothing.'[36] (His own wife was nothing like this imaginary flippertigibbet, he observed gratefully elsewhere, not trusting her maids to oversee the outhouses but happy to 'wet her own shoes to see it done herself.'[37])

The fact that conduct books were full of exhortations for wives not to be proud, not to seek to 'have their owne rule',[38] not to nag or gossip or speak hastily to their hen-pecked husbands, suggests that real wives were less easy to control than on paper, less worried about the humble feminine ideal presented in Scripture and more concerned with getting on with their daily lives. Just as subjects could not always be relied upon to obey their king, wives could not always be expected to be meek and silent.

In practice, the best kind of wife – as acknowledged in the letters of husband after husband throughout this period – was what historian Amanda Vickery calls the 'sexy battleaxe': an intelligent, energetic woman capable of acting independently, decisive and knowledgeable and fully in command of her own spheres of influence. 'I know I cannot have a better steward than thyself to manage our affairs,'[39] writes one; another calls his wife 'the saver of my estate';[40] 'pray put on the breeches until I come home,'[41] requests another fondly.

Marriage was a seventeenth century woman's career and many of them devoted their considerable talents and energies to succeeding in it, not just in serving their husbands and bringing up their children but in promoting their families' interests, managing their households and estates, and working in their communities. Virtuous wives and widows might feign modesty but many enjoyed playing a more executive role when they got the chance. Margaret Cavendish (stepmother of the playwrights Jane and Elizabeth) said that although her own widowed mother 'would often complain that her family [estate] was too great for her weak management, and often prest my Brother to take it upon him, yet I observe she took a pleasure and some little pride in the governing thereof; she was very skilfull in leases, and setting of Lands, and Court-keeping [presiding over manorial courts], ordering of Stewards, and the like affaires'.[42]

Ann would have no need for these skills in wartime Oxford: no country house with its household staff and tenant farmers to oversee in Richard's absences, no London mansion to fill with evidence of her good taste and throw open for influential guests. Echoes of their happiness can be heard in their few surviving letters to one another, years later, in which they address each other as their dearest soul or life. 'Once more and ever, God bless us all,' Richard concluded one. 'Dearest only love, thine ever.'[43]

Ann conceived her first child the month after their wedding, although not until August or September would she have felt her belly swell and the baby quickening inside her. Young and inexperienced, without her mother to watch over her, she might not at first have recognized the symptoms: no 'courses', cloudy urine, growing 'dull, careless and qualmish, [and] longeth after strange things'.[44] Once she did know she was expecting she would have drunk ginger infusions to relieve morning sickness and endeavoured not to work too hard – or, perhaps more pertinent for the Cavalier bride, dance too energetically. Sex was frowned upon, at least until the last months, and, because babies were thought to be shaped by what their mothers saw and experienced while they were pregnant, funerals were to be avoided – not easy in the Oxford of 1644, living in cramped lodgings in St John's College.

Expectant mothers must have been particularly fearful at this time. It was an era, after all, in which Parliament removing bishops from the Church of England was imagined by Royalist satirists as a whore giving birth to a headless baby; a 1648 play was entitled *Mistris Parliament Brought to Bed of a Monstrous Childe of Reformation*. Lurid accounts of a real baby said to have been born without a head interpreted this foetal abnormality as the reflection of a sinfully disordered society and portent of worse tragedies to come.

Thankfully Richard wasn't a soldier, for the wives of men in service had daily to fear for their lives, too. Poor Cary Verney's husband was killed in a skirmish in July 1645, leaving Cary, at eighteen, not just a widow but seven months pregnant and penniless. She was thrown upon the mercy of her in-laws and, when her baby was born a girl, it was almost a relief because it meant that they would not insist on her raising it in their house and she could go back to her brother's.

Absorbed in her new love and the new life stirring inside her, Ann would have been insulated from outside events but it was impossible to be entirely protected from them. Her sister-in-law Joan's husband Sir William Boteler was killed in late June, barely a month after being a guest at Ann and Richard's wedding, and Richard's ruddy-cheeked, libertine (Ann's word) brother Simon was taken prisoner at the Battle of Marston Moor on 2 July. He had no children of his own but he did have an eight-year-old stepdaughter, Katherine Ferrers, whose mother – Simon's wife – had died the previous year. Richard and Ann arranged for the little girl to be made a ward of court (as an heiress she was valuable) and sent to live with his sister, Alice, Lady Bedell, 'a most worthy woman, and eminently good, and wise, and handsome'.[45]

Earlier in the year, the two sides facing one another at the Battle of Cheriton, for King and Parliament, had chosen the same cry: 'God With Us!'[46] Two months later the Parliamentarian Bulstrode Whitelock (a friend and contemporary of Richard and Sir Edward Hyde as a law student in the early 1620s) spoke at a debate on whether to pursue peace. 'The land is weary of our discords,' he said. 'The creatures are weary and groan to be delivered from them. Children are weary being robbed of their beds and food and of their parents. Women are weary of them being robbed of their children, their chastity and of their husbands. Old men are weary of them being robbed of their rest, of their goods and of their liberty. Young men are weary of them being robbed of their strength, of their limbs and of their lives...'[47]

His appeal was eloquent but it went unheeded. Apparently unwearied by discord, both sides remained determined to defeat their enemies whatever the cost, as this tub-thumping sermon, preached by the Royalist vicar of Barton the same year, shows:

> Let horror and amazement take hold on them, and keep them in a perpetual alarm... Their sons and their daughters that were the joy of their hearts, let them be cut off in the flower of their days; and the wives of their bosoms, let them be given into the bosoms of those that hate them. And when they have seen all this, and a world of misery more than all this, let their last end be like the rest, let them go down to the grave with a tragic and disastrous death.[48]

In December, Agostino, the Venetian ambassador, wrote to the Doge imploring him to summon him home. 'Of my uninterrupted stay of seven years in England two have passed, since I occupied this post, amid the perils of a rude Civil War among an inhuman and barbarous people, with the unbearable expense through the loss on the exchange, the scarcity and the exorbitant taxes, from which none of the foreign ministries is exempt'.[49] It was an impossible situation, he wrote a week later, which not even talk of a truce could ease. 'Into the furnace of these dissensions, the King breathes peace, which only kindles it the more'.[50] If Ann dared hope the times would be more settled when her baby was born, her hopes would be in vain.

CHAPTER 3

1645
Mrs Fanshaw of Jenkins, her receipt to make a Sacke posset, the besst that is

Take 12 eggs, leave out 2 or 3 of the whites, take out the threds and beat them very well, putt them into the basin you make the posset in, halfe a pound of sugar a pint of sack, a nutmeg sliced, mingle them well together sett the basin upon a chafing dish of coals till the liquor is more than bloud warme. Take a quart of cream and when it boyles up skim it and pour it into your basin covering it with a warme plate, setting it upon embers till it be that thickness you like.

Midwives had many methods for telling a baby's sex: the shape of the mother's belly and how she carried it; the clarity or cloudiness of her urine; how (and how nimbly) she got out of a chair; whether the shadows under her eyes were more pronounced on the left than the right. The doctor and herbalist Nicholas Culpeper's guide for midwives suggested the mother squeeze a drop of her milk into a basin of water. 'If it drops in, round as a drop, 'tis a Girl she goes withal, for if it be a Boy, it will spread and swim at the top.'[1] I can picture Ann Fanshawe, like so many expectant mothers, before and since, intent on divining whether she was going to have a girl or a boy, her dark head bent over the bowl as she tried to make out whether the drop had sunk or spread.

When she felt the first contractions, or throws, in her back and belly towards the end of that cold February of 1645, Ann entered the darkened room prepared for her lying-in. Only women were allowed into the lying-in chamber. Special sheets, hangings and nightclothes would have been gathered together, bought or borrowed, whatever could be found to make do in this crowded city far away from home, so that the room was warmly swathed in draperies, the windows and doors covered and a fire blazing, with everything that would be needed – blankets, baby clothes, towels and basins – ready to hand. Even keyholes were covered and, according to custom, all the knots in the room were loosened.

Childbirth linen was precious, handed down from mother to daughter, and often had great sentimental value. A year earlier, a desperate Lucy Heath wrote to a friend from Oxford that everything had been taken from their sequestered estate, even 'denying so much as might bury my deare babe I have now newly lost and to this is added this time when I most neede them being big with childe the takeing away of all my lennin even to my very baby clouts and mantels all of which I confess I much more prize in regard they were the gift of my deare mother'.[2] The first child she referred to, Robert, had just died at nurse; the child she was expecting, John, was born in October 1644 and would die in November. At the same time she wrote to beg official passage for a servant to go to a three-year-old daughter, living with the nurse where little Robert had just died and about whom she had not heard since his death. Lucy's story was tragic but hardly unusual. She would die the following year, aged twenty-seven, leaving a single surviving daughter who would, thirteen years later, marry Richard's cousin, Sir Thomas Fanshawe of Jenkins, and as his wife contribute recipes to Ann's receipt book.

If her mother had been alive, she would have travelled to be by Ann's side, particularly for this first birth, bringing her linen with her. In her shabby rented room in Oxford, Ann must have felt her absence keenly; but she had her receipts, and her sister Margaret, her constant companion through these years, would have been with her, along with her maid and a midwife.

Much of her time before labour began in earnest would have been spent in prayer: for herself, that she survive – fifteen or sixteen of every thousand women died in childbirth at this time[3] – and for her baby, that it be born whole and healthy. Imperfections in a newborn were seen as divine punishment for the parents' sins. 'Lay no more on me than thou wilt enable me to beare,'[4] begged Elizabeth, countess of Bridgewater – the young playwright Elizabeth Cavendish, as a married woman – in a prayer written in time of labour and a reminder that there were no effective painkillers in the seventeenth century. 'Sweet Christ bring me out of this my extremity, and fill my mouth with honour and praise to thee, that I may see this my dear child without any deformity, which sight is of the wonderful mercy of my God, far beyond my sins'.[5]

Death could feel very close. One contemporary and friend of Ann's, Elizabeth, Lady Mordaunt, prayed the Lord would 'grant my child life and opertunety of babtisme, and Lord preserve it from all deformity what soever, give it a cumly body, and an understanding soule, and thy Grace from the Cradell to the Grave'[6] – however long that might be. Mothers prepared themselves in case they did not survive labour, setting their affairs in order and often writing letters to be read by their children if they died. In New England, the poet Anne Bradstreet wrote 'Before the Birth of One of her Children', to tell her unborn baby she loved him in case he never knew her:

> How soon, my Dear, death may my steps attend,
> How soon't may be thy lot to lose thy friend,
> We both are ignorant, yet love bids me
> These farewell lines to recommend to thee,
> That when that knot's untied that made us one,
> I may seem thine, who in effect am none...
> And if change to thine eyes shall bring this verse,
> With some sad sighs honour my absent hearse;
> And kiss this paper for thy love's dear sake,
> Who with salt tears this last farewell did take.

In the warm, candlelit chamber, the midwife would have offered Ann herbal medicines to calm her fears, ease her pains and hasten delivery. Oils of lilies, roses and columbine were all thought to be effective, as was a drink of powdered myrrh in white wine or even, according to one receipt book, a porringer-full of the father's urine. Purgatives like cyclamen – dangerous at any other time – might also be used. The women attending Ann would have mopped her brow with scented cloths, given her sips of caudle, warm spiced ale, and encouraged her labours. Brilliana Harley's receipt book suggested the use of 'hysterick water' during labour, a mixture of black cherry water, surfeit water (a drink to relieve the symptoms of eating and drinking to excess), mugwort water and spirit of castor that would calm panic or fainting fits.[7]

Ann's little boy, whom she named Harrison for her father, was born at nine o'clock at night on 23 February. The midwife would have bathed him in warm water and rubbed him with oil, dabbing his umbilicus with powdered frankincense, an astringent, to stop it bleeding. She would have swaddled him neatly and presented him to his anxiously waiting father before returning to attend to Ann as her shift and sheets were changed and she was made comfortable by her maid and sister. If she had after-pains, one folk remedy involved grilling the afterbirth over a fire until it was dry and then laying it on the woman's belly, wrapped in a coarse cloth. The windows and doors, closed throughout labour, would have been flung open.

Perhaps at first Ann hoped he would flourish, but poor Harrison, who was at least a month premature, must have been sickly from the start, for he would die fifteen days after his birth. About a quarter of children born in this period would die before their first birthday. Like another bereaved mother, Anne Bathurst, Ann may have imagined her baby's soul rising up to heaven, like a bright spark, entering 'into this great Light and [becoming] one with it'.[8]

He'd been baptized the day after he was born, with his uncle Sir Thomas Fanshawe and his grandfather John Harrison as his godfathers and Joan Boteler, Richard's youngest sister who had been present at their marriage, his godmother. Baptism would have been especially urgent if Harrison was not well. It was thought that babies were born in a state of original sin, 'wrapped up in uncleanness', and could not enter heaven unless they had been christened. In a 1618 sermon on the miracle of baptism, John Donne wondered whether any man could 'bring a clean thing out of filthiness?'[9] Only God could cleanse a being conceived in sin and born bathed in blood.

Christenings were, as the historian Diane Purkiss notes, an ideological battlefield during the civil wars. A month before Harrison's birth the newly reformed church had banned godparents at christenings and forbidden vicars from making the sign of the cross over a baby's head; some Puritans were even refusing to baptize babies on the grounds that the children of devout Christians were automatically saved and baptism was something the child needed to be old enough to understand. Families were 'made miserable by the difficulty of getting vulnerable infants baptized by their preferred rite,' explains Purkiss. 'Worried parents tried to do their own homework, anxiously poring over the Bible and pamphlets much as modern parents might agonize over vaccination.'[10] Against Parliamentary strictures, traditionalists like Ann persisted in appointing godparents and held christenings with friendly priests at home, where they could be sure of having the ceremony they wanted.

As the Royalists' position becomes ever less secure, the king decides to send the young Prince of Wales away from Oxford, accompanied by his council, in March 1645. Parliamentary forces unsuccessfully lay siege to the city of Oxford that May. A series of Parliamentary victories, beginning with Naseby in June, all but destroy the king's army. From mid-1645 Royalist defeat

seems inevitable. Prince Charles and his small court retreat further and further west as the Parliamentary forces advance.

Harrison's death was made more dreadful by the fact that Ann had to endure it without Richard by her side. 'Only the argument of necessity' could have persuaded him to leave Oxford on 8 March, following his royal master, the Prince of Wales, to Bristol. It was the first time they had been parted and Richard was 'extremely afflicted, even to tears' to leave his young wife 'with a dying child… in a garrison town, extremely weak and very poor'.[11]

Harrison died two days after Richard's departure and Ann, devastated, stayed in bed. Child mortality rates were so high and so accepted a part of life that her loss was almost commonplace, something she was expected to put behind her: a misfortune rather than a tragedy. Even so, more than twenty years after Harrison's birth and death, her recall of the details is crystal clear: it can't have been easy to forget. 'It cost me so dear,' she wrote, 'that I was ten weeks before I could go alone [get up]'.[12]

With the support of her father and sister and with the aid of 'cordials', little by little she recovered her strength. Ann mentions half a dozen waters in her receipt book that she might have taken as a general cure, from a 'cordiall to be given at the beginning of a sickness' to 'a good restorative after a long sickness', both from her mother, to 'the precious water of wallnutt', which had a myriad uses from infertility to palsy to healing wounds and soothing sore eyes. Surprisingly, only one specifically mentions recovering from labour, though several are credited with raising depressed spirits.

Instead I've chosen for this chapter spiced posset, 'the besst that is', because a good sack posset was not just something for celebrations – it was given to brides and grooms on their wedding night and was always on the menu at lyings-in – but, enriched with egg yolk and cream, was also a nourishing drink for invalids. Sack is fortified white wine, a version of modern sweet sherry, its English name derived from the Spanish verb *sacar*, to draw out, as in drawing wine out of a barrel. Possets were drunk out of posset pots, shaped a little like a teapot made of pottery, the finest ones painted blue and white in the Dutch style (silver would have conducted heat), with a lid and spout, so they could easily be sipped lying in bed.

The receipt came from a cousin of Richard's, a sign of Ann's acceptance and absorption into the Fanshawe family, although with Richard gone it was her father and sister Ann turned to in her illness. As a centre for displaced Royalists, Oxford was full of family and friends, so when she was well enough, Ann had plenty of visitors. Even secluded in her chamber, she was learning about life at court. They came to see her, she said, out of kindness but also because Richard was in such 'good employment' – by which she meant so close to the royal family – that 'they found him serviceable to themselves'.[13]

Sometimes, too, she was fortified by letters from Richard, though correspondence was not easy across battlelines. A Royalist prisoner in London wrote to his friend at court the previous year that 'the Times are so ticklish, that I dare not adventure to send you any London intelligence',[14] that intangible but most valuable of commodities. Susanna, the mother of fifty-two-year-old Edward Nicholas, Secretary of State to the king in Oxford, complained that she hadn't been able to write to him for a long time because she couldn't find anyone to carry her letters from their house in Wiltshire. She was keeping his valuable greyhound locked up, she added, because 'the troopers steal dogs and horses'.[15]

In May, Ann was well enough at last to leave her chamber and go to church, accompanied (by tradition) by the midwife who had delivered her baby. This was her official re-entry into society, the moment she was cleansed from the impurities of childbirth and, crucially, could resume sexual relations with her husband. After the service, Sir William Parkhurst, Warden of the Mint and a friend of her father's, approached Ann with a letter from Richard along with fifty pieces of gold.

Almost overcome with 'inexpressible joy', she and her father went to sit in the spring-filled garden of St John's College and together they read Richard's news. The Thursday following, wrote Richard, he would send two men with horses to accompany Ann, her father and her sister to meet him at Bristol, and Lady Capel and Lady Bradford (wives of other members of the prince's council) would meet them on the way. The gold, wrote Ann with feeling understatement, 'did not so much revive me as his summons'.

Hearing regimental drums beat beneath the garden wall, Ann and Sir John went up onto a hill to watch the soldiers march past, knowing they belonged to their friend Sir Charles Lee's company of foot. In compliment to his audience (one can imagine him doffing his feathered hat with a flourish), Sir Charles ordered his men to fire a volley of shots. One of the muskets was loaded and two bullets went into the tree against which Ann was leaning 'not two inches above my head... for which mercy and deliverance I praise God'. They set off the next week 'very merry, and thought that now all things would mend, and the worst of my misfortunes past', Ann remembered, 'but little thought I to leap into the sea that would toss me until it had racked me'.[16]

For fear of being captured by the enemy, quartered along their route south-west, they planned to ride through the night. They had ridden twenty miles when, as night fell, a troop of horsemen came towards them, bridles jangling through the dim light. These were Cavaliers led by Sir Marmaduke Rawdon, a countryman from Hertfordshire, who, hearing Ann and her party were approaching, had ridden out to conduct them safely past his garrison. Sir Marmaduke rode with them about twelve miles before 'with many thanks we parted, and having refreshed ourselves and horses, we set forth for Bristol, where we arrived on the 20th of May.'[17]

When Ann and Richard were reunited, joyfully he took her in his arms and gave her a hundred pieces of gold, saying, 'I know thou that keeps my heart so well, will keep my fortune, which from this time I will ever put into thy hands as God shall bless me with increase'. It was not avarice that made Ann mention this detail. By trusting her with his 'fortune' Richard was acknowledging her for the first time as a partner in their marriage, transforming their relationship from one between superior and inferior or master and dependent (as the law would have it) to one (at least behind closed doors) between equals, in which both worked lovingly towards a single goal with shared debate alongside individual responsibility.

'Upon which confidence,' Ann confessed, addressing her son, 'I will tell you what happened.'[18] Thinking herself 'a perfect queen' to be doted upon by so wise and good a man, she wrote, Ann had allowed her head to be turned by one of the older, more sophisticated women at court. Elizabeth, Countess Rivers, a Catholic kinswoman of Ann's who had been attacked in her home by a Parliamentary mob in Suffolk in 1642 and had given, so Ann said, thousands of pounds to the king's cause, took Ann aside and 'tacitly commended the knowledge of state affairs', telling her the most fashionable women at court 'were very happy in a good understanding thereof'. News was a commodity, which could be bought (one informative letter-writer was paid £20 a year in the 1630s for his weekly correspondence), but was more valuable when it came from friends and allies, and as such fitted into the system of clientage as a form of exchange, creating and cementing friendships. It was especially suited to the soft power women could wield: Lucy Hay (née Percy), countess of Carlisle, an active intriguer at court, urged her provincial sister to write to Henrietta Maria, reporting back that the queen was pleased to have her intelligence, or news.

She knew, Lady Rivers continued, that a post had just come from the queen in Paris for the king. If Ann could get her husband to tell her what 'the Queen commanded the King', she could tell Lady Rivers. Ann, 'young and innocent, and to that day had never in my mouth "what news", began to think there was more in inquiring into public affairs than I thought of'.[19]

As the notion of Henrietta Maria sending her orders to the king shows, women were very much involved in the civil wars from the bottom of society up. 'Adventurous women'[20] travelling on foot through the countryside brought Royalist newsletters, books and messages to printers and agents in London. In besieged towns, women helped strengthen defences, organized garrison administration and even took part in the fighting; defending Royalist

Chester later in 1645 the women were 'all on fire, striving through a gallant emulation to outdo our men and will make good our yielding walls or lose their lives. Seven are shot and three slain, yet they scorn to leave their undertaking'.[21] Women went in person to submit strongly worded petitions to Parliament, making their voices heard despite the knowledge that they would be dismissed as 'lewd women'. Female spies, like the woman known as 'Parliament Joan' who worked for the earl of Essex, seeking to disrupt the network of underground Royalist newspapers, and whose husband was hanged as a parliamentary spy in Oxford, roamed the armies of Parliament and king to bring intelligence to their friends on either side.

Richard's friend Edward Hyde described the queen in Oxford in 1643 as taking 'pleasure in nothing but knowing all things and disposing all things'.[22] Gathered around her at court were a group of clever, ambitious women who acted as intelligencers, spies, campaigners and fundraisers, not always in the queen's interest: Lucy Hay, countess of Carlisle, and Susan Feilding, countess of Denbigh, were just two of Henrietta Maria's Ladies of the Bedchamber with pronounced political agendas. The power of these women was regarded as dangerous because, predicated on their allure and sexuality, it was wielded in private, behind closed doors, and was therefore impossible to quantify or refute except by seeking to undermine the possessors of it by 'exposing' them as promiscuous.

Lady d'Aubigny, née Lady Catherine Howard, whom Lady Rivers used as an example of this type to Ann, was one of the most prominent of these women. A few years older than Ann, a celebrated beauty married in thrilling secrecy to one of the king's cousins in 1638, she had long been a court celebrity. Her husband was mortally wounded, aged twenty-four, at Edgehill, but Lady d'Aubigny continued to plot on Charles's behalf, obtaining permission after he died to travel to London to settle her affairs and instead trying to raise the city in the king's name alongside the poet and MP Edmund Waller and other conspirators in May 1643. Two were executed while she and Waller were star prisoners in the Tower for a few months – a propaganda coup for Parliament – before being released, upon payment of fines, and fleeing (separately) to Paris to join the queen, who had escaped England in 1644. When Lady d'Aubigny died in 1650 even Sir Edward Hyde, who loathed women interfering in politics (as he saw it), admitted that she was 'a woman of very great wit, and most trusted and conversant in those intrigues which at that time could best be managed and carried on by ladies who with less jealousy could be seen in all companies'.[23]

The other woman mentioned by Elizabeth Rivers was Lady Isabella Thynne, the older sister of Dorothy Osborne's friend Diana Rich. She was a fêted beauty, like Catherine d'Aubigny, but had a bad reputation. Her miserable marriage, according to Osborne, had made her think she could not 'be more undon whatever course' she took, 'O 'tis ten thousand pitty's... in Earnest shee was then the lovlyest thing that could bee lookt on I think'.[24] (Dorothy was writing from a distance of thirteen years; Isabella had been married in 1640 aged eighteen.)

Her name has sometimes been associated with Ann's. In his *Brief Lives* John Aubrey described the vast and ancient president of Trinity College, Dr Kettle, patrolling Trinity Grove which had become, since the court was in Oxford, the Hyde Park or Spring

Gardens of the town, 'the Daphne for the ladies and their gallants to walke in'. Dr Kettle, who kept a pair of scissors in his muff, poised to snip at students' ringlets, heartily disapproved of courtiers invading his domain. Isabella Thynne was lodging next door at Balliol and came often to Trinity Grove 'with a theorbo or lute played before her. I have heard her play on it in the grove myselfe,'[25] remembered Aubrey mistily, who was at Trinity, aged seventeen, in 1643. Isabella was a noted musician; Dorothy Osborne also recalled her speaking and looking and singing and playing 'and all so prittily'[26] and her portrait at Longleat, by Van Dyck, shows her holding a twelve-stringed lute.

> I remember one time this lady and fine Mistress Fenshawe, her great and intimate friend who lay at our college (she was wont, and my lady Thynne, to come to our Chapell, mornings, halfe dressed, like angells) would have a frolick to make a visitt to the President [Kettle]. The old Doctor quickly perceived that they came to abuse [tease] him; he addressed his discourse to Mistress Fenshawe, saying, 'Madam, your husband and father I bred up here and I knew your grandfather; I know you to be a gentlewoman, I will not say you are a whore; but gett you gone for a very woman.'[27]

Much as the story-teller in me would love Aubrey's playful Mistress Fenshawe to be our Ann Fanshawe, the facts don't add up. When Dr Kettle died in 1643, Ann was still Harrison; neither Sir John Harrison nor Richard Fanshawe went to Trinity (Richard was a Jesus College, Cambridge man); they lodged in St John's College, not Balliol. The woman Aubrey refers to was almost certainly Dorothea Fanshawe, wife of John Fanshawe of Parsloes – a cousin of Richard's who did go to Trinity – and daughter of Sir William Kingsmill, who also studied there under Dr Kettle.

But the incident is revealing, nevertheless. It gives a flavour of the courtly world imported to the hallowed groves of academia and the clash between the two cultures. It shows the reverence shown to young and beautiful women, in Aubrey's response to Isabella and Dorothea, and the fury of others at their sway, in Kettle's frustrated and defensive diatribe. Ann herself may not have appeared in Van Dyck or Lely-esque undress at church, like the angels Aubrey remembered, but she would have known them and, being a little younger, perhaps admired them.

Inspired by Isabella Thynne and Catherine d'Aubigny, Ann went to Richard the evening after Lady Rivers spoke to her, when he returned from council, following him into his study. 'He turned hastily, and said, "What wouldst thou have, my life?"' Ann asked what had been in the packet from the queen, which she guessed was in his hand. 'My love, I will immediately come to thee, pray thee go, for I am very busy.' When he emerged, she asked again; he kissed her and changed the subject. At dinner she sulked, even though he repeatedly toasted her, like the gallant Cavalier he was, and was full of conversation with their guests. 'Going to bed I asked again, and said I could not believe he loved me if he refused to tell me all he knew… he stopped my mouth with kisses.' Ann cried herself to sleep.

The next morning he woke, kissed her while she pretended to sleep and drew the bed curtains back around her before leaving for work. That evening he took her in his arms and told her that, although nothing on earth could afflict him like seeing her troubled, and his life, fortune and every thought of his heart were hers, he could not preserve his honour if he communicated royal affairs to her. 'Upon consideration it made my folly appear to me so vile, that from that day until the day of his death I never thought fit to ask him any business but what he communicated freely to me in order to his estate or family.'[28]

Some historians have interpreted this anecdote[29] as evidence of Ann's complete submission to the role of wife, her unquestioning acceptance of the patriarchal times in which she lived – and it is true that she never dreamed of challenging the rules by which her world was organized. I see it, though, as an initiation into adulthood, a spiritual test she needed to pass. Other writers of her age and background included in their accounts of their lives incidents like this,[30] when they were tempted by an older person whom they respected, perhaps for the wrong reasons, into doing something they later regretted. Having learned their lesson, they developed into a more virtuous adult. 'From this moment on,' went the narrative, 'I would be wiser, more discreet, better...'

Lacking her mother to guide her first steps into independent adulthood, Ann always responded strongly to older women who took an interest in her. Her sisters-in-law, Alice Bedell and Joan Boteler, were both more than eighteen years older than Ann and acted as mentors to her; later she would admire several of Henrietta Maria's ladies in waiting, similarly of an older generation, who provided receipts for her book. When she met the Portuguese queen mother in the early 1660s she called her honourable, ambitious and magnificent, observing that 'she loved government and I do believe the quitting of it did shorten her life'.[31] Lady Rivers may have fitted into this pattern of relationship, with twenty-year-old

Ann seeking to emulate a more mature, powerful woman she respected.

Finally, I think Ann also wanted to distance herself from any accusations of intrigue and interfering in politics specifically because those charges would later be levelled against her. For me, she protests a little too much about her discretion and detachment, when frequently in the memoirs and elsewhere we can see the marks of her being fundamentally involved in her husband's career, for good or ill. It is significant that immediately after relating this incident and her Damascene moment in Richard's arms, she described Richard gaining the prince's favour at the expense of his ambitious rival, Sir Robert Long, who had been placed on his council by Henrietta Maria. When Long was discovered to be in communication with the Parliamentarian earl of Essex he fled to France and, as Ann had hoped, Richard briefly became secretary to Prince Charles's council in his place. Mentioning Long a few pages earlier, when she related how he had become secretary initially rather than Richard, she'd added tartly that, though the queen had a great fondness for him, 'the consequence will show the man'.[32] These are not the words of a submissive woman who dared not speak her mind.

Ann's later letters reveal the honesty and directness of their partnership as well as her involvement in Richard's work: writing in the 1660s she needed a code, she said, to tell him privately everything she had to communicate. 'Now, my sense upon the whole business is this,'[33] she began one anecdote, denouncing someone's 'canting language' and calling another 'that foul [fool]';[34] in another letter she warned him to 'take great care what thou sayest to FP, who is to play a double game'.[35] But she was careful not to drop her feminine guard to outsiders: when someone else tried to speak to her about Richard's affairs, she assured her husband she had demurely replied 'that I was very sorry that I was not capacitated to understand the things of state'.[36]

Ann and her family had escaped Oxford just before Parliamentarian troops briefly laid siege to the city, but in Bristol they found another danger: plague. The small court removed to Barnstaple in Devon – 'one of the finest towns in England' – with Ann and Richard following the prince after two days, 'for during all the time I was in the Court I never journeyed but either before him, or when he was gone, nor ever saw him but at church, for it was not in those days the fashion for honest women, except they had business, to visit a man's Court'.[37] How that fashion would change over the next few years.

They stayed in a house belonging to a merchant called Mr Palmer, who owned a hundred-year-old parrot, and tasted the local delicacy – pies made with massards, or mazzards, the native English cherry (as opposed to the sweet cherries and sour cherries which are imports; black cherries were used for medicinal drinks while Morello were eaten for pleasure), and eaten with clotted cream. Ann remembered them as the best she ever ate. A weakness for cherries, like Ann's, was a familiar refrain in seventeenth century writing.

While Ann enjoyed the ripe mazzards and the sea air in Barnstaple – and Prince Charles, aged fifteen, enjoyed being seduced by a ripe beauty called Christabella Wyndham, formerly his nurse – across the country Royalist fortunes were disintegrating into ashes. The siege of Oxford was abandoned in early June as the Parliamentarians, under Sir Thomas Fairfax and Oliver Cromwell, began to amass their forces near Naseby in Northamptonshire.

Defeat at Naseby on 14 June 1645 was conclusive. The Royalist army was all but destroyed and the king suffered the humiliation of losing his personal baggage, including his correspondence. 'And all places, like ripe figgs without pulling [from the tree], fall into the eater's mouth; so disastrous are the consequences of a great battle lost… Now the king, like a hunted partridge, flitts from one garrison to another'.[38] Since he refused to leave England, now Charles could only put off the inevitable day of his capture.

Naseby was memorable too for its aftermath. The victorious New Model Army (a Parliamentary force comprised of professional soldiers rather than part-time militiamen, noted for their Puritanism and political radicalism) massacred over a hundred female camp followers, justifying their violence on the grounds that their victims were Irish (they were in fact mostly Welsh[39]) and thus whores, papists, viragos or even witches. Parliamentarians were enthusiastic pursuers of witches – this was the heat of the witch craze, during which perhaps three hundred men and women in East Anglia were interrogated for being witches and more than a hundred put to death between 1645 and 1647[40] – and the Irish, whom they credited with all sorts of barbaric wickedness. Parliamentary pamphlets before the battle had repeatedly warned of Irish women who wanted to cut the throats of Englishmen with their signature weapon, the skein, a long dagger. Many more women following the Royalist camp had their noses slit, the traditional punishment for whores.

I have been surprised during my research by how infrequently rape is mentioned as an element of the civil wars. During a conflict which killed 190,000 people out of a population of five million[41] – 3.7 per cent of the total, a greater proportion than during World War One – I find it hard to believe it was only seldom used as a weapon of war, even though historians on the whole seem to have accepted that it was rare in this conflict on the grounds that rape is a crime of hatred and violence, and thus less likely to be used where the ideological and ethnic gulf between sides is small;[42] I'm not convinced by this argument. The oblique references I have come across make me think rather that perhaps it was so integral a part of normal life even in peacetime, a daily hazard for women of the lower classes especially, that it was considered worthy of mention only in exceptional circumstances.

As we saw in the previous chapter, even men of God might pray that the wives of rebels 'be given into the bosoms of those that hate them', while in Parliament speakers bemoaned the women who were being robbed of their chastity by the war as if it were a fact of which everyone was aware, as obvious as men losing their lives on the battlefield. One Royalist banner depicted a naked man with an erect penis, holding an unsheathed sword; the motto declared, *In Utrumque Paratus* (Ready to Use Both).[43]

Three months earlier, Sir Marmaduke Langdale – not to be confused with the Marmaduke Rawdon who had so chivalrously accompanied Ann and her party past his garrison that May – had led an army into Parliamentarian-controlled Pontefract. 'This march of theirs was accompanied with many unheard-of cruelties,' wrote Sir Samuel Luke, Parliamentary intelligencer, to his superior officers, in a rare account of sexual violence.

> They robbed all the country people of their goods and took away their cattle. They ravished the women, and bound men neck and heels together and ravished their wives before their faces, and tied women in chairs and ravished their daughters in their sight. One woman they ravished was within a week of her time. A gentlewoman and her daughters travelling along [alone] were ravished by them and the soldiers said frequently that the war was but now beginning.[44]

Two facts were seen as particularly noteworthy – one that a heavily pregnant woman was raped, the other that several gentlewomen were – which indicate that Ann's status would probably have served as some kind of protection from assault, in most cases. Still, the knowledge of violence like this, even if it was largely unspoken, surely served as a menacing backdrop to the times for women of her background – and a very real threat to most women.

The issue of gender during the civil wars is a complex one. Both sides described prominent women on the opposing side as unnatural and on their own as courageous and virtuous. There are exceptions to every rule in this period but, in the main, the Puritan/Parliamentary group, while more egalitarian on its extreme fringes – with, for example, female preachers speaking the word of God – was more likely to view women in general, and Royalist women in particular, as licentious, interfering and ungodly. Female Royalists, starting with Henrietta Maria and including women like Ann, were eager to portray themselves as submissive wives because maintaining the integrity of traditional gender roles was an essential reflection of a well-ordered society:

good wives obeyed their husbands and cared for their children and servants just as good people obeyed their king and fulfilled their roles in the world. The popular image of each side is also revealing: Roundheads were stereotyped as lowborn, humourless cuckolds, while Cavaliers were assumed to be at once effeminate, with their flowing locks and penchant for romance and womanizing, and casually violent.

But through the romance tradition, with its tales of true lovers triumphing over suspicion and separation and wronged rulers regaining their kingdoms, Royalists accepted the parallel between political obligation and the marital bond, both founded on love. This association empowered women within marriage – as Ann was empowered by Richard's love and trust in her – and, where the husband was not as strong or virtuous as Richard (at least as Ann portrayed him), was seen as feminizing men.[45] Parliamentarians drew parallels between dangerously disordered households and dangerously disordered societies.

As a famously uxorious husband, Charles I was especially vulnerable to this criticism. In the last masque held at the Caroline court in January 1640, Henrietta Maria had appeared as an Amazon, the incarnation of the king's conscience, showing her preparedness to risk all for her husband by placing herself firmly in a tradition of warrior queens. His political appeal to women was also considered dubious. Women had been under suspicion less than usual, reported Ambassador Agostino to the Doge early in 1643, although when the earl of Leicester's daughter's house was searched and a catalogue of all Charles's 'partisans' was found there, attitudes hardened: 'the king could not escape the mischief done which is considerable'.[46]

After Naseby, when his private correspondence, much of it with Henrietta Maria, was captured and published by special order of Parliament as *The King's Cabinet*, Charles's image as a weak ruler in sway to his foreign, Catholic, domineering wife appeared set in stone. But Royalists quickly laid out their own interpretation of the royal relationship, transforming the king's flaws into virtues. *A Key to the King's Cabinet*, also published in 1645, argued that the secrets revealed by his letters showed Charles not as tyrannical, duplicitous or ruled by his wife but, on the contrary, the possessor of a loving, noble soul. Gender was irrelevant where political loyalty endured, as this pamphlet defending the queen demonstrated:

> For sirs forbear, do not the world perplex:
> Reason and judgement are not things of sex.
> Souls and their faculties were never heard,
> To be confined to the doublet and the beard.[47]

Ideology aside, Henrietta Maria's greatest impact over the civil war years was on personal feuding between Royalist factions. As early as 1643 her favourites, Lords Jermyn, Digby and Culpeper (no relation to Nicholas, the politically radical herbalist), were ranged against Charles's partisans, of various opinions but broadly speaking headed by Sir Edward Hyde, Chancellor of the Exchequer, and, through him, Richard Fanshawe as well as Edward Nicholas and, usually, Prince Rupert. Simply put, the queen favoured retreat from England and the use of foreign money and armies to invade and take the country back without compromise; the others, more sympathetic to the king's opponents, argued for peace by accommodation with Parliament. It was these internal debates (as well as her private ambitions for her husband) that Ann reflected when she crowed about Richard replacing the queen's man, Sir Robert Long, as Prince Charles's secretary.

But even in 1645 there was more to life than war and politics. By the end of the year, having followed her husband and the Prince of Wales's fugitive court across the country and living out of her couple of trunks at lodgings in Truro, in Cornwall, Ann would have known she was expecting another baby – a baby that, this time, might live.

CHAPTER 4

1646
An excellent Water Gruell for Cleansing a Childbirth Woman

Take a quart of spring water, half a pint of Rhenish wine, 3 spoonfull of whole groots, 2 handful of candied oringo [orris] root, 2 handfull of maydin hayre, boyle this close stopt in a pipkin: You must take this at 3 times, Viz: in the morning early fasting, at 4 of the clock in the afternoon, and when you are in yr bed at night.

As the king evaded capture in England at the start of 1646, his elder son, Charles, Prince of Wales – now the great hope of Royalists of all stripes – backed further and further south-west, away from the Parliamentary forces. Accompanying him was his small council and in its train travelled Richard, Ann, her sister and her father.

From Barnstaple they went to Launceston, where Ann and Richard lodged at Truro, twenty miles beyond, and where Ann boldly defended a small trunk containing the prince's jewels against thieves. From Launceston in February 1646 the small court continued on to Pendennis Castle and Ann, Margaret and their father lodged in Penzance with Richard's brother Thomas and his family. Once again, joy sat alongside despair, for Sir

Thomas and his wife Elizabeth (née Cokaine) buried a daughter in Madron churchyard in December, the month before Ann's father, John Harrison, then fifty-five, got married for the second time to Mary Shadbolt, a Hertfordshire girl who was part of the Fanshawe household.

From Penzance Sir Thomas and Elizabeth Fanshawe and Sir John and the new Lady Harrison set sail for Brittany (narrowly surviving a shipwreck on the way) while Ann, at the beginning of April, followed her husband and the court to St Mary's, the largest of the Isles of Scilly. It was an ill-starred journey from the start. They left what she called their 'house and furniture', worth £200, with a Captain Bluet, taking only two trunks on the sea journey; but when they sent for their possessions later the captain 'said he had been plundered of them, notwithstanding it was well known he lost nothing of his own'.[1] Trust had been dissolved in these upside-down times.

On board the ship taking them from Land's End to St Mary's the sailors mutinied and, with the captain discredited, Richard was forced into the role of mediator, using his own money to pay their wages. 'That night following they broke open one of our trunks and took out a bag of £60 and a quantity of gold lace, with our best clothes and linen, with all my combs, gloves, and ribbons, which amounted to near £300 more. The next day, after having been pillaged, extremely sick and big with child, I was set on shore almost dead in the island of Scilly.'[2]

Ann went straight to bed and woke to find herself in a bed so vile 'that my footman ever lay in a better', in a house partitioned into four, two rooms and two little lofts reached by a ladder, with one room a store for dried fish, in which slept Richard's two clerks, one for Margaret, one for Ann and Richard and one for the servants. Not only that but it was freezing and her 'bed was near swimming with the sea': the landlord insisted weakly that his house only ever flooded at a spring tide. They had no clothes, no food – St Mary's was usually provisioned from Cornwall, which had just been taken by the Parliamentary army, so they were forced to send to France for supplies – 'and truly we begged our daily bread of God, for we thought every meal our last'.[3]

Finally, after three weeks, the little court and its followers, a bedraggled group of some three hundred people from the prince down to his tailors, grooms, laundresses and dwarfs, sailed for Jersey, arriving there thanks to another spring tide, which swept them safely over the rocks in the treacherous harbour ('God be praised'). Sir George Carteret, the island's Governor, was waiting to welcome them 'with all plenty and kindness possible'.[4] (Ever susceptible, Prince Charles immediately fell in love with Carteret's cousin Marguerite.) Ann and Richard and their few servants found good lodgings with a widow in the market place, a stocking merchant called Madame de Pommes, and it was here in early June 1646 that Ann's second baby, a little girl she christened Anne but always called Nan, was born. They would have had to borrow everything: sheets, blankets, bed and wall hangings, baby clothes. Perhaps the midwife gave little Nan something Brilliana Harley recommended for newborns, a few drops of cat's blood in wine, to 'keep it from convulsions though all [babies] she has had before have died as soon as they were born':[5] a kind of sympathetic magic perhaps seeking to harness the cat's supernatural energy.

It was not very unusual to travel immediately before having a baby, though there were always risks – one of John Evelyn's nieces miscarried in the coach on her way home to give birth, and Isabella Twysden, whose Royalist husband was in prison in London in 1645, rode pillion behind her servant George Stone from Peckham to Kent at eight months so she could be at home for her lying-in. (The baby, when he came, was named Charles.) Writing twenty years later Ann seems unfazed by what was clearly quite an ordeal; but then this baby was born healthy, which surely was all she remembered afterwards.

Nan was given over to the care of a wet nurse, as babies of women of status almost always were, while Ann remained in bed for a few days before she would be allowed to begin 'upsitting' (as it was known), when she could get up, though not leave her room. After another few days, depending on her health, she would begin to move around inside the house and finally, when she was churched, she would receive communion and once more take her place in society, and in her husband's bed. By tradition each stage of lying-in was accompanied by celebrations and special food and drink for the women who had been with her at the birth.

Remaining in their lying-in chamber allowed women to recover from labour and let their milk dry up. This 'gruell' is one of the least legible recipes in Ann's receipt book but it is the only remedy of over a hundred she includes that mentions recovering from childbirth. (There is one other, a 'vulnerary liquor' supplied by Sir Kenelm Digby, of whom more later, made of powdered crabs' eyes in vinegar, recommended as a 'great strengthener of the inner parts' and for expelling gravel, or small kidney stones, for ulcers and 'for women in labour', rather than recovering afterwards.) It is almost impossible to read some of the ingredients for the gruel but they include maiden hair fern, traditionally used to reduce inflammation and expel heat and phlegm, orris root, or iris root, a raspberry-flavoured diuretic that can help ease swelling and inflammation, and 'groots', probably groats, or nutritious whole oats.

It wouldn't have been difficult to make, if the ingredients were available in remote Jersey, and along with caudles and possets and broths would have strengthened Ann as she prepared to follow Richard wherever he needed to go next. Happily, she wasn't ill. Avoiding infection was key in the period of recovery after labour: puerperal or childbed fever and milk fever were ever-present fears in the first week or so after birth in this pre-penicillin age. Tight corsets, worn by women from early childhood, often caused inverted nipples, which could add to the danger of infection and, potentially, gangrene. Calamine plasters were used to soothe engorged breasts, or plasters of linseed oil, honey and butter; midwives told women to wear black wool in their armpits to help their milk dry. Sage ale and possets would also help her milk stop flowing.

Not breast-feeding meant that a woman could more easily become pregnant again as soon as she was churched and resumed sexual relations with her husband, rather than once the child was weaned. (Apart from breast-feeding delaying the return of ovulation, sex with a breast-feeding woman was thought to spoil her milk.) There was no concept of contraception as we'd understand it today: a woman's role in life was to bear children, and interfering with God's divine plan by seeking to control when and how many children she might have would have been not just sinful but unthinkable. For gentry families like the Fanshawes in particular, to whom family and inheritance meant everything, the more children a woman had, the greater the chance a son and heir might make it to adulthood.

Very few people seemed to realize that babies sent to nurse had a higher mortality rate than those nursed by their mothers. One in five boys born to the British aristocracy died in their first year as compared to one in seven born to lower-status families between 1550 and 1700; about a quarter of children born under the Stuarts would die before the age of ten.[6] It wasn't that their health suffered from being nursed by another woman, but wet nurses couldn't always be relied upon to care for their charges as they would their own baby: malnutrition was a risk, albeit not well understood, and 'overlaying' – where a sleeping nurse rolled onto a sleeping baby and smothered it – was frighteningly common. Missing out on colostrum, popularly rejected as witches' milk, with its richly immunizing properties, aggravated these risks.

Almost every seventeenth century writer who mentioned this topic had lost children at nurse themselves, from the doctor and herbalist Nicholas Culpeper to John Evelyn. The countess of Lincoln, whose 1622 treatise on breast-feeding was inspired by the deaths of 'one or two of my little Babes [she had eighteen in total]... by default of their nurses', argued passionately that noblewomen ought to nurse their own children. It was unnatural to thrust your own child away and entrust it to a 'lesse tender heart';[7] besides which it was wrong to hire others to do the work you ought to do, causing another poor woman to banish her own child in favour of yours, for the sake of making a living.

But for a woman like Ann the arguments against breast-feeding were more persuasive. As Lady Lincoln admitted, many women found it 'troublesome... noisome to ones clothes, [and]... makes one look old'. Others protested it would damage their health and, perhaps more pertinently, it was seen as unfashionable and lower class. Lady Lincoln, who had not nursed her own children, admitted, 'partly I was overruled by anothers authority, and partly deceived by some ill counsell, & partly I had not so well considered of my duty in this motherly office'.[8] There may have been a more modern aspect to this as well, in that a breast-feeding mother might have been a less independent and thus less effective wife to her husband and manager of her estate; if she wasn't nursing a baby she could be more active – concentrating on her career as a wife by delegating her responsibilities as a mother.

Giving a child to a wet nurse did not mean its parents didn't love it: Stuart parents were accustomed to the idea of living apart from their children, especially in their early years. A healthy wet nurse and fresh country air were believed to give a child the best possible start in life; it would then return home aged two or three ready to become a full member of the family. A baby girl, sent out to nurse in 1630, brought with her more than a hundred articles from home, from sheets and pillows and counterpanes to gloves and a whistle. Another nurse received 4 shillings a week and two loads of firewood, to ensure her house was warm; the little boy's mother reported to his father that though the nurse looked 'like a slatterne... truly she hath toe as fine children of her owne as evor I sawe,' adding fondly that theirs was a 'lovely baby'.[9] For all the horror stories of overlaying and neglect there were many cases of profound affection on both sides, with nurses becoming valued members of households and adults remembering their nurses in their wills or providing them with homes or a pension in their old age. (Prince Charles's subsequent relationship with Mrs Wyndham was, presumably, highly unusual.)

Choosing a wet nurse was notoriously difficult since her traits were thought to be communicated to the baby through her milk. Women who squinted or had crooked posture or bad teeth were inadvisable; ideally she should be young and healthy, with 'a merry, pleasant, cheerful countenance, a ruddy colour, very clear skin that you may see her veins through it' and an evident love for children which would make her the fittest carer for them. A wet nurse should be a recent mother, preferably with a baby of her own younger than two months old; she should also suckle a boy if she had a boy of her own, and a girl if she had a girl. Let her exercise, recommended Nicholas Culpeper, for exercise caused 'good digestion, good digestion good Blood, good Blood good Milk, good Milk a thriving Childe'.[10]

Nan must have thrived, for unlike Harrison a year earlier her christening was held a week after her birth, without any sense of urgency. There was no question for Ann of christening her children 'with out gossips [godparents], the nue waye'.[11] Instead little Nan would have worn a white robe – fashioned out of something someone had in their baggage or perhaps borrowed from Ann's new friends, the Carterets – and presided over a small feast that usually included marchpane and marmalade (a dense jelly rather than a loose jam), wine, sugared biscuits, cakes and comfits. Her godfather was Sir Edward Hyde, Richard's old friend and colleague on the council, and her godmothers were the countess of Brentford – the wife of the Prince of Wales's Chamberlain, a notorious drunk whose nickname was Rothwein, a pun on his surname, Ruthven – and Lady Carteret, a friend of only a few weeks, married to the welcoming Governor of Jersey; the same sort of age as Ann, married about the same length of time. Nan's three guardians would have done their best, despite the difficult times and living out of trunks and cloak bags, to give her something traditional like a porringer or an apostle spoon or a piece of coral mounted in silver, which served a dual purpose both as a teething ring and a protection from witchcraft.

The king flees Oxford in disguise just before it falls to the Parliamentarian army in June 1646. He hands himself over to the Scots Presbyterians, formerly his enemies, and opens negotiations for an alliance with them against Parliament. His younger son James, duke of York, is captured and taken to London a prisoner. In Jersey the Prince of Wales considers his options.

Once the prince's court was settled on Jersey his council met to discuss his future. Lord Culpeper argued on behalf of the queen that the Prince of Wales should join his mother in exile in Paris, where she had apparently secured the support of Cardinal Mazarin, the French king's Chief Minister, but Hyde and Lords Capel and Hopton did not believe the prince should leave British soil. The debates 'begot some warmth and contradiction between persons,' wrote Hyde with evident understatement, soon afterwards, 'inso much as the Prince thought it very necessary to suspend the debate until the next day'.[12] Even once Charles had expressed the desire to go to France, convinced by his father's argument that there he would at least be safe, there were 'sharp replies between the lords of different judgements, which made the council break up the sooner'.[13]

The prince departed for Paris on 25 June, having signed an order for Richard to be repaid 2008 *livres* (as opposed to English pounds) he had lent him and written to the marquess of Ormonde, Lord Lieutenant of Ireland, recommending Richard for employment in his service. Abroad, the young prince had no need of a council; with the council disbanded, Richard needed a new job. Also unemployed and, despite their loyalty to the king, out of favour with Henrietta Maria, Lords Capel and Hopton and Sir Edward Hyde planned to remain on Jersey for the moment, staying with the Carterets.

Hyde was to be there almost two years, working on the first part of his *History of the Rebellion*, begun in Scilly that March. The future earl of Clarendon was one of Richard's oldest friends; they had been students together at Middle Temple in the late 1620s. While Richard turned away from law to poetry and diplomacy, Hyde persevered, although his scholarly interests – historical and literary – would always remain preeminent. Witty as well as learned, he was, according to Samuel Pepys, the best speaker of his generation.

Like Richard, he was not an unquestioning Royalist, beginning his Parliamentary career as a critic of the king. By 1642, however, he had become a valued royal advisor and his devotion was unswerving, though his politics always remained moderate and conciliatory. Where some of Charles's favourites encouraged him to hope he might somehow return to the throne with absolute power like European monarchs – that was why Henrietta Maria and her friends were so willing to rely on foreign aid, rather than negotiating with Parliament – Hyde was always in favour of a constitutional system. He ascribed Charles's downfall to the fact that he listened to men (and women) whose judgement was worse than his own. As a man, Hyde was defined by his integrity and moral certainty; as an advisor, by his scholarship; as a friend, by his charm and loyalty. His enduring weakness was for food, attested by his plump face in portraits and the hungry descriptions scattered through his extensive, endearingly affectionate correspondence.

Although Hyde opted to remain in Jersey, Richard and many other friends began to scatter into exile. There was no future for them in a Parliamentary England and scant hope, for the moment, in a captive king or his teenaged heir. Endymion Porter, formerly one of Charles's Gentlemen of the Bedchamber, was sent to Paris with letters for the queen, but found he was greeted coldly. He had arrived in the riding suit in which he'd left England, with no money and no thought of where he might end up. 'Here in our court, no man looks on me, and the queen thinks I lost my estates from want of wit rather than from my loyalty to my master,' he told Sir Edward Nicholas, then in Caen. But he had no regrets: 'God be thanked, I know my own heart, and am satisfied in my conscience, and were it to do again I would as freely sacrifice all without hope of reward as I have done this'.[14]

Some went alone and in haste, like Porter, taking just the clothes they stood up in; others disguised themselves for fear of capture and trial for treason; still others could afford to travel in some style, bringing their families and retinues with them. Many believed, more through hope than conviction, that they would be home before too long, either once the king had come to terms with Parliament and the Scots or if, by some miracle, a force of Royalist Scots and Irish soldiers could be assembled to sweep him back onto his throne. No longer young, Edward Nicholas wrote to yet another fellow exile the following year to express his 'hope that it will not be long before we hear that peace in England is in so good forwardness, as that honest men may return in comfort to their homes'.[15] He could not have guessed that he would remain away from his beloved Wiltshire farm for another thirteen years, quite something for a man already in his fifties.

The decision to abandon their homes and possessions, their country, their past and their looked-for futures, was never easy. 'I pray send word what shall be done with your trunk which lies buried at my house,' Edward Nicholas's brother Matthew wrote to him from Wiltshire early in 1646, 'for I expect every day to have my goods carried away and my wife and children turned out of doors, my estates being seized on'.[16] He could still find someone he trusted to bring Edward £100, if he needed it, but for himself he dared not leave home. Propertied royalists had their estates sequestered, or confiscated, by Parliament: goods seized, houses leased to tenants, rents and thus income taken, sheep and cattle sold, trees cut down and pasture ploughed up. The only way to get them back was by compounding (literally, to accept a financial settlement in lieu of prosecution for treason), paying a fine and formally submitting to Parliament with an oath of loyalty.

Sir John Harrison returned to England before October 1646, when his and Mary's son was born (named Richard for his uncle), and compounded for Balls Park, the confident expression of his self-made wealth commissioned and built less than a decade earlier, before (as the Royalist ballad went) the world turned upside down. Compounding fines – usually about a tenth of an estate's value, sometimes as much as a third – were on top of any money spent, given or loaned, for example to the crown or to displaced or unemployed relations, in the Royalist cause. Dorothy Osborne reckoned her father's income had been reduced by ninety per cent from £4000 to £400 per annum during this period and it would not be unreasonable to estimate that Sir John's had been reduced by a similar proportion. But £400, in a world where an annual rent for a comfortable house in the country might be £60 and a maid's annual salary was about £3, was still enough to live like a gentleman. Extravagances like laced and embroidered silk court clothes, which might cost up to £100, were no longer possible; essential marks of status like family portraits, which might cost £10, were still just affordable.

Ralph Verney, who had defied his loyal father to side with Parliament in 1642, had changed sides within a year of his father's death on the battlefield as the king's standard bearer by refusing to sign the Covenant, an oath of loyalty to the Parliamentary regime, and attracting an order of sequestration, or confiscation by Parliament, on the family estate, Claydon, in Buckinghamshire. The following year he fled England as a delinquent (a term used by Parliament to describe dissenters to its rule, interchangeable with malignant), under the name Ralph Smith, taking with him his wife Mary, their two elder children, Mun (Edmund) and Peg, and a 'man and mayde'.[17] Their four-year-old, Jack, was left with servants at Claydon, which was vested in trustees to avoid sequestration; their London house was 'leased' to four friends, also 'to prevent sequestration',[18] as he wrote in a secret legal document; their valuables were hidden in London; and they took with them fifty-one parcels of linen, pictures and personal items.

When the order of sequestration was imminent, in late 1645, Ralph was warned by a friend still sitting as an MP – Roger

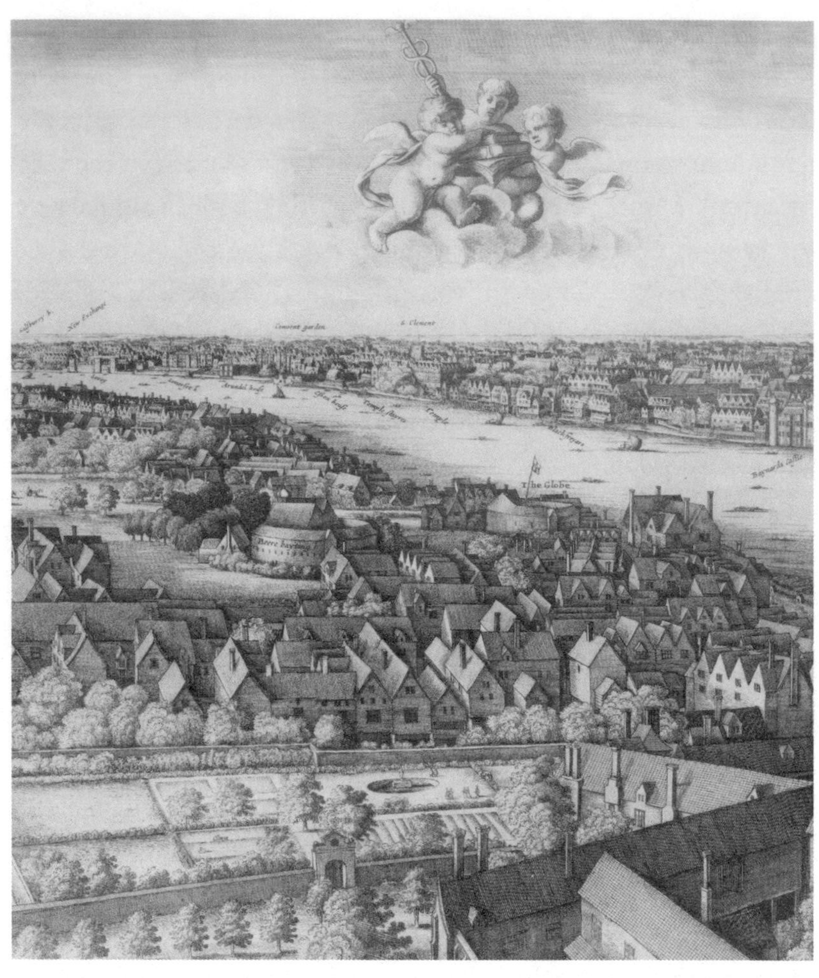

Part of Wenceslaus Hollar's panorama of London from Bankside, made in Antwerp in 1647. He relied on old engravings: 'The Globe' was actually the Hope Theatre and the Bear Garden (or 'Beere Bayting') was the Globe.

Burgoyne, code-named Mr Good in Ralph's correspondence with his wife – in time to send Mary back to England to petition against the order. 'Certainly it would not do amiss if shee can bring her spirit to a soliciting temper and can tell how to use the iuyce of an onion sometimes to soften hard hearts,'[19] wrote Mr Good. Ralph's uncle echoed this a few months later. 'Women were never so useful as now', pleading before the Parliamentary committees for compounding: 'their sex entitles them to many privileges'.[20]

After much thought, Richard Fanshawe decided to go to Caen, where his brother Thomas, to whom he was devoted, was seriously ill. Entrusting Nan to a nurse under the guidance of Elizabeth Carteret, who had quickly become so fast a friend that Samuel Pepys later described her and Ann as 'like sisters'[21] at this time, they left Jersey for France in early August. After two weeks in Caen, Ann, accompanied by her sister Margaret and her maid, boarded a small merchant ship headed for Cowes on the Isle of Wight and arrived in London two days later. The plan was that she would raise what money she could and procure a pass for Richard to join her in England. 'This was the first time I had taken a journey without your father, and the first manage of business he ever put into my hands,' she wrote, 'in which I thank God I had good success.'[22]

She lodged with Richard's recently widowed sister Joan Boteler in Fleet Street, in rooms belonging to a watchmaker called Mr Eates. Mary Verney, also in London on her husband's business in the autumn of 1646, found a chamber for herself and another for her maid for 12 shillings a week, with breakfast, washing, candles and firewood all extra. 'All provisions are most extreamly dear... Fammin is very much feared,'[23] she reported to Ralph. London was packed and, although she was pregnant, she was walking everywhere because taking a sedan chair or a hackney coach was 'infenett dear',[24] eighteen pence for a coach for an hour's hire.

Ralph and Mary Verney felt the pain of being apart keenly, as Ann and Richard must have done. Struggling to find a patron who would argue their case with the powers that be (Ralph's Parliamentary-inclined godmother, the countess of Sussex, was proving unhelpful and Mary had not given her the guitar and watch she had brought as sweetening presents for her), Mary wrote despairingly to Ralph, her 'dearest Roge [rogue]', 'my dear heart I must tell you if I had known what it had been to me to be parted so far from thee I should never have done it'. 'Dear Hart, dear Budd,' Ralph wrote back, 'were I to meet thee there [at Blois, where they hoped to be reunited] I should ride night and day: for till now I never knew the sorrow of separation'.[25] He still managed to boss her about, even from a distance, telling her which present should be given to whom and reminding her to practise her guitar and her French and to read her devotions daily.

Private devotions were a necessity, because London's churches were so crowded that Mary found on Sundays she had to drive (in one of those maddeningly expensive coaches) from church to church to find one that had a spare seat, and then 'when one getts roome, one heares a very strange kind of sarvis, and in such a tone that most people doe noething but laughe at itt'. Truly, she said, 'one lives like a heathen in this place'.[26]

Like Mary, Ann sought out a family friend with Parliamentary connections, in her case a Colonel Copley, 'whose wife had formerly been obliged to our family'. These sorts of relationship became hugely important during this period, a spider's web of favours sought and given up and down the social scale as well as horizontally across it to friends, family and more distant kin. The seeking of advantage was a constant refrain throughout Ann's memoirs and must have felt constant throughout their lives, something that made people feel they were important and active in the world as much as something to be complained about. It was a necessary adjunct not just to court life but to life in general. When they were in Oxford in the early 1640s Richard was managing the attentions of people who wanted something from him as secretary to Prince Charles's council, but (as Ann proudly observed) no one was better than him at distinguishing between true friends and opportunistic ones.

The colonel arranged for Richard to petition to compound for £300, 'but it was only a pretence, for your grandfather was obliged to compound for it [pay it], and deliver it us free'.[27] While he waited to hear of his own fine, Sir John still had enough ready cash to help his daughter; that would not always be the case.

By Christmas, Ann and Richard were reunited in London, though any merriness would have taken place behind closed doors and shuttered windows, with festivities, celebrations and even sermons, when the 25th didn't fall on a Sunday, banned by Parliamentary order. In 1646 there would be no eating of mince pies or plum pudding, no holly- and ivy-trimmed houses or churches, no playing of cards or bowls, hawking or hunting, no money given to the servants or apprentice boys, no gifts of food or drink sent to friends.

Probably this enforced joylessness suited Richard and Ann. 'In daily fears of being imprisoned before he could raise money to go back again to his master,' Richard remained 'very private'.[28] At least they had another baby to look forward to: Ann was expecting once again.

CHAPTER 5

1647
The Flowre of Oyntments

Taken Rosen and parozen of each halfe a pound, Virgin Waxe & Frankincense of each a quarter of a pound, of Harts Tallow a quarter of a pound, of Camphire two Drams, of Mastick once ounce. melt that which is to be melted, and make powder of that which is to be made in powder, boile it well & straine it into a Bottle of white Wine & all the other stuffe together. Let it coole a while, then put thereto of Turpentine a quarter of a pound. Stirre it well together till it be cold. Keepe for the best oyntment or Salve on warrantize.

The Vertues of this Oyntment: 'Tis good for all manner of wounds, for the Head Ache, for ye singing in the Braine, for all Imposthumes in the Head or Body, for Sinews that be shrunke or sprained, it draweth out any thorne or broken bone from a wound, It is good for the biting of any evill Beast, for Festure, Canker or Nole me tangere, it draweth out all ache from the Liver, Spleen or Reines [kidneys], it breaketh the Imposthumes, good for swelling in the Members, easeth the Fluxe and of the Emrodes [haemorrhoids] & healeth them very faire and is spetiall good to make a Seare Cloth.

Ann and Richard stayed quietly in London, at lodgings in newly built Portugal Row, along the south side of Lincoln's Inn Fields (near where Richard had studied as a young man), until October 1647, living 'upon thorns',[1] as Ann put it, of guilt, worry and fear of exposure.

On 14 January, with the help of Ann's Parliamentary contact Colonel Copley, Richard's petition to compound for a fine of £300 was approved. Copley must have been an effective agent, because despite his well-known delinquency Richard's case went through the House with impressive speed, although perhaps this was as much to do with his lack of property as Copley's guidance; the Verneys, pursuing their suit at the same time but for an extensive estate, found it dragged on and on.

For Ann and Richard the process of compounding seems to have been relatively straightforward; the decision behind it must have been the hard part. Both options open to them were bleak: stay abroad, away from home and penniless, in the train of a prince who could not afford to maintain even a skeleton court and, as a minor, remained in the care of his overbearing mother with whose opinions on the nature and limits of royal authority they disagreed; or submit to an enemy regime that was determined to keep them if not imprisoned then confined, poor, impotent and idle. Ann and Richard's solution was to compound and lie low in order to rejoin Charles when they could; Richard found a way to swear his oath of loyalty to Parliament with his fingers metaphorically crossed.

Although many anxious Royalists came to this decision, others deeply disapproved of making any settlement with Parliament. Sir Edward Hyde wrote angrily to Lady Dalkeith, little Princess Henriette's governess in Paris, that there was 'no news from England or France but that of a multitude of men of honour running to compound'.[2] This was October 1646; he may well have had his honourable old friend Richard Fanshawe in mind. By January 1647, just after Richard heard the decision of the compounding committee, Hyde was writing impatiently to find out where he was as the Prince of Wales's council was due to meet once again to debate what his next move should be.

While Ann was preparing for the birth of her third child, Richard distracted himself by writing poetry: an account of the ordeal of his friend and former master, the earl of Strafford, whom Richard had served in the late 1630s and whose execution Charles I had reluctantly approved in 1641 and bitterly regretted to his dying day, and the translation of *Il Pastor Fido*, an Italian pastoral written in the 1580s. It was privately published as 'The Loyall Shepherd' in 1647, with a commendatory verse by John Denham, a poet who also worked as an encipherer for Prince Charles, and dedicated to the prince as a 'tribute for my hours of vacancy'. Even away from his master, Richard felt himself to be serving him. It was only a light play about shepherds and their loves, Richard wrote, but it could be looked upon as a parable for their times; and he expressed the hope that its happy ending might be reflected in 'the sad Originall… [with] your self a great Instrument of it'.[3]

One consolation was a healthy son, Henry, born at the end of July, but 'this was a very sad time for us all of the King's party'.[4]

In January 1647, the king is handed over to Parliament by the Scots in exchange for withdrawing from Newcastle, which they have captured, as well as £100,000 in cash and the promise of further payments. Charles is held prisoner at Holdenby Hall in Northamptonshire until early June, when he is seized and taken in the name of the New Model Army to Newmarket. There he summarily rejects the Heads of Proposals, a surprisingly generous offer of amnesty from prominent Parliamentarians Oliver Cromwell and Henry Ireton which promises religious toleration and to dismiss the Long Parliament, with new parliaments elected every two years. Still Charles hopes that some miracle might make him truly king again, in deed as well as name. He refuses to compromise. From Newmarket he is taken to Hampton Court where he is held prisoner through the autumn of 1647.

Throughout that summer of 1647, fruitless negotiations continued between the king and his captors and Richard was often with Charles at Hampton Court, the king 'pleased to talk much [to him] of his concerns'.[5] Soon after his last council meeting Charles told Richard he should go as his ambassador to Spain, one of his last diplomatic acts. Richard could not, of course, hope to be paid; Charles was reduced to promising him, for his maintenance, the proceeds of a consignment of fish sent to Bilbao nearly a decade earlier, if only he could track down the merchant involved and extract the money from him.

Ann saw the king three times, 'both as I was the daughter of his servant, and wife of his servant'. The man she met can be seen in his last portrait by Peter Lely, once his official portraitist. The earl of Northumberland was the Parliament-appointed guardian of Charles and Henrietta Maria's middle children: Princess Elizabeth and Henry, duke of Gloucester, aged ten and five, were living at Northumberland's house, Syon Park, not far from Hampton Court; the eldest and youngest, Charles and Henriette, were with their mother in France; fifteen-year-old Princess Mary was living in Orange with her husband, William. Twelve-year-old James, duke of York, was based at St James's Palace, under close watch, but was allowed to come often to Syon when his father was at Hampton Court. Northumberland commissioned portraits of the royal children and a double portrait of the king with James, which was apparently painted on his visits to Syon and for which he paid £20.

Storm clouds billow behind them. Charles holds a folded letter and is either giving or receiving something, perhaps a key, from his son; they stare intently at one another, locked in their own world, excluding the viewer. Charles is no longer the radiant mounted sovereign or the warrior-king in armour of earlier portraits but an exhausted man, sad and apprehensive. He has not lost his royal dignity but it is hard to see any hope in his face. To his followers, the nobility of his 'grief triumphant' and 'victorious sorrow' (as the Cavalier poet Richard Lovelace described his expression in 'To My Worthy Friend Mr Peter Lilly') only enhanced the glory of his 'clouded majesty', deepening their commitment to him and his cause.

At her last visit, bidding him farewell before they embarked on their mission to Spain, Ann could not hold back her tears as she wished her king a long and happy life. Charles stroked her cheek and said, 'Child, if God pleaseth, it shall be so, but both you and I must submit to God's will, and you know in what hands I am.' Then he turned to Richard: 'Be sure, Dick, to tell my son all that I have said, and deliver those letters to my wife; pray God bless her! I hope I shall do well.' He took Richard in his arms. 'Thou hast ever been an honest man, and I hope God will bless thee, and make thee a happy servant to my son, whom I have charged in my letter to continue his love, and trust to you… I do promise you that if I am ever restored to my dignity I will bountifully reward you both for your service and sufferings.'[6] The 'both' is important: their loving, gentle master was recognizing the service and suffering of Ann as well as Richard.

Then 'by the folly, to give it no worse name', of a group including Sir John Berkeley and John Ashburnham (the only names Ann gave), in November 1647, Charles allowed himself to be persuaded to escape from Hampton Court after receiving a letter, possibly genuine, threatening his life. It's likely that Parliament knew of the plot to free the king from the start: Ann was in no doubt that 'the cursed crew of the standing army for the Parliament'[7] had drawn the conspirators in. Through misadventure as much as anything else, the weak, beleaguered king ended up in Carisbrooke Castle on the Isle of Wight an enemy prisoner rather than the gentleman captive he had been at Holdenby and Hampton Court.

Across the Channel in France, the king and queen's frustrated supporters were splintering into rival factions. Grievances and resentments dating back to wartime Oxford between partisans of Henrietta Maria and those hostile to her but loyal to Charles, like Prince Rupert, sparked into duels: picture the swish of angrily flounced capes, the tossed heads of curls, the booted footsteps striding away down long corridors. On one occasion Prince Rupert challenged his old foe Lord Digby to a duel. Hearing of the argument, Henrietta Maria sent her favourite, the deeply unpopular Henry Jermyn (feelingly described by Andrew Marvell as being 'full of soup and gold'[8]), to stop Digby going to meet him. George Digby managed to insult Lord Jermyn so grievously that Jermyn ended up offering his services to Prince Rupert as his second. In the end, it took Prince Charles turning up with guards to the appointed place, a remote crossroads in a forest near the palace of Saint-Germain-en-Laye, to stop the fight.

At about the same time, Ann and Richard packed their trunks again and began their journey to Spain, loyally obeying their captive, impotent king. Ann did not say how they expected to leave England, given that Richard was well known to Parliament as a malignant; nor did she comment on the quixotic nature of Richard's role as 'ambassador' to a prisoner rather than a monarch.

While they waited for their ship they went for a walk along the shore. Bullets fired from a Dutch ship (sent in support of her father by Charles's daughter Mary of Orange), in a skirmish with Parliamentary ships just off the coast, whizzed past them so close they could hear them whistling through the air. Terrified, Ann started to run back, calling to Richard to make haste; unruffled, Richard continued to walk, saying calmly, 'If we must be killed, it were as good to be killed walking as running.'[9] They embarked the next day, stopping at Jersey to collect fifteen-month-old Nan from Lady Carteret, but on their arrival in France they decided to return home, for the moment abandoning their plans to go to Spain.

At Ware, preparations for a family wedding were under way, a reminder that for all the upheavals and tragedies of the civil wars normal life would still endure. Richard's brother Simon's ward, the young heiress Katherine Ferrers, who had been living with Lady Bedell, Richard's sister Alice, at Hamerton in Huntingdonshire, was betrothed aged thirteen to a Fanshawe nephew, Thomas, son of Thomas – a neat way of keeping her inheritance in the family.

Richard's other sister, Joan Boteler, recently widowed by the wars, was also celebrating her marriage to Sir Philip Warwick, then serving as secretary to the king in his captivity at Hampton Court and Carisbrooke. Other families might cross party lines, with siblings or parents and children choosing different political allegiances, but there were no divided loyalties among the Fanshawes.

Ann was close to both of Richard's sisters, as evidenced by the number of receipts she included from them in her receipt book (they are second and third to her mother), but thoughtful, honest Sir Philip seems to have become a particular friend. He contributed four medical receipts to Ann's book, including the alarming sounding 'opening pills' and a drink 'admirable against a cold', packed with hyssop, liquorice, raisins and aniseeds, evidence that sharing recipes was not exclusively a feminine domain but something that crossed gender barriers. Family ties, background and political associations were far more important in establishing these links, which men and women seem to have enjoyed on equal terms.

This was a time when gift-giving – in which are included the sharing of receipts – had a special significance. In a society shaped, as the historian Susan Vincent writes, 'by the networks of patronage and clientage, and where the personal merged with the official, gift exchange was a strongly cohesive force. The offering and accepting of gifts both created and fulfilled obligations and in some sense bound giver and recipient together. The giving and receiving of objects, and the objects themselves, thus gave material expression to relationships'.[10]

The wonderfully named Flowre of Oyntments was given to Ann by Richard's sister Joan. There are fourteen receipts from Joan in the book in total, six medical remedies and eight cookery recipes, in addition to her new husband Philip's four. Over the years, Ann would often stay with Joan and Philip at their house, Frogpool, in Kent, and they must have spent time together in Frogpool's still-room and kitchens making up receipts, perhaps this very one. It assumes quite a high level of competence with its 'melt that which is to be melted and make powder of that which is to be made powder of', no mean feat when dealing with various gums, resins, tallows and turpentine.

Its active ingredients are fragrant frankincense (anti-inflammatory and antimicrobial), camphor (used in Tiger Balm: antimicrobial and a gentle local anaesthetic, with that wonderful warm smell, and good for circulation) and mastic (antioxidant, antibacterial and antifungal, as well as a binding agent) in an oily base. Its virtues, according to the receipt book, were multiple. A familiar feature of contemporary receipt books (Culpeper found a version dated 1513), sometimes known as the 'yellow salve', the Flowre of Oyntments was 'good for all manner of wounds' including animal bites and broken bones, for headaches, tinnitus, sprained muscles, aching liver and spleen, abcesses, cankers and dysentery. If only there had been an ointment like this for healing the broken body politic.

Back in Hertfordshire for a few months, Ann would have been close not only to the Fanshawes but also to her beloved father and his new wife and son. Their fate was a reminder that although friends and family could be a consolation for the war, times were still bleak for those on the losing side. John Harrison's compounding case was settled in December 1647, with his fine levied at £10,745, half the value of his estate. With debts of £25,000 on top of this, he was a ruined man. Perhaps preferring a lower sum that might be paid to a huge penalty that would languish in arrears, the following summer Parliament agreed to reduce his fine to £1000. His wife petitioned to take possession of Balls, which was standing empty (wives were permitted to apply to rent their husband's former homes, with a fifth of their income for support), but it would be several years before they were able to move back in.

Without a house of their own, Ann and Richard did not have this safety net to fall back on. As the year ended, they were living with one relation or another with little hope of finding somewhere of their own to settle and bring up their children. It is hard to trace exactly how they coped financially, with the only surviving record of their accounts being Ann's memoirs, but the best explanation I can give is that though their circumstances were vastly reduced, like the rest of their friends and families, there was still just enough money collectively for them to maintain a lifestyle that they would have considered essential for gentility. In the 1630s, Richard had been left £50 a year and £1500 in cash by his parents, though he'd eaten into this capital by the time he met Ann; even if she only received half of her promised dowry of £10,000 she was still a substantial heiress. It was this joint income that meant Ann could proudly claim that throughout their exile neither she nor Richard had ever had to borrow money – although without owning a house or land it meant they spent everything they had in the king's cause.

Neither in her memoirs nor her receipt book did Ann ever think to explain her – and Richard's – devotion to the Stuart cause: her Royalism was as integral a part of her as her responsibilities as a wife and mother, something she did not need to analyse or evaluate. The lives of her father and husband were caught up entirely in service to the crown and thus hers was too. This is not to say that Richard was uncritical of Charles. His political poetry shows that, like his friend Edward Hyde, he believed a king could govern well only if he was well advised. But despite his links to some on the Parliamentary side – Ann wrote that Oliver Cromwell, her husband's distant cousin, would have loved to have had Richard among his allies – turning his back on the king would have been inconceivable and the passage of events only crystallized his loyalty. By the late 1640s, though, the royal cause seemed hopeless and Charles's friends and supporters contemplated the dissolution of their world and everything they held dear.

What the Cavaliers did still have was each other. The network of Royalists either living in exile or trying to avoid attention at home wrote eagerly to one another, their friendship the most potent reminder of what they were working to restore. This charming letter, dating to November 1647, demonstrates the affection that held this group of refugees together as they learned to endure the hardships of defeat. It's from the former courtier Endymion Porter in Brussels to Sir Richard Browne, the English ambassador in Paris: 'I write not often to you for fear of troubling you. But I wish myself often in your company, because I love it as you do pie… I beseech you buss [kiss] my sweet country-woman [Lady Browne came from a village in Gloucestershire close to Porter's] for my sake, with such a buss as made the lass turn nun.'[11]

Whether at home or abroad, Royalists were desperately nostalgic for happier days, as Sir Kenelm Digby (a cousin of the duelling lord mentioned above, and a kinsman of the Fanshawes) wrote to a friend from Calais, also that November, with the hint of a Cavalier wink: 'Those innocent recreations which your lordship mentioneth, of tabours and pipes, and more innocent dancing ladies, and most innocent convenient country houses, shady walks, and close arbours, make me sigh to be againe a spectator of them, and to be againe in little England, where time slideth more gently away than in any part of the world.'[12]

CHAPTER 6

1648
To Make Gascoigne Powder

Take 4 ounces of the black tipps of Crabbs clawes, taken when ye Sunne is in Cancer in June, or the beginning of July (for then they have much more Vertue then at other times) and one ounce of Magister of Pearle, both made into fine Powder: then take Snake Skins cutt in pieces as long as ones finger, put them in a Pipkin filld with fountaine water; have another Pipkin stand by with fountaine water upon the Embers, & as the water of Snakes consumes still supply it with the other, let it stand over the Embers 36 Howers, & when it will jelley take it of, straine it through a strainer, and when it is cold make up your powders with it, and have by Saffron strained in Orange Flower water, and as you make up the little Balls, dipp your Fingers in the Saffron water, so make them up and keepe them for your use.

Ann and Richard spent the spring of 1648 in Hertfordshire. There in rural seclusion they were able to avoid being swept up in the resumption of conflict that became known as the Second Civil War, when disenchanted Presbyterians united with Royalists to rise against Parliament alongside the Scots in one last attempt to change the passage of events, now moving firmly in Parliament's favour. Instead the Fanshawes quietly celebrated the marriages of Richard's sister and his nephew, and awaited the birth of their fourth child.

Little Richard, called Dick, was born on 8 June and left, with his one-year-old brother Henry, at nurse in Hartingfordbury, close to both the Fanshawes' Ware Park and the Harrisons' Balls (still empty, but they were living nearby), when his parents and two-year-old Nan went to London at the end of July. As their little party passed through the town they saw the Parliamentarian commander Colonel Montagu (later earl of Sandwich) '[de-]spoiling [it]... for Parliament and himself',[1] having defeated the forces of the Royalist earl of Holland (father of Diana Rich and Isabella Thynne) and taken him prisoner.

They had by no means abandoned politics, though. In London Ann hastened to pay her court to Elizabeth, marchioness of Ormonde, wife of the man to whom Prince Charles had recommended Richard for employment the previous summer and who was then in Paris with the queen and prince. She and Ann already knew one another – Lady Ormonde's father had owned the house in which Ann grew up – and Lady Ormonde received her warmly, telling her 'she must love me for many reasons, and one was, we were both born in one chamber' (ten years apart) in the house near St Olave's Church. 'When I left her, she presented me with a ruby ring set with two diamonds, which she prayed me to wear for her sake, and I have it to this day.'[2] They never saw each other, Ann wrote later, without her giving Ann a present.

The friendship between Ann and Lady Ormonde, demonstrated by this ring, was a complement to and reflection of the fond working relationship between Richard and her husband, the honourable, splendidly loyal marquess, commander of the Royalist forces in Ireland until 1647. Together, he and Richard had served their mutual friend the earl of Strafford in the late 1630s and they had both been much with their ill-fated master at Hampton Court the previous autumn, advising Charles as he contemplated defeat. Richard was no soldier; with Ormonde as his patron, his wagon was hitched to Prince Charles's star. Serving and supporting him in exile, when at last he was able to join him, would be the best way he could further his master's cause.

1648 was the coldest, wettest summer in living memory, even coming after a series of damp summers and failed harvests. Rivers overran their banks and haycocks floated up and down water-filled valleys. 'I conceive the heavens were offended with us,'[3] concluded Sir John Oglander on the Isle of Wight, recording scarce three dry days together from May to September. As 'for news, it is printed as fast as started'.[4]

Early in June, Lord General Thomas Fairfax, at the head of an experienced Parliamentarian army, failed to take Colchester by storm and prepared to lay siege to the town, which was occupied by Royalist forces under the earl of Norwich but had until this point been sympathetic to Parliament. By 2 July the Essex town was completely encircled by Fairfax's fortifications, with its water supply cut off; by August the townspeople were eating cats and dogs, soap and candles rather than starve, begging an unyielding Norwich to surrender. One of Norwich's lieutenants inside the besieged town was Lord Capel, a neighbour and kinsman of the Fanshawes and member of Prince Charles's council alongside Richard in 1645 and 1646. He had helped Henrietta Maria flee

England in 1644 and assisted in the king's flight to the Isle of Wight the previous year.

Impatient to conclude the siege, Fairfax ordered that no mercy should be shown, even to women and children begging at the town gates. When Norwich sent a group of women of the town to the army lines to plead to be let out, the Parliamentarian commander ordered them stripped naked and sent back, much to the amusement of his soldiers. Norwich, hoping to force Fairfax's hand, initially barred the gates against them and they were forced to beg to be allowed back into the starving town. Richard and Ann must have paid anguished attention when the Parliamentarians, holding their heavily pregnant friend Lady Capel and her invalid son hostage, paraded young Arthur Capel around the town's fortifications, part of the campaign to force the Royalists to surrender. Only intensive lobbying from Lady Fairfax, never shy of speaking her mind, and other female relatives brought the boy safely away.

When the news of Oliver Cromwell's victory over the Scots at Preston reached them on 24 August, Norwich and his companions finally understood they would not be relieved and could no longer hold out. They surrendered, accepting Fairfax's non-negotiable terms – he demanded their senior officers as prisoners with no guarantee of their fate at the hands of the victorious forces. Norwich, Lord Loughborough and Lord Capel were taken to the Tower to await trial by their peers while two more junior commanders were found guilty of treason and shot on the spot.

With the suppression of a flurry of Royalist uprisings over the spring and summer of 1648 and the final defeat of the Scots at the end of August, Parliament is in a commanding position during its negotiations for a settlement with the captive king. From September Charles begins meetings with fifteen Parliamentary Commissioners at Newport, on the Isle of Wight, though his heart is not in it: secretly he sends word to the marquess of Ormonde telling him not to abide by whatever he might agree. The same month, Ormonde lands in Ireland to try to raise a Royalist army there.

Ann did not say how or why, but in September Prince Charles summoned Richard to his small navy, lying off the south coast, leaving Ann and Nan in London. He had taken control of the fleet from his younger brother James, duke of York, who had recently escaped from Parliamentary control in London. The bold 'boy in buffe', just eighteen years old, Charles hoped to fight the remainder of the navy loyal to Parliament – perhaps he dared dream of rescuing his father, whom he had not seen for two years but whose island prison was within his sight as he waited in the Channel for his enemy to sail close enough to engage.

Believing they were about to do battle, 'which if they had, would have been the most cruel fight that ever England knew', Richard wrote to Ann in London, 'full of concern for me', urging her to patience if he should die 'with so much love and reason that my heart melts to this day when I think of it'.[5] The prince's fleet was betrayed to the enemy but a storm rose up in time to separate the two navies without a shot being fired. Charles returned to Holland, Richard continued to Paris 'on his master's business'[6] and from there, early in November, he sent for his wife.

Ann raised £300 in cash 'of his money' (as opposed to from her dowry) and rushed to Richard's side: a day's ride to Dover from London, perhaps with little Nan, her constant companion, sitting in front of her on the saddle, a quick crossing (waiting for favourable conditions to cross the Channel might be a matter of hours but could take weeks and the Channel was also full of pirates, some of them privateers belonging to the Prince of Wales), and then a few days from the coast to Paris. The road from Calais to Rouen, along the route to Paris, was notorious for highwaymen, preying on travellers laden down with all their worldly goods, as well as, in winter, hungry wolves: John Evelyn described travelling along this route with his guns loaded. Rouen in 1648 was full of English exiles waiting 'till they might upon some good change return to their own country'.[7]

In Paris Ann and Richard 'passed away six weeks with great delight in good company'.[8] It was a light-hearted interlude and Ann would remember it fondly after more than two years divided between difficult travel in Prince Charles's train or living in enforced seclusion, in both cases mostly either pregnant or with a newborn.

While the king had been in Carisbrooke Castle, immersed in an ever-shrinking world of coded letters hidden in close-stools or sewn into the linings of clothes, of files and aqua fortis (nitric acid) smuggled into his cell in laundry baskets and hopeless fantasies of regaining his throne, his queen ruled over an increasingly impoverished and irritable court at Saint-Germain-en-Laye, just outside Paris. Duelling continued to flourish among her followers, an epidemic born of impotence and anxiety. Leaving England in 1644, Henrietta Maria had imagined being embraced by her French family and provided with money and soldiers who would spirit her and Charles back to power; in fact she and her small band of followers were tolerated rather than welcomed. She was given an allowance by her sister-in-law Anne of Austria (almost all of which she sent back to England) and apartments at the Louvre, as well as the use of the palace of Saint-Germain-en-Laye in the summer, but no real diplomatic, military or financial exertions were made on her behalf.

When Prince Charles had arrived at court the previous summer his younger cousin, the new king Louis XIV, had been unable for several weeks to find time just to receive him and, by the summer of 1648, Cardinal Mazarin had his own rebels to cope with: the *parlement* of Paris was refusing to pay its taxes, the first scene in the drama of the five-year rebellion known as the Fronde. 'The troubles and distractions in this kingdom increase daily and very fast,' commented one English exile a few months later. 'They are here as eager upon rebellion against their Governors and Government as ever our wretched English were.'[9]

Having lost so many of her belongings over the past few years, Ann must have been eager to visit the boutiques of the Palais Royal, looking forward to being 'trim in all the new fashiones'[10] available there. The Verney letters are a wonderful source of information about shopping in Paris, because Ralph Verney was a keen errand-runner and present-giver for female friends and relations. Even as a young man his bossy godmother had entrusted him with buying all sorts of things for her in London – wine glasses, pens and papers, spangled lace, a 'fasyonable mofe [muff]'[11] – and in Paris the retail opportunities were dazzling.

Ribbons, hoods, scented gloves, patches and enamelled patch boxes, tweezers and wooden combs were all good presents to send home (although pins and fragrant orris powder were better quality in London) and Ralph bought a friend one of the newfangled little brushes 'for making cleane of the teeth, most covered with sylver and some few with gold and sylver Twiste'.[12] It was not just women's fashions that were tempting: Ralph was persuaded to change the style of his wig from the English to the French fashion, 'well curled in great rings and not frizzled',[13] incurring a flurry of bills not just for the wigs but for ribbons, pomade and white powder, scented with Cyprus or *chypre*, a citrus top-note and woody base-notes, so heady it had to be mixed with plain powder so it didn't give him a migraine. Later he bought Flanders lace in white and black and was hunting down an ebony cabinet for someone, though he could only find tortoiseshell. Perhaps he went to a shop John Evelyn described 'cal'd Noahs-Arke, where are to be had for mony all the curiosities naturall or artificial imaginable, Indian or European, for luxury or use, as Cabinets, Shells, Purselan [porcelain], Dried fishes, rare Insects, Birds, Pictures, & a thousand exotic extravagances'.[14]

If shopping was one welcome Parisian distraction, the company of exiled courtiers was another. A pamphlet published on the theme of 'Parliaments of Ladies' satirized the public role of Royalist women, many of whom were in Paris in late 1648. The upside-down Parliaments met, amusingly, in Spring Gardens or Covent Garden and the names are familiar: Lady Rivers, who had tried to persuade Ann to wheedle secrets out of Richard, was Chancellor; Moll Cutpurse, a cross-dressing pickpocket notorious on the streets of London, was Sergeant-at-Arms. Lucy Hay, countess of Carlisle, and Lady d'Aubigny were also featured. Both were active at this time: Lucy Hay was selling the pebble-sized pearls in which she had been painted by Van Dyck to raise money, acting as intermediary between the king and queen's clandestine letters and seeking to create an alliance between moderate Royalists and Presbyterians; Lady d'Aubigny, by now married to Viscount Newburgh, was devising an abortive plan to spirit the king out of his prison. That unhappy beauty, Lady Isabella Thynne, and her mother, Lady Holland, wife of the Royalist commander defeated and captured earlier in the year, were mentioned too.

This was the world into which Ann was afforded a glimpse in Paris, a shadow of its former glory at Whitehall in the 1630s but still giving off a residual gleam of glamour and influence. The three women Ann remembered being most kind to her were Lady Morton (Ann spelled it Norton, as did the author of the 'Parliament of Ladies'), governess to little Princess Henriette; her aunt Susan, Lady Denbigh, another court lady featured in the pamphlet; and Susan's daughter, Elizabeth, Lady Boyle (whom Ann calls Lady Guildford, a title she was given in her own right for her lifetime in 1660). Anne, countess of Morton, also known by her earlier title of Lady Dalkeith, was a great friend and correspondent of Sir Edward Hyde, who described her as the best woman he knew. Like Susan Denbigh, she was part of the Villiers clan, niece of the one-time heartthrob of the Stuart court, the divinely handsome George Villiers, duke of Buckingham, beloved by James I and afterwards bosom friend of Charles I.

Although he'd been murdered twenty years earlier, Buckingham's presence at court and in council was still strong thanks to the members of his family who had profited by his stratospheric rise during his lifetime. As a young lawyer, Edward Hyde had first come to royal attention through the Villiers family; the affectionate letter-writer and former courtier and diplomat Endymion Porter's wife Olive was a niece of Buckingham's; his son and heir, the young duke, was Prince Charles's childhood companion, sharing his distinguished tutors, among them the political theorist Thomas Hobbes, the physician and anatomist William Harvey, and the sweet-natured classicist and future Bishop of Salisbury, Dr John Earle. The death of Buckingham's dashing younger son, Lord Francis Villiers, in a skirmish in 1648 aged nineteen, was noteworthy enough for Ann to include it in her memoirs written twenty years afterwards.

Buckingham's sister, Susan Denbigh (or Danby, as Ann spelled it), was Lady of the Bedchamber to Henrietta Maria and one of her most loyal friends. Although her elder son, Basil, had broken her heart by fighting for Parliament, her husband and second son had died fighting for the king in 1643. She'd followed the queen into exile in 1644 and was accompanied by her daughter Elizabeth, another Lady of the Bedchamber, a little older than Ann and a widow since 1642, when her husband, son of the dynamic Richard Boyle, first earl of Cork, had died in battle beneath Charles's standard. Like the queen and many of her circle, both were Catholic; Susan's mother Mary had converted in the 1620s and her daughter and granddaughters followed her. No fewer than sixteen of Lady Denbigh's receipts would make their way into Ann's book, mostly culinary rather than medical, among them a hasty pudding made with cream, several marmalades (one used Ann's favourite cherries), pheasant pie and pickled lemon peel.

Perhaps because she had her toddler Nan with her – two years younger than Princess Henriette – Ann found Anne Morton a particular friend, receiving Ann and presumably Nan in four-year-old Henriette's apartments in the Palais Royal and visiting Ann in her lodgings. Ann also kissed the queen's hand, 'who promised her favour, with much grace, to us both'[15] – that important 'both' again – and she gave Richard letters to deliver to Prince Charles, then in Breda and lacking the credit to borrow £200 from a banker in The Hague.

They left Paris on Christmas Day, travelling to Calais with a merry party including the rich and amusing poet and former MP Edmund Waller and his wife, another name from the 'Parliament of Ladies'. After conspiring to turn London over to the king in 1643 (aided by Lady d'Aubigny), Waller had avoided execution with a florid public apology accompanied by payment of a fine of £10,000. (His cause was surely helped by the fact that he was related to two prominent Parliamentarians, John Hampden and Oliver Cromwell.) Banished to France, he managed to live in splendid contrast to most impoverished exiles, keeping table for his companions by selling his wife's jewels. He was a particular fan of the beautiful lutanist Isabella Thynne, eulogizing her several times in verse.

Richard had travelled from Calais to Paris with the Wallers a few months earlier. They had many friends in common, most particularly John Evelyn, who considered the two older poets to be mentors. Poets were valued by the Stuart court not just for their literary talents but also as coders, for while secret information needed to be communicated, letters were freely opened and read by postmasters and spies. Abraham Cowley, a cryptographer as well as a poetic prodigy who'd published his first work aged fifteen, served Henry, Lord Jermyn, as private secretary while William Davenant and John Denham had also followed their mistress into exile, Denham acting as an intelligence officer for Henrietta Maria. Earlier in 1648 Denham had helped James, duke of York, escape imprisonment in St James's Palace and flee to France and he was a particular friend and literary collaborator of Richard's.

Though the Cavaliers had been defeated on the field, they were still winning the war of words: literary sophistication was a badge of Royalism. Richard's poetry – his translation of *Il Pastor Fido* was reissued in 1648 with a dedication to Prince Charles – exemplifies the way Royalist poetry could be read as being about at once contemplative retreat and public duty and service.

In Calais Richard and Ann met more old friends – the young earl of Strafford, son of Richard's former patron executed at Parliament's behest in 1641, and Sir Kenelm Digby – and were feasted at the Governor's table in the castle where 'much excellent discourse passed'.[16] Digby, who held his audience spellbound with an account of how barnacles grew into seabirds, was considered by his contemporaries to be one of the seventeenth century's great characters. 'He was such a goodly handsome person, gigantique and great voice, and had so gracefull Elocution and nobel addresse, etc., that had he been drop't out of the Clowds in any part of the World, he would have made himself respected,'[17] said John Aubrey.

His father had been executed for his part in the Gunpowder Plot and, apart from a brief period of conversion to Anglicanism for career reasons, he was a lifelong Catholic and devoted Royalist. In the late 1640s, after a spell in the Tower of London and an extended

European tour (he was a renowned linguist) during which he was variously joined by John Evelyn, Edmund Waller, Andrew Marvell and the duke of Buckingham's two teenaged sons, Digby was living in Paris. He was a familiar figure on the city's streets, extravagantly bearded, wearing a high hat, swathed in a long grey coat and always accompanied by his large mastiff. Ann was fond of Sir Kenelm, whose 'extraordinary stories' were met with applause and laughter at the dinner she described and whose only 'infirmity, though otherwise a person of most excellent parts, and a very fine-bred gentleman',[18] was an inability to tell the truth. (Even so, she swallowed his account of how barnacles became birds.)

One of the seven receipts he gave Ann was for Gascoigne Powder, a regular feature of later seventeenth century receipt books. His receipts would not be published until after his death in 1669, but Gascoigne Powder was one of the few Ann included in her book that appeared in other receipt books, either manuscript or published. An almost identical receipt was the Countess of Kent's Powder, published in the *Choice Manuall* of 1653, two years after the death of Elizabeth Grey, countess of Kent; it would come out in nineteen editions over the next thirty-four years. A granddaughter of the fabled Bess of Hardwick, she had been a Lady of the Bedchamber to Henrietta Maria and was well known for her medical expertise as well as being a noted linguist.

Sir Kenelm's receipt is a mixture of the homely and the exotic, with the ground powder of pearls and the crab claws to be gathered, like plants, in late spring when they were at their most potent, laced (to modern eyes) with a dash of wizardry – those snake skins, which like crab claws were actually a fairly common ingredient in seventeenth century receipts. It took skill to jellify the liquid: Sir Kenelm was an eager collector of receipts (especially for mead) and a keen experimenter, with an elaborate still-room, an early modern laboratory, in his rooms at Gresham College in Bishopsgate.

He was perhaps most famous during his lifetime for his wound remedy, which involved putting an ointment on the weapon which had caused the wound, rather than the wound itself, in order to heal it. Strangely it could be effective, because the wound was cleaned and dressed simply – no other medicines were applied – and often healed better than a wound smothered in some other, stronger ointment which might cause infection; but his theory was that some kind of sympathetic magic took place whereby the weapon was in some kind of communion with the wound it had created. Ann did not include this receipt, which called for moss from the skull of an unburied man, in her book.

Not everyone took Digby's ideas seriously (after discussing chemistry with him John Evelyn concluded, 'the truth is, Sir Kenelm was an errant mountebank'),[19] but he and his contradictions were at the heart of seventeenth century intellectual life. As a young man he'd studied mathematics, alchemy and astrology at Oxford with Thomas Allen, a disciple of John Dee. Alchemy was an interest he shared with his friend Van Dyck and he was an early follower of Descartes, whose *Discours* (containing the immortal line, 'I think, therefore I am') he sent to Thomas Hobbes in 1637. In Paris, like Evelyn and other well-connected exiles, he pursued his interest in the natural world with chemistry courses at the Jardin des Plantes.

Ann didn't record what the pills were meant to cure, but perhaps this was because Gascoigne Powder was so renowned a medicine that it required no explanation. It was widely hailed as a cure-all, effective against poxes of varying kinds, fevers, measles, plague and pestilence and, finally, melancholy (a bodily humour as well as a mood, indicating torpor, stiffness and wistfulness) – this would have been the ground pearls, thought to combat depression as well as purify the blood. The herbalist Nicholas Culpeper said the flesh of vipers was good for the sight, as well as being effective against snake-poison – the thing which causes the wound being the best cure for the wound itself.

Gascoigne Powder is a good illustration of the stimulating crossover between domestic medicine, like that practised by housewives and mistresses of the house across England, and the study of the natural world through philosophy and experiment that would become modern science. Natural philosophy was the subject studied by Sir Kenelm and the men who would found the Royal Society in 1660, with the support of amateur scientist Charles II. Fellow founders included John Evelyn, Christopher Wren and Robert Boyle. But in the 1640s and '50s the subject was not very far from the expert distilling, medicine-making and diagnosis practised by women like Ann Fanshawe and the countess of Kent. Evelyn, like Sir Kenelm, kept a receipt book (although he didn't share any receipts with Ann) and his diary records working alongside his wife at experimentation; a few years later, still in exile, Edward Hyde would ask Evelyn to tell Edward Nicholas's wife 'that the stills are up and they spend their time wholly in making strong waters'.[20] Digby's book also records receipts from female contributors, including a note from Lady Fanshawe, who must be Ann, about fattening poultry with sweetened barley and strong ale.

The relationship between Robert Boyle and his sister Katherine, countess of Ranelagh, is a case in point. Boyle, who studied with Galileo in Florence in 1641, is considered the first modern chemist and a pioneer of the experimental method in science. He lived for most of his adult life with Katherine, at her house first in Queen Street and then in Pall Mall, and the siblings apparently worked side by side in 'his' still-room, or laboratory, there. Although two other sisters, Lettice Goring and Mary Rich, also featured in contemporary receipt books as sources of remedies, Katherine was especially renowned for her intellect, an important member of the circle writing letters informally communicating information and discoveries to the publisher Samuel Hartlib in the 1650s. Even as a girl she was praised to Ralph Verney's father as having 'a memory that will hear a sermon and goe home and penn itt after dinner verbatim',[21] the great contemporary encomium for intelligent women.

Katherine Ranelagh's closest female friend was Dorothy Moore, another Hartlib letter-writer, and Hartlib's *Ephemera* contains numerous references to the pair passing on receipts, distilling and experimenting together, working on 'Paris chemistry'[22] and trying out the Countess of Kent's Powder. Another friend was Elizabeth Ormonde, also Ann's friend, who gave Katherine an interesting 'watch dial without a clock to bee hung on a wall'[23] in 1653. Katherine's receipt book records an unusually catholic variety of sources for receipts and ideas, about equal male and female, from both sides of the political divide and from social inferiors as well as equals, and contains a complete mixture of recipes, from '*spirit* of roses my brother Robert Boyle's way' to waters for the face and remedies for rickets mixed in with 'orange pudden'[24] and lemon cream.

A handwritten manuscript in the British Library entitled 'My Lady Ranelagh's Choice Receipts' and valued by its unnamed copyist 'above gold' is slim and pocket-sized, evidently copied from Katherine's own notes. You'd need to be knowledgeable to use it, as it's full of Latin, abbreviations, shorthand and scientific symbols; some of the pages are singed, as if they've come too close to an experiment. Sir Kenelm contributed a few receipts, as did William Harvey, the anatomist who first described how blood circulates around the body and served as tutor to the Stuart princes.

Katherine Ranelagh may have been exceptional, but she was not unique. Mary Sidney, countess of Pembroke, is more celebrated today for her poetry and literary patronage but in the early seventeenth century she was also known as a 'great Chymist'[25] and a patron of men of science. In the 1630s, the young Princess Elizabeth was taught by Bathsua Makin,* reputed to be another 'good Chymist' with an interest in astronomy who believed that an educated woman should understand 'Physick and Chirurgery'.[26] Ann Fanshawe was not as well educated as these women, but their example must surely have been known to her and contributed to her collection of receipts and interest in science and medicine, albeit in a domestic context.

But although women like Katherine Ranelagh and Mary Pembroke were respected and celebrated by their contemporaries, from the middle of the century, while women were still encouraged

* Makin observed, in a 1673 essay entitled 'An Essay to Revive the Antient Education of Gentlewomen', that if God had 'intended women only as a finer sort of cattle, he would not have made them reasonable'. (Otten 6.)

to practise medicine at home, they were increasingly excluded from the study of natural philosophy. The prestige of the Royal Society, from its foundation in 1660, meant a corresponding decrease in the diversity of scientific experimenters.[27] Although Digby, Evelyn and Boyle were founding members, they did not consider it an appropriate place for the women in their lives, regardless of their intelligence and interest in scientific matters; not until the twentieth century would a woman be elected a Fellow.

And so we leave Ann and Richard in Calais at the year's end, enjoying the company of their friends, stimulated by the exchange of ideas, receipts, poems and laughter. It was a moment of happiness and good cheer to be enjoyed all the more because it was so rare.

Although Hollar engraved this in 1649, the year his father was executed, when Charles was nineteen and in exile, a king without crown, he was copying Van Dyck's pre-1641 portrait in which the young prince was still at Whitehall, his troubles ahead of him, looking like a lost and distrustful child.

CHAPTER 7

1649
Mrs Cokain's Drink for the King's Evil

Take 100 quarts of running spring water, one handful of whit archongele flowers, sweet fennell seeds, & annisseeds of each an ounce bruised, sassafranilla and sassafras, of each a quarter of an ounce, cut in smal peeses, of Cloronwort, one good handfull, one ounce of Liquorish scraped, & sliced thin, put all these into a pipkin and boyle them on a very soft fier, till a third part bee consum'd, them strain it and put to it 60 ounces of [illegible] of roses, take a quarter of a pint at a time, in the morning fasting, at 6 a clock in the afternoon and when you goe to bed, for 6 weeks Spring and Fall, at least a chill May take less.

The clownwort, and archangel flowrs, must bee gatherd in their Season and kept dry.

In January 1649, having purged itself of those who might have argued for moderation, the House of Commons indicts the king for treason and summons him to be tried before the House. The trial begins in Westminster Hall on 20 January. For the first three days, Charles refuses to enter a plea on the grounds that he does not recognize the authority of the court. He is dismissed at the end of the third day and two days follow during which more than thirty witnesses testify against him. He is condemned to death, says goodbye to the two of his children who remain in England in Parliamentary custody on 29 January, Princess Elizabeth, aged thirteen, and Prince Henry, aged eight, and is executed at Whitehall the following day. For Parliamentarians, England becomes a republic; Royalists, at home and in exile, hail his elder son, then eighteen, as Charles II.

At Charles's trial, as the judges prepared to read their sentence, two women in masks – commonly worn to protect ladies' delicate faces from sunshine, dust or excessive cold – cried out from the gallery in response to the words 'in the name of the people of England', 'It's a lie… Not half, not a quarter of the people of England. Oliver Cromwell is a traitor!' One of these hecklers was Lady Fairfax, famously strong-minded wife of the Parliamentary general, Cromwell's colleague. As they were bustled out the soldiers in the hall lowered their muskets threateningly, the muzzles so close to the gallery that, according to a lady who remained, 'we were very hush'.[1]

The king went to his death with all the composure, dignity and gravitas for which his followers might have hoped, famously wearing two shirts to ensure that he would not shiver on the scaffold and give his enemies cause to think he was afraid. John Evelyn refused to witness 'that execrable wickedness' and ever after, like many Royalists, kept the day of Charles's 'martyrdom'[2] a fast. Ann and Richard's brother-in-law Philip Warwick was told by a friend who saw the execution that Charles was 'very majestick and steddy... [he came] out of the Banqueting-house on the scaffold with the same unconcernedness and motion that he usually had, when he entered into it on a Masque-night.'[3] When his head was severed the crowd let out a long, collective, involuntary sigh of shock, perhaps, or sympathy.

Women were particularly moved by Charles's fate and their devotion to him was strengthened and reinforced by how harshly he was treated at the end. Ann was still passionately angry about his death, writing nearly thirty years later, still passionately committed to the cause for which she and Richard had risked everything: 'that glorious sun [who] was tormented and afterwards barbarously and shamefully murdered, as all the world knows'.[4]

In the days before his trial and death, about the time Evelyn got himself into the 'rebell Army at Whitehall [and]... heard horrid villanies',[5] the Abingdon prophetess, Elizabeth Poole, told the General Council of the Officers of the Army that the king should be imprisoned but not executed. 'You never heard that a wife might put away her husband as he is the head of her body,'[6] she warned – and was dismissed from her role as unofficial advisor to the army. Ralph Verney's uncle reported to him in France after the execution that 'the women generally are in mourning for him, ye men dare not, only some few'.[7] Pamphlets were published specifically consoling bereaved Royalist women for the 'burthen of those tender thoughts that are in you towards his sacred Majesty' and offering solace in parallels with Christ and the thought that Charles had 'died so good a KING'.[8]

The only place in England that proclaimed Charles II king after his father's death was Jersey, where the loyal Governor, the

Fanshawes' friend George Carteret, waved his hat and shouted '*Vive le roi!*' as the drums rolled,[9] although the Scots proclaimed him king in February, opening the way for negotiations over their future support for Charles's rule. Elsewhere the country had become a republic: the House of Lords was abolished within a week of the king's death and the 'office' of king the next day. In April, the poet Richard Lovelace emerged from a second spell in prison to find 'the dragon hath vanquished St George':

> Now the Sun is unarmed,
> And the moon lies as charmed
> And the Stars dissolved to a Jelly,
> Now the thighs of the Crown,
> And the arms are lopped down,
> And the body is all but a belly.[10]

The receipt for this chapter, a remedy for the King's Evil, is thus a remedy that reflects the practical, everyday ways the English world changed when Charles died. Traditionally the king or queen, as a mark of their divinely appointed status, had been thought to be able to cure scrofula, or the King's Evil, by laying their hands on the swollen and distorted necks of sufferers. Scrofula is almost always associated with tuberculosis (it is thought to be transmitted in the milk of cows with bovine TB) and causes the lymph glands to swell, horribly but largely painlessly, although tubercular symptoms, of fever, chills and malaise, often accompany it.

This is one of two preventatives against the King's Evil in Ann's receipt book, a herbal water containing archangel flowers (deadnettle, a wild herb related to mint, often used as a wound herb and associated in herbalism with the throat), fennel, aniseed, liquorice and some kind of rose extract in a spring water base. It contains sarsaparilla, a powder taken from the roots of a Central American tree thought to have powerful analgesic and antiseptic properties, and sassafras, also from the Americas and similarly newly in use in English remedies. I have not been able to identify cloron or clownwort; the closest I can get is coral wort, a kind of violet Culpeper said was cleansing and good for inward wounds, or something called clown's ringwort or clown's all-heal, mentioned in one of Sir Kenelm Digby's receipts.

Mrs Cokain's drink came from Richard's elder brother Thomas's wife, a Mistress Cokain; Ann was using her sister-in-law's maiden name as she often did. In her memoirs, Ann dismissed her tartly as 'a very good wife, but not else qualified extraordinary in any thing'.[11]

Her receipt is in the tradition of the Queen of Hungary's water, one of several widely known receipts Ann included in her book. The Queen of Hungary's water, made from stimulating, antimicrobial rosemary, considered especially effective for reducing putrefaction, and sometimes other herbs distilled in brandy or aqua vitae, was a plague remedy dating back to the Middle Ages (though under which Hungarian queen it originated is unclear) to be drunk and used as a wash. It did not fall out of fashion until the advent of eau de Cologne, another herbal drink/wash/scent concoction, in the early eighteenth century. The other remedy Ann included for the King's Evil, which was also a wound drink and came from her brother-in-law Philip Warwick, is a similar herb water but with white angelica rather than the archangel flowers Elizabeth Cokain used.

Having referred to Charles's death in her description of visiting the king for the last time at Hampton Court in 1647, Ann did not describe where she was when she heard the news of his execution, or indeed what she felt: that was a given. It is easy to imagine people of the mid-seventeenth century, of whatever ideological stripe, remembering where they were and what they were doing when they heard the news of Charles's death and with it the knowledge that, for good or ill, the body politic had been severed.

Ann had departed Calais in early January, with little Nan, her sister Margaret and Mrs Waller, landing at Deal instead of Dover in a great storm with their hoy half full of water and carried ashore 'up to the middle in water and very glad to escape so'.[12] 'Though nothing was so grievous to us both as parting, yet the necessity both of the public and your father's private affairs, obliged us often to yield to the trouble of absence,'[13] she wrote of this separation.

Over the next months she 'had the good fortune, as I then thought it' to sell the largest part of her dowry, an annuity of £300 a year, to an Essex man, Judge Archer, for £4000 in cash. At the time, she said, she 'thought [it] a vast sum; but be it more or less, I am sure it was spent in seven years' time in the King's service, and to this hour I repent it not'.[14] This would give them an annual income, over those seven years up to 1657, of over £500: more than enough for a comfortable life on the road even factoring in travelling and the expenses of being unpaid servants of an unthroned king.

By the king, Ann already meant Charles II, of whom she had after all been thinking as king for decades by the time she was writing. Though she didn't make the connection explicit and perhaps she and Richard had already decided that they had to commit to exile and their prince, I can't help thinking that the final prompt for her selling her valuable annuity was Charles I's death. Before his death there was still hope that everything might return to the way it had once been; after it, nothing would be the same again. There would be no use having money tied up, untouchable, while she, Richard and their family needed to devote themselves afresh to returning the English crown to their master, their young king without a kingdom.

Other Royalists decided to cut their losses, too, either making plans for an indefinite exile, like the Fanshawes, or returning to England because they could not bear being away from home any longer. The earl of Hertford wrote to his son in March 1650, on hearing that he was bringing his family to live near him in Netley, that it was 'neither unpleasant nor unsafe, if any place in England be safe, for all are now alike… [but at least it is] out of all roads'.[15] That writer of delightfully affectionate letters, Endymion Porter, whose request to compound had been rejected in 1647, was permitted to return to England in April 1649 following his wife's successful petitioning on his behalf; he died a few weeks after his last appearance before the Commission for Compounding in July.

For many, though, there was nothing left in England without the monarchy. 'If this madness in England cease not,' wrote Edward Hyde at about this time, 'no man can live innocently there.'[16] 'Not only the family I am linked to [married into] is ruined,' lamented Margaret Cavendish, born Lucas, 'but the family from which I sprung, by these unhappy wars.' For their loyalty to the king, one of her brothers was killed (he was shot for treason after the siege of Colchester) and her other brothers and mother were plundered 'of all their goods, plate, jewels, money, corn, cattle and the like; cut down their woods, pulled down their houses, and sequestered them from their lands and livings'.[17] The engraver Wenceslaus Hollar, returning to England from the Low Countries in 1649, 'found the Countenances of the people all changed, melancholy, spightfull, as if bewitched',[18] quite unlike the cheerful population he had observed when he first came to England in the 1630s.

Ann was not prepared to remain anywhere without Richard for long, and anyway, without an estate, there was not even the fifth of its income, as granted by Parliament to the widows of Royalists and the wives of exiles, to live on there. It was better to take their cash abroad. Margaret Cavendish, wife of the rich marquess of Newcastle and thus among the most prosperous of exiles, described the constant round of borrowing, pawning, selling and begging that became second nature to Royalist refugees on the Continent. Although when she, her husband and their six gentlemen attendants and servants moved to live in Antwerp they travelled in a coach accompanied by a small carriage and three wagons containing their belongings, still they could be reduced to selling paintings, jewels, clothes or, at one particular low point, toys belonging to Margaret's maid's child, 'to procure a dinner'.[19]

With £500 in cash and the remainder deposited with her father's agent, Ann gathered her trunks and boxes together with her small household – Nan (nearly three), her sister Margaret, three maids and two men, one of whom may have been the secretary Joseph Avery, the other a boy of all work who could run messages, walk by a horse and do odd jobs. Henry, almost two, and his younger brother Richard, almost one, would remain in Hertfordshire with their wet nurse.

Not knowing how long they would be away, Ann must have packed carefully: several lockable trunks, maybe with her initials picked out on them in brass nails like Mary Verney's, containing bedlinen, pillows and wall hangings; a small writing case carrying blank paper, an inkhorn and quills as well as important letters – and receipts – seals and financial documents, a knife for trimming pen nibs and fine sand for blotting wet ink; a travelling cabinet, or small chest, in which her glass bottles of rosewater and salves, green and yellow, and other essential medical supplies would have fitted neatly, to endure the jolts and bumps of the road (carriage-springs weren't invented until the 1660s); various small silver boxes containing precious spices like nutmeg to grate over a creamy posset or glowing, scented resins like frankincense, not easily available on the road; perhaps some miniature portraits of family members left at home or lost to death; good quality candles,

The accoutrements of mid-seventeenth century womanhood by Wenceslaus Hollar: kid gloves, fur muffs, a fan tied with silk ribbon, laced-edged handkerchiefs and a mask.

well wrapped up (rats and mice found wax delicious). Ann had learned the lute and virginals as a girl and Nan must have too, so probably a child-sized lute or guitar; almost certainly some of Richard's poetry books. Her money would have been in gold, silver and perhaps promissory notes (though these were still rare), carefully squirrelled away, maybe in a small strong-box; when Richard had travelled in Europe as a bachelor in the 1630s, he'd carried his gold pieces (eighty of them) 'quilted in his doublet'.[20]

Clothes for herself and, in miniature, for Nan: fresh white linen smocks, caps, 'handkerchers', collars and cuffs, all embroidered with an F for Fanshawe, to make them easy to find on laundry days; but no drawers, not then in common use. Gowns, bodices and petticoats, some light for summer wear, some quilted for winter, one at least of silk for best and two or three of wool for everyday. Shoes, stockings – silk for best, linen for everyday, knitted garters to hold them up beneath the knee – hats and hatbands, kid gloves (the most valuable were lavishly embroidered), cloaks (fur-lined for winter; a velvet cloak cost £8 10 shillings at about this time). She would have needed extra ribbons, lace, buttons and buckles, needles and thread: there was a gold bodkin in Ralph Verney's travelling sewing kit.

Together Ann and her small 'family' journeyed to Bristol in the spring of 1649, to await Richard's instructions. They went perhaps by post-coach, perhaps in a more expensive coach privately hired, a wagon carrying their trunks trundling behind, travelling about five miles an hour or forty miles per eight-hour day, and stopping each of the three or four nights at coaching inns along the way. The dust or mud – by turns – of the dangerously pot-holed roads would have meant nothing to Ann, behind the protective mask or vizard women of gentle status commonly wore for travelling, since she was headed 'very cheerfully towards my north star, that only had the power to fix me'.[21]

Richard had rejoined Charles in Holland in February and almost immediately departed on his orders for Ireland to join the marquess of Ormonde as Treasurer of the Navy, which in practice meant Treasurer of the Irish war effort. Ormonde and Prince Rupert were raising an army there to invade England. Richard's Latin would be invaluable since English was not yet widely spoken in Ireland, especially in administrative matters. From Ireland, he sent for Ann, though his letters to his colleagues didn't get through the watching Parliamentary spies, 'swarming all over England as Lice and Frogs did in Egypt',[22] as easily. Loyal but querulous Sir Edward Nicholas, Charles's Secretary of State and, along with Sir Edward Hyde, one of the lynchpins of the older generation of Royalists abroad, was waiting in Le Havre in April for news of Ormonde from Richard to communicate to the king; Richard's letter was 'still much expected'[23] on 3 May.

It was about May when Ann, Margaret and Nan, having endured the 'very hazardous voyage',[24] braving treacherous tides, fog and pirates, arrived in Youghal in Cork to meet Richard. 'So soon as he heard I was landed he came to me,' she wrote, 'and with mutual joy we discoursed those things that were proper to entertain us both'.[25] There followed six months of lush green summer in which Ann, Richard and their small household lived at Red Abbey, a pleasant medieval friary belonging to Dean Boyle, future Archbishop of Dublin and Lord Chancellor of Ireland, in the seaside town of Cork. Their life at Red Abbey was 'so much to our satisfaction, that we began to think of making our abode there during the war, for the country was fertile, and all provisions cheap, and the houses good… and the country seemingly quiet'.[26]

In England, life was far from satisfactory for prominent Royalists who had remained behind. Lords Holland and Capel were executed in March (Capel's dramatic escape attempt having failed) alongside the leader of the Scottish Royalists, the duke of Hamilton. Lady d'Aubigny and Isabella Thynne fled to Holland and France respectively (Lady d'Aubigny would die the following year), but Lucy Hay, who had agitated on both sides for peace without winning the trust of either, was imprisoned in March, weeks after her cousin and possibly lover Lord Holland was executed, and shown the rack in May. Although she begged the gaolers not to hurt her, promising to confess everything, she would not be released for eighteen months.

Two days after Charles died Parliament had begun debating what to do with his 'goods', all of which had passed into Parliament's hands and for which, naturally, they wanted to get the best price. With the king-in-exile planning an invasion by sea from Ireland, the Parliamentary navy was in urgent need of funds. Eleven trustees were appointed to oversee the inventory and sale of Charles's possessions, which would have the dual advantage of raising money and diminishing the mystique of his majesty.

Charles was back in France in June 1649 and in September made it as far as Jersey, whence he planned to go on to Ireland to meet Ormonde, Prince Rupert, Richard Fanshawe and an army, at the head of which he hoped to sail for England. He did not know that at the same time, Oliver Cromwell was setting out for Ireland himself, bracing his men for brutality by telling them to think of themselves as Israelites embarking on a mission to stamp out idolatry in Canaan.

Oliver Cromwell lands in Ireland in August and captures Drogheda in early September, taking no quarter: only sixty-four English soldiers are killed while 3500 Irish die. He travels south to Wexford where his men slaughter 200 women as they beg for mercy. On he marches along the south-east coast towards Cork, leaving a trail of blood in his wake.

Terrifying tales of Cromwell's ruthlessness preceded him, as he intended they should: later, in a letter to Charles, Ormonde listed the towns that fell to Cromwell as he swept through Waterford, one after the other, 'all betrayed to him without one stroke struck'.[27]

In Cork, her illusion of domestic security shattered, Ann wondered 'what earthly comfort is exempt from change?' As ever, as soon as they settled somewhere that felt like a home, she had dreamed of making it permanent; as ever, fate had conspired against her. Having just heard of the death of her elder son, three-year-old Henry, from his nurse in England, they then learned of Cromwell's landing, 'who so hotly marched over Ireland'. Prince Rupert and his small fleet were forced to flee, his brother Prince Maurice's ship 'with many a brave man' and 'hundreds of thousands of pounds'[28] of treasure was lost in a storm, while Richard remained behind, awaiting instructions from Charles and hoping they would reach him before Cromwell's army.

As Cromwell approached Cork early that October Ann was pregnant and in bed with a painfully ill-set broken wrist, after falling from a stumbling horse (expecting a baby evidently did not mean taking it easy). Richard had gone to take care of some business at the garrison in Kinsale, ten miles away, when, at midnight, she heard great guns and the 'lamentable shrieks of men, women and children'. Discovering that Cork had been taken in Cromwell's name overnight and the people were 'stripped and wounded, and turned out of the town', Ann wrote a note to her husband telling him not to worry about them or his papers and sent it with a servant 'let down the garden-wall of Red Abbey'.[29]

She packed Richard's papers up in his cabinet, a travelling desk, along with about £1000 in silver and gold, and 'all other things both of clothes, linen, and household stuff that were portable, of value'. Out in the dark market square with a candle, at three in the morning, she found Cromwell's commander surrounded by soldiers with their swords in their hands, a Colonel Jeffries whom Richard had known 'whilst he was loyal' – before he had abandoned the king to support Parliament. She asked Jeffries for a pass to leave the city; 'instantly' he wrote her one, for herself, her family and her goods, 'and said he would never forget the respect he owed'[30] Richard, who had shown him many civilities in the past. Once again, across the lines, friendship and favours were remembered when it really mattered.

Back she went 'through thousands of naked swords' to hire the neighbour's cart and have it loaded up with 'all that I could remove'.[31] With her sister Margaret, Nan, three maids, two men and two horses, which they rode by turns, fearfully they set out through the chill November dawn towards Richard in Kinsale. They found him 'the most disconsolate man in the world... but his joys exceeded to see me and his darling daughter' and hear of their 'wonderful escape'. Adding piquancy to their relief was the news that Cromwell, on being told of Cork's surrender, immediately asked where Mr Fanshawe was. When he was told Richard was safely in Kinsale he demanded to know where his family and papers were, to which no one could reply. 'It was as much worth to have seized his papers as the town,'[32] stormed the frustrated general. Ann's delight at having outwitted him glows off the page.

Within a few days they heard from Charles, who instructed Richard to meet Hyde and Lord Cottington, formerly ambassador to Spain under James I and an ardent Catholic, in Madrid, where, as his envoys, they were hoping to raise funds from Philip IV. This was something of a blow for Richard, who thought Charles I had promised him the ambassadorship two years earlier. There was nothing he could do but comply. For his part, now that the plans for invading England with an Irish army had collapsed, Charles II had no choice but to begin humiliating negotiations with the Scots, a line long advocated by Henrietta Maria and her court in Paris but bitterly opposed by Hyde, Ormonde, Nicholas and Fanshawe.

Eikon Basilikon, a collection of Charles I's writings compiled while he was held captive at Holdenby House and Hampton Court, was published immediately after his execution in January 1649. Apart from being a justification of Charles's rule and behaviour, establishing him (to his supporters) as a martyr, it offered a programme for the future, a book of counsel for his young successor from beyond the grave. It expressed very clearly Charles's antipathy to an alliance with the Scots – perhaps reflecting the influence of the marquess of Ormonde and Richard Fanshawe, both of whom had spent a great deal of time with the imprisoned king at Hampton Court – and would become an embarrassing reminder of Charles II's betrayal of his father's memory in making such a deal.

For the moment, though, Ann and Richard could not leave Ireland. Because the Lord Chancellor, Lord Roscommon, had died in an accident, Richard had to remain with the broad seal of Ireland until he could hand it to Roscommon's replacement; they would need to wait until Charles could be informed and had sent back word of what to do. While Ormonde went to Holland and his army dispersed, 'every person concerned in that interest shifting for their lives... Cromwell went through as bloodily as victoriously, many worthy persons being murdered in cold blood, and their families quite ruined'.[33]

Ann suffered privately alongside the Irish through Cromwell's bloody rampage. She does not say when she lost the baby she was carrying as she fled Cork in early October, but her next child would be born in late July the following year, indicating she was conceived in late October or very soon thereafter. The likely progression of events is a mid-term miscarriage (she had, after all, been living with Richard for six months) almost immediately after their flight followed by getting pregnant again within weeks.

They stayed first with Ormonde's sister, Eleanor Muskerry, at Macroom. With her customary attention to gift-giving, Ann noted that Lady Muskerry presented her with a 'great Irish greyhound' while Ann returned the favour with a fine bezoar stone, evidence of her interest in medicinal matters and identification as a woman with an interest in healing. Bezoar stones, undigested matter found in the stomachs of animals, were thought to act as antidotes to any poison, protect against the plague and were considered especially effective as amulets for labouring women. Highly valued, they were often encased in gold or silver, sometimes with a loop attached so they could be worn dangling from a belt or purse like a pomander.

From there they went to Limerick, thence to Lord Inchiquin's, and on to stay with Lady Honor O'Brien, an unmarried lady 'that went for a maid, though few believed it'. Although Cromwell was 'pursuing his conquests at our backs', everywhere they went they were entertained with great kindness and hospitality.

The only exception was their stay with Lady Honor. On the first night Ann awoke to see a pale woman with red hair and a 'ghastly complexion' leaning in through their window in the moonlight. Three times the woman said, 'A horse', in a strange voice, and disappeared, 'her body more like a thick cloud than a substance'. Ann was 'so much frightened that my hair stood on end, and my night clothes fell off'.[34] Richard, naturally, had slept through this apparition and Ann's 'disorder' but she shook him awake and told him what she had seen, and they lay together, companionably unable to get back to sleep, while Richard told her how much more common ghosts were in Ireland than in England and they agreed it was the Irish want of faith that allowed the Devil to work among them in this dangerous manner. In the morning they discovered that an O'Brien cousin had died unexpectedly that night and this ghost, of a woman 'got with child by the owner of this place' and thrown by him into the river long ago, always appeared when a member of the family was dying. Lady Honor apologized, saying she'd put them in the best room not knowing her cousin was ill. 'We made little reply to her speech,' concluded Ann, 'but disposed ourselves to be gone suddenly.'[35]

Their theory of the credulity of the unsophisticated is corroborated by John Aubrey, who believed that 'in the old ignorant times, before woomen were Readers', fabulous stories of spirits and fairies were handed down from mother to daughter. 'When the warres came, and with them Liberty of conscience and Liberty of inquisition, the phantoms vanished. Now children feare no such things, having heard not of them'.[36] These new beliefs had evidently not yet reached Ireland; in England, though, the 'warres' had brought modernity in all its guises pell-mell in their wake.

CHAPTER 8

1650
An Oyntment for Burning with Gun Powder or Scalding with Hot Water

Take a Quart of Boares Grease, 2 Handfulls of Groundsell, and 2 or 3 Heads of Houseleeke, stampe them together, then putt to it 2 handfulls of new Sheepes Dung, 2 handfulls of Goose dung, stamp them all together and fry them and straine them when they are hot through a Cloth into a Earthen Pott, and with the Liquour anoint the burnt or scalded Place.

At the beginning of the year word arrived from Charles instructing Richard to leave the Irish seals of state with Lord Inchiquin and set sail for Spain. Having handed over the seals and written to his old rival Sir Robert Long, momentarily reinstated as Charles's secretary at Henrietta Maria's instigation, in Breda to tell him of the 'mutual jealousies between the English and Irish',[1] Richard and Ann turned their minds to the problem of leaving Ireland, by this time almost entirely controlled by Cromwell's men.

They headed towards Galway, because they had heard that a Dutch ship bound for Malaga was waiting in its harbour, but Galway was itself as frightening a prospect as turning back to face the Parliamentary army. Its population had been decimated by the plague that had raged there the previous summer and still lingered on, leaving the pleasant buildings, fine marketplace and paved and colonnaded walks beside the 'noble harbour' admired by Ann almost empty, its 'streets grown over with grass'.[2]

The guards at Galway's walls permitted them to enter the city only because they said they would be leaving by ship and had rented rooms in a well-known merchant's house by the seafront, but they had to leave their horses at the gates. A friendly footman led them down through the deserted town on foot, 'all on the back side of the town, under the walls, over which the people during the plague, which was not yet quite stopped, flung out all their dung, dirt, and rags, and [unable to turn back] we walked up to the middle of our legs in them'.[3]

When their tired, mucky little party of ten, accompanied by Ann's new greyhound, reached the house, the merchant was there to greet them. Although he was assisted by just one maid, his house was clean and he gave them a good supper before they went to bed, entertaining them with tales of aristocratic perfidy (a locked chest, supposedly filled with jewels, which had been left by a marquess as security for a large loan, was later found by his creditors to contain rocks). It was not until they bade their host farewell that they were startled to hear him say how glad he was 'you are all gone safe from my house, notwithstanding I have buried nine persons out of my house within these six months'.[4]

On they went, 'with prosperous winds' at their backs, south towards the Straits of Gibraltar. As they came into the Mediterranean they saw, heading straight for them 'with full sails, a Turkish galley well-manned'.[5] Wild and moustachioed Turks, from an Ottoman empire whose lands stretched at its peak a century earlier from Belgrade to Babylon, were the bogeymen of the seventeenth century, the villains whom mothers warned their naughty children would seize them and spirit them off into a frighteningly alien world from which there could be no return. 'We believed we should be all carried away slaves,' wrote Ann, for although their ship had sixty guns it was so heavily laden with goods for Spain that they were useless.

The captain called for brandy and drank deeply while he thought. Emboldened, he resolved to fight rather than lose his £30,000-worth of ship and cargo, cleared the decks and sent his passengers to their cabins. The women of the ship were specifically ordered to stay below decks; if the Turks did not see women on board they were less likely to think it a passenger or merchant ship with a rich cargo and try to board. Slung about with his gun, bandoliers and sword, standing on deck surrounded by his 200 men, the captain prepared to defend his floating world.

This captain, 'the greatest beast I ever saw',[6] had taken the precaution of locking Ann into her cabin. Judging by her furious description of him, it seems likely that he had seen a flash of defiance in her eyes earlier in the voyage. In tears, Ann 'knocked and called long to no purpose', until at last a cabin boy took pity on her and opened the door. She pressed half a crown into his hand for his 'blue thrum cap… and his tarred coat… Flinging away my night clothes', slipping into the cabin boy's jacket and tucking her hair into his knitted cap, she crept up on deck to stand 'by my husband's side, as free from sickness and fear as, I confess, from discretion; but it was the effect of that passion, which I could never master'.[7]

I think that by the passion she could never master Ann meant her desire always to be at Richard's side, but it reads to me as if she also means her impetuosity, that longing for adventure and the feel of the wind in her hair that marked her attitude to her life with Richard and her enthusiastic adoption of their life of exile. You can almost see her on deck in the cabin boy's shaggy cap and unwashed jacket, her face damp with spray and shining with excitement. If she had lived her mother's life, or even one of her daughters', she would never have found herself dressed as a boy, looking out at a Turkish galley in the Mediterranean sunshine with her hair whipping into her eyes, listening to the inexorable splash of its oars as it approached (thrillingly, with possible murderous intent).

In the end, the two captains parleyed and went their separate ways, both unwilling to engage. Richard turned and, to his astonishment, saw Ann behind him. He 'snatched me up in his arms, saying, "Good God, that love can make this change!"' Though seemingly, he 'chid me, he would laugh at it often as he remembered that voyage'.[8] He adored his young wife as much for her nerve and resourcefulness as for her desire to be near him.

Had they entered into an engagement with the Turks, they might well have had need of Ann's sister-in-law's burn remedy. This is one of the receipts in her book that reads very strangely: no one now would dream of using dung in medicine, although the boar's fat would have been soothing and groundsel was commonly used in poultices. It recalls some of the old-fashioned folk remedies Royalist diarist John Oglander included in his commonplace book earlier in the century: leeches to calm haemorrhoids; boars' urine, hung for a month in its bladder, to anoint gout-ridden feet; fried horse dung for a bruise; powdered fox's lungs for consumption;

stroking a cyst with the hand of a dead person (it was important, apparently, for a woman to be stroked with the hand of a dead man, and for a man, a dead woman).[9] Culpeper's *Herbal* included an entire section on medicinal ingredients made from animal products and excrement. Some of these remedies would have been effective – in Chinese medicine, as noted earlier, earthworms are still used and their active ingredient is haemostatic, impeding the flow of blood – but others would have been sympathetic medicine, working as placebos.

One of the more outlandish seventeenth century medicinal ingredients, at least to modern eyes, is snails, often used in conjunction with worms. Oglander seethed them in badger's grease to make a salve for aches; others used them in dressings to diminish swellings. Roasted and ground with pilewort, they were used to relieve haemorrhoids. The one receipt Ann had for Snail Water was a drink to be taken for liver problems like jaundice; it was also thought to be effective against 'hectick' fevers, being innately cooling. London snails were especially prized for their glutinousness.

Ann, Richard and their party landed in Malaga in March, 'very well, and full of content to see ourselves delivered from the sword and plague, and living in hope that we should one day return happily to our native country'.[10] They knew the odds were small, she added, considering how things stood, but they trusted in God, whose ways were as mysterious as they were powerful. Mysterious indeed: they had not been on land three days when they heard that, by the negligence of a cabin boy, the ship they had travelled on had been blown up in the harbour with a hundred sailors on board – perhaps the very cabin boy whose 'negligence' had allowed Ann up on deck in his cap as an enemy approached.

Travelling up through Spain towards Madrid they were tourists, taking a leisurely month over their journey to enjoy the scenery and the spring. Their first stop, past 'the highest mountains I ever saw in my life [and]... the finest valley that can be possibly described, adorned with high trees and rich grass, and beautified with a large deep clear river', was Granada, where Ann marvelled at the Alhambra palace. Here her writing took on the tone of a travel book, the most popular reading of the time, rhapsodizing over the landscape, architecture, sculpture and textiles they saw: the palace, she wrote, had 'many courts, many fountains, and by reason it is situated on the side of the hill, and not built uniform, many gardens with ponds in them, and many baths made of jasper, and many principal rooms roofed with the mosaic-work, which exceeds the finest enamel I ever saw'.[11]

In Madrid, Edward Hyde was anxiously awaiting their arrival. He had arrived as one of Charles II's 'ambassadors' (agent is a more realistic description of their role) to the Spanish court with Francis Cottington the previous October, only to find that Philip IV would not officially receive them. In March, Hyde had written to Edward Nicholas worrying that he had not heard from 'poore Dick Fanshaw'[12] (of whom, as a fluent Spanish speaker, he was in desperate need), but a few weeks later he was informing his wife of the Fanshawes' approach.

'That thou mayst see how ill a husbande I am in comparison with others, wee have a whole English family comminge to this town,' he began; Frances Hyde and four of their six children had been living in Antwerp for the previous few years. 'Dick Fanshaw, whom I gave over for lost in Ireland, this last night writt to me, that he and his wife are landed at Malaga, 12 dayes journy from hence, and are comminge hither as fast as they can. What they will do heare, or how they will be able to lyve, God knowes; that woman will undoe him; if he had come by himselfe, he should have bene with us, and wanted nothinge, but he had neede have brought good store of money with him to keepe such a trayne [train].'[13]

Ann always sensed the high-minded Hyde's disapproval of her (later her resentment of his treatment of Richard would become overt) and she was not wrong to suspect him of writing Richard off because he distrusted the influence of his much younger wife. In the abstract, Hyde actively disapproved of women having anything at all to do with politics, noting in his commonplace book in the late 1640s that women were 'not fitt for secretts'. Four years later he would explode in frustration to Nicholas, after an argument with Charles's sister, Princess Mary of Orange, 'I swear to you heartily I have almost contracted so much prejudice to the whole sex that I would have as little to do with them as may be.'[14]

In Ann's case his distrust was personal, too. She and Hyde had contrasting ideas about the role a good wife should play. Although he always wrote to his wife with great fondness and by all accounts they had a happy enough marriage, they had been married ten years longer than the Fanshawes and the narrative of their relationship was a pre-war, peacetime one. His preferred endearment for her, 'deere little Rogue',[15] is affectionate but for me the most patronizing of the commonly used marital endearments of the time. He ended this letter to Frances assuring her that, although he would pay any price for her company, he did not wish her with him in Spain because he thought it 'the most uncomfortable place, for women to lyve in, that is in the world'.[16]

Richard and Ann, by contrast, had embarked on married life as an adventure, embracing exile in partnership. But Hyde thought, possibly with good reason, that Richard's duty to his master could best be performed unencumbered: he could not forgive Ann for hindering Richard from fulfilling it. 'That woman will undoe him': it may not just have been her presence, and her expanding brood of children, that exasperated Hyde; perhaps her independence of mind and the openness of her relationship with Richard – her insistence on being present and heard – also grated.

The financial problems of living in exile were also much on Hyde's mind as he contemplated Richard's imminent appearance with his expensive family. 'Never in my life [have I] known so absolute a want of money as I have done since I came hither,'[17] he wrote to his friend (and Ann's), Anne Morton, in June. Later he wrote to his wife again, urging her not to lose faith in their cause. He had been living on credit and until he could send her money, 'thou must not be ashamed to be in debt… and thou must write into Englande to anybody that thou thinkest will lende; at least let your frends ther know the necessityes you are all in [Frances had her parents with her, as well as four of their children], and if that mooves them not, they will lyve to be ashamed of it'.[18] Elsewhere he told her to remember to 'be as merry as poore, honest, undone people can be'.[19]

Hyde needed to encourage his colleague Edward Nicholas in The Hague, too, stiffening his resolve to remain abroad in Charles's service. In October, as news of even more compounding 'rogues' filtered through to them and they waited in vain for word from the young king, he had to remind Nicholas (then nearly sixty) that they 'must die in the streets first of hunger,' before either of them could give up and go home. 'We have hitherto suffered for doing what our consciences obliged us to do, and those obligations continue though our party should be lessened to three men... I think with as much pleasure as these miserable times will admit, upon living a year together with you, studying hard and mending one another upon recollection of all that is past, and I hope yet we shall live to enjoy one another in our own country.'[20]

Nicholas wrote back despairingly that his wife Jane, who had been back in England for two years, could not get a pass to travel without signing the new Commonwealth's Oath of Engagement and could raise no more money from their friends, all 'being weary of her'.[21] Her experience was increasingly common: another Royalist, a friend and colleague of Richard, Nicholas and Hyde, Christopher Hatton, told a friend that he would have starved in exile 'had I not left all to my wife to manage, who gets something by living there [in England] and haunting some of her kindred and what ways I know not'.[22]

Ann faced different challenges. By the time she and her family arrived in Madrid in the middle of April, she was heavily pregnant. Only Nan, now four years old, was with them in Spain: their sole surviving other child, little Richard, aged two, was at nurse in Hertfordshire. Their time in Madrid was brief and dominated by the birth of their fifth baby, Elizabeth, on 13 July 1650.

Little Elizabeth's godmothers were Ann's sister Margaret and her own older sister, Nan; her godfather a Mr Avery, a secretary of Richard's who must have been with the family at least a year, since they had been in Ireland, the same 'Joseph Auerie' who would later copy out Ann's receipts. He is mentioned twice in Ann's papers – once as godfather in 1650, in her memoirs; once as scribe of her receipt book the following year – and I have been able to find out nothing more about him.

The paucity of their new baby's godparents, all three coming from their household of ten (Hyde was already godfather to Nan), was a measure of how isolated their small party was. She was baptized by Dr Bell or Beale, Master of Jesus College, Cambridge, who had once been Richard's tutor and, by coincidence, was living in Madrid as a chaplain to an English family. He would also perform the burial ceremonies when she died fifteen days later, perhaps because she was premature. She was buried in the Chapel of the French Hospital, the third burial site for a Fanshawe child.

Not until their next visit to Madrid, in the mid-1660s, when Richard really was ambassador (and Charles really was king), did Spain feature in Ann's memoirs, but it made such an impression on her then that it is worth describing its fabulously exotic glamour in brief here. Philip IV, king and emperor of vast swathes of the known world, ruled over a court notable for its formality and magnificence – a far cry from the shaky French and English regimes in the 1640s and '50s. Diego Velázquez had been Philip's official painter since 1624 and he would paint his enigmatic masterpiece, *Las Meninas*, six years after Ann and Richard's first stay in Madrid.

She visited galleries containing the finest art of the day, splendid Catholic churches (so different from the Puritan austerity they had left behind in England), lush gardens and, at the Escorial, the apothecary's shop and 'the finest stillatory I ever saw'. This still-room was very large, paved with black and white marble and shelved around with crystal and glass bottles 'sized and sorted'[23] on the shelves. In the centre of the room was a huge furnace with 500 glass bottles, pyramid shaped, with glass stoppers, standing around it. The apothecary's shop was richly adorned with gilt and marble, with all the vessels and surgical instruments made of silver.

Her gold-embossed receipt book could have been bought while they were in Spain in 1650 since Spain was celebrated for its fine leather-work. Its receipts include the Spanish methods for perfuming skins with jasmine, for glove leather, and making amber beads, scenting rose petals to keep in bags among clothes and making rose-scented pastilles to burn as incense, as well as Spanish hippocras, a spiced wine 'which exceeds all other'. The earliest, stitched into the centre of the book, are all Spanish, written out I think in Ann's very neatest hand, and dated to 18 June 1650.

It was perhaps here that Ann first tasted chocolate, a new import from South and Central America to which Spain, whose empire encompassed all chocolate-producing lands, had almost exclusive access. In the 1630s, the diplomat and courtier Sir Toby Mathews, recently returned from Madrid, had offered to make Henrietta Maria some chocolate, amusing everyone by absentmindedly on-purpose drinking it all himself. In 1650 it was still hard to come by. From exile in Blois Ralph Verney sent to England to get hold of 'the quite new drink chocolate' for his ill wife, which his uncle sent with instructions because 'the thinge itself is not knowne in France'.[24] With typical confidence in 1649 Edward Hyde, himself always comfortably round, recommended his slender wife keep up her strength and spirits by drinking 'soculate'[25] for breakfast. (He did not mention how she should pay for it.) Ann's receipt, 'To Dresse Chocolate', accompanied by a drawing of a West Indian chocolate pot and frother, dating to 1665, is the earliest known recipe for hot chocolate in English, though crossed-out and illegible.

Ann and Richard's time in Madrid was marked by private tragedy and Richard's official mission was no more successful, even though with his arrival Charles's envoys could at last communicate confidently with their hosts. France and Spain were still at war, the Habsburg lands in Germany were still recovering from the devastations of the Thirty Years War: this was no time to be asking Philip IV to embark on an expensive campaign to help an impoverished prince from an insignificant land when his victors seemed determined to create a stable regime.

Furthermore, while they were there, the small English population of Madrid was in disgrace because the man sent by the Commonwealth as envoy to the Spanish court, Anthony Ascham, was murdered that June by a gang of young English exiles including a member of Lord Cottington's household, an English merchant and four adventuring mercenaries in the Spanish army. Ann, evidently sympathetic to the motives of the murderers (if not their methods), described them being furious about the 'impudence of that Askew [*sic*], to come a public minister from a Court where there were two Ambassadors [Hyde and Cottington] from his king'.[26] Mr Sparks, the merchant and the only one of the gang who was a resident of Madrid, was executed for this crime.

'The Spaniards will not express what offices of friendship they intend to perform, as their own necessities increase upon them daily,'[27] wrote Hyde and Cottington, in a dispatch to Charles at the end of July, confessing their failure on his behalf. All they had been able to elicit from Philip was 'good words and professions'.[28]

The young king accepts humiliating terms for Scottish support including swearing the Presbyterian Oath of the Covenant and betraying his loyal servant the earl of Montrose, a superb military tactician whose victories in Charles's name in Scotland had kept the Royalist cause alive there through the late 1640s. Montrose is hanged days before Charles lands at Speymouth at the end of May 1650. Under Oliver Cromwell, the New Model Army defeats the Scots at Dunbar in September.

Hyde thought Charles's alliance with the Scots 'folly and atheism'[29] but his loyalty never wavered. He and Cottington begged Charles to write back letting them know how he had been received by the Scots, 'and of any other access of good fortune which may advance your service, in which no men can labour with more duty and affection how unprofitably soever, than we'.[30]

There was very little good fortune for poor Charles to report. He was so wretched in Scotland, kept a virtual prisoner, forced to denounce his parents and practise a religion he despised, that he was said to have cheered Cromwell's victory over his so-called allies at Dunbar that September and made his first, vain, attempt to escape the following month. Life there, he said afterwards, was miserable: 'there was not a single woman; the people were so backward that they thought it a sin to listen to violins; and he had been terribly bored'.[31]

Before they left Spain, Hyde told Richard he wanted to send him to Scotland, partly because Charles needed a secretary, partly because a quarrel between Charles and his younger brother James, the future James II, also in Scotland, threatened Royalist unity and he hoped Richard would be a good mediator: Charles was after all still a teenager, very much in need of guidance, and Hyde feared any jealousy between the brothers could be exploited. James was actively sympathetic to the Catholic cause, a position Hyde distrusted, and he favoured a French alliance over the Spanish one Hyde hoped to promote. Hyde and Cottington beseeched Charles, still in their letter of 27 July, 'to hear him [Fanshawe], whose integrity and devotion to your service and his great ability to serve you, your Majesty well knows'.[32] Privately they distrusted the extravagant, easily offended Viscount Newburgh, recently widowed husband of the intriguing Lady d'Aubigny, who had accompanied Charles to Scotland; they hoped Richard would temper his influence.

For the moment, Richard does not seem to have shared Hyde's plans for him with Ann. Leaving Madrid at the end of July they travelled to San Sebastián, a journey of fifteen days (the last three by mule) that Hyde had taken the previous year in the opposite direction. Travelling in seventeenth century Europe was uncomfortable at the best of times, but rural Spain, as Hyde reported wearily to his wife, was so primitive that none of the houses had chimneys (meaning fireplaces) and only the very best had glass windows, and 'never travellers saw lesse of a country to satisfy our curiosity then wee doe'.[33] He had been up every day at dawn and stopping after dark, with a two-hour break for dinner 'as much for the horses' sake as our owne', on 'so wearysome a journy as thou canst not imagine'.[34]

Like Hyde, Ann and Richard found San Sebastián and its people uncomfortable and uncivilized and they remained there only two days before hastily taking ship for Nantes. After a day at sea they sailed into a violent hurricane in the Bay of Biscay that lasted three days until finally they were washed ashore, miraculously unharmed and with all their possessions intact. They managed to find some mules to carry them and their goods to Nantes, after a night during which they 'sat up and made good cheer; for beds they had none, and we were so transported that we thought we had no need of any, but we had very good fires, and Nantz white wine, and butter, and milk, and walnuts and eggs, and some very bad cheese; and was not this enough, with the escape of shipwreck, to be thought better than a feast? I am sure until that hour I never knew such pleasure in eating, between which we a thousand times repeated what we had spoken when every word seemed to be our last'.[35]

On they went through Nantes, where they hired a boat to carry them up the Loire to Orléans. This, remembered Ann, was the most pleasant journey they ever took, a surprisingly contemporary barging holiday complete with sightseeing, shopping at local markets and an on-board barbecue: 'Every night we went on shore to bed, and every morning carried into the boat wine and fruit, and some bread, with some flesh, which we dressed in the boat, for it had a hearth, on which we burnt charcoal; we likewise caught carps, which were the fattest and the best I ever eat in my life . . . we saw the finest cities, seats [houses], woods, meadows, pastures and champaign [fields] that I ever saw in my life, adorned with the most pleasant river of Loire'.[36]

They arrived in Paris, this time crossing over with John Evelyn, with whom they dined (according to his diary).[37] Once again, Evelyn was enjoying himself; perhaps the Fanshawes joined in with some of his activities. Paris was full of English exiles. Soon after his arrival, 'My Lady Herbert invited me to dinner; Paris, and indeede all France being full of Loyall fugitives'.[38] He went to the theatre, watched riding exhibitions, sat to a sculptor, saw the young king Louis XIV dancing in a masque, even witnessed a thief being tortured at the Châtelet ('the spectacle was so uncomfortable, that I was not able to stay the sight of another').[39] Highlights included seeing a dromedary, 'a very monstrous beast',[40] being shown around the laboratory belonging to the physician and apothecary Friar Nicholas and marvelling at the shells, minerals and botanical drawings of Monsieur Morine.

At dinner in Saint-Germain-en-Laye, Evelyn met a gentleman called Sir Lewis Dyve who kept the company entertained with his account of escaping prison in Whitehall the night before he was due to be executed, despite being guarded by six musketeers. Leaping 'down out of a jakes [lavatory] 2 stories high into the Thames at high water', he swam to a waiting boat. Disguised variously as a woman and a coalman he made it to Scotland and thence to France. He showed Evelyn the dented coins that had saved his life 'by receiving a Musket bullet upon them'. 'This knight was indeed a valiant Gent,' observed Evelyn, 'but not a little given to romance, when he spake of himself.'[41]

Even in Paris, though, Evelyn thought of home – and home meant receipts. He wrote to his sister Jane asking her for recipes for pork, for syrup of violets and for surfeit water (the drink for overindulgence – useful in Paris, then as now); later he would ask for his grandmother's green salve for wounds (similar to Ann's King of France's Balsome) and her burn remedy. His wife Mary would become renowned among their friends for her skill in the still-room and her famously good preserves. A 1655 letter from Evelyn to Elizabeth Carey (later Mordaunt) conveyed receipts for a vomit and a posset for her ill sister from his wife, along with his own instructions to keep the 'pretty Patient'[42] warm, indicating a shared expertise. Their immaculately kept receipt book ends with a verse of doggerel, sadly water damaged, beginning, 'In this book is recorded many a cure/Of oyntments & plaisters for every sore'.[43]

As soon as they had ordered themselves some appropriately rich clothes for court, something that would have taken a large hole out of their finances, Ann and Richard called on Henrietta Maria (and Nan's friend, little Princess Henriette) who received them graciously. The queen mother, as she was known, gave Richard letters to take to her son and as autumn turned to winter they continued on to Calais, with the plan that Richard would go to Holland to await orders from Charles and Ann would return home to raise more money. Their long journey from Ireland through Spain and France had cost them 'all we could procure: yet this I will tell you,' she continued proudly, addressing their son directly, neither 'your father nor I ever borrowed money nor owed for clothes, not diet, nor lodging beyond sea in our lives'.[44]

This claim was quite a contrast with most exiles – Hyde had travelled to Spain the previous year borrowing money for 'coach, horses, wagons and dyett',[45] and Endymion Porter, a year after his arrival in France, wrote to his old friend Nicholas that he was still wearing 'that pore riding suit in which I came out of England, which shows I am as constant in my apparel as I am in my respects to your Honour'.[46] From her position of relative comfort, Ann looked down on other exiles' poverty and continual borrowing without much sympathy, believing it redounded 'much to the king's dishonour and their own discredit'.[47] It was easy for her to think so.

Hyde and Nicholas had not given up hope of Richard joining Charles in Scotland. In England it was almost impossible to raise money, as one agent lamented, finding 'in all so great an apprehension of the difficultye of returne without discovery of persons that I could not presume of any certainty in that kind'.[48] Their European options were closing down, with France in crisis, Spain not interested and the recent death of William of Orange, married to Charles's sister Mary (their son, also William, would later become King William III of England, married to his cousin, James II's daughter Mary). Despite its grave disadvantages, an alliance with Scotland was their only chance of foreign aid. Sir George Radcliffe wrote to Nicholas in November, just as the Fanshawes were kissing Henrietta Maria's hand at Saint-Germain-en-Laye, repeating how ideal Richard was as an envoy to Charles in Scotland. 'He shall deny us stiffly if he go not, for no man is so fit; it is of huge importance to send one that may probably do the business he goes for'.[49]

In Calais, Richard confessed to Ann that he had agreed to join Charles in Scotland. As soon as she sent him money from England he would leave. 'Here I will show you something of Sir Edward Hyde's nature,' she wrote, still smarting at this betrayal of their decision to remain together. Hyde, she said, feared Richard 'might come to a greater power than himself, both because of his [Richard's] parts and integrity' and because Hyde had failed Charles in Spain. Hyde 'begged my husband to remember the King often of him to his advantage... promising, with all the oaths… that he would make it his business all the days of his life to serve your father's interest'.[50] These were promises she did not think Hyde kept.

And so Ann returned to England alone – or rather, with four-year-old Nan and her sister Margaret and their several maids and men – to retrieve two-year-old Richard from the wet nurse in Hertfordshire, find a place to stay in London and raise yet more money. 'God knows how great a surprise this [was for] me,' Ann wrote of this unexpected separation, 'being great with child [she was about three months' pregnant] and two children with me not actually in the best position to maintain them… but I did what I could to arm myself [with patience], and was kindly visited both by my relations and friends.'[51]

SVMMER

Phebus doth now grow hott, and with bright Rayes
By Courting Summer doth prolong the dayes

Like Loues plump hills her naked brests lye bare,
Her Fann protects her from Sunburning ayre.

2

CHAPTER 9

1651
A Vinegar to Wash the Teeth for the Scurvy

You are to take 4 good handfulls of the tops of Firre and you are to take a pottle of the best white wine Vinegar you can get. You are to boyle the said Vinegar till it comes ye 3rd part. These tops of Firre are not to be had in any place in England but at Roe-Hampton near Putney. When you have boyled these together you are to wash your mouth Evening & morning but in the day as often as you please.

The little circle of Charles's servants in Europe buzzed with the news of Dick Fanshawe's imminent departure for Scotland in January 1651, a measure of their anxiety about their impressionable young master, dependent on demanding hosts without their guidance in a strange, unsophisticated land of religious fanatics. Using the alias Mr Lloyd, Hyde wrote to Richard's first cousin Christopher Hatton (under the name Simon Smith) from The Hague on 4 January to say that 'your cousin Fanshawe' was preparing to leave, having been summoned 'for settling a clear understanding between the Duke of York and the King'.[1]

Richard set off from Breda, where he had stopped to collect letters from the marquess of Ormonde for Charles, in the last week of January. As he embarked on his journey he wrote to Ann, already in London, 'to arm myself with patience in his absence' since frequent letters would be impossible. 'He hoped, that when we did meet again, it would be happy and of long continuance, and bade me trust God with him, as he did me'.[2] When he arrived he was received by Charles 'with great expressions of great content',[3] who gave him the broad seal and signet, the symbols of his government, to keep, a mark of immense favour.

Hyde, Nicholas, Ormonde and their friends followed Richard's progress closely. In early March, Hyde wrote to Ormonde to express the hope that Richard would be back by Easter, with 'more certain measures how to judge of the King's condition and affairs in Scotland, which I have some reason to doubt [suspect] are not in so prosperous a state as some relate them'.[4] By 'some' he meant the queen and her 'Louvrian' friends, who had pinned all their hopes on an alliance with the Presbyterian regime in Scotland, a policy of which Hyde and the others were deeply distrustful. Ormonde was reduced to telling 'them openly that they were there [in Paris] all turned Presbyterians';[5] testily Nicholas reported that the beautiful Isabella Thynne had converted a Mr Coventry to Presbyterianism, 'which has put him in favour at the Louvre'.[6]

In April, a letter Richard had written from Dundee reached Nicholas. The following day Nicholas received a letter from Ormonde saying how much he was hoping to hear of Richard's safe return, adding, '& receive testimonies of the King's kindness to you',[7] because Nicholas – living miserably in The Hague and increasingly unpopular with the queen and her friends at the Louvre – was considering giving up the struggle and going home.

Henrietta Maria had made clear her dislike of Nicholas, who

had served her husband steadily for so long. He was waiting for Richard's return to decide whether to continue in Charles's service or to compound. He wrote to Hyde, his closest friend and correspondent among the exiles, that if he didn't receive any fresh commands from the king through Richard – Charles had written to him directly only once since he arrived in Scotland the previous year – 'I shall then consider what course to take for the subsistence of myself and poor family, being reduced even to the last bit of bread. I do not conceive I am obliged to suffer my wife and children to starve in the streets'.[8]

Richard, with his steady loyalty and clear head, was much in demand that spring. As well as Hyde and Nicholas, James, duke of York, sent away from Scotland by his brother, wrote to Charles from Holland begging Richard be allowed to join him 'that I may find my rest', because he needed 'help to repair me against some that would ruin me and do your Majesty no good'.[9] (James apologized that he hadn't been able to raise enough money in Holland to get to France, whence Charles had asked him to go; even members of the royal family were finding it nearly impossible to muster the funds they needed.)

The person who missed Richard most, though, was Ann. She had picked little Richard up from his wet nurse and, with him and Nan, coming up for five, found lodgings in Hundson House, Blackfriars. The three of them, still with Margaret and presumably two or three maids, lived there nearly seven months, from December 1650 until June 1651, and 'in that time I did not go abroad [out] seven times, but spent my time in prayer to God for the deliverance of the King and my husband, whose danger was ever before my eyes'.[10] Intimately aware of the 'animosities amongst themselves in Scotland', she was in 'daily fears'[11] for Richard's safety.

So although she was settled in London, and still only twenty-six, for her there were no jaunts to Spring Gardens (despite the times, John Evelyn had taken some female relatives there the previous year; Cromwell would shut it down in 1654), no feasting on cherries, no shopping or calling on friends. Time spent in prayer was a regular feature of every seventeenth century matron's life, for everyone had much to pray for, but this was a moment of crisis. Traditionalists like Ann continued to use the Book of Common Prayer in private, though a certain amount of public attendance at Parliamentary-approved churches was required to avoid unwanted government attention. Pious women might have spiritual books read to them while they dressed; they transcribed sermons after hearing them to contemplate them again at their leisure and composed prayers and meditations for support in moments of specific hardship like childbirth or disease; they performed their own devotions several times a day and led their households in worship, often in morning and evening prayers. In this role, Royalist women were particular guardians of Anglican traditions.

Friends and family who rallied round Ann were another great consolation: 'all had compassion on my condition'. Her father was her kindest and most frequent visitor, sometimes staying a week with Ann and the children, and even in these straitened circumstances she could pride herself on being 'seldom without the best company in the town'.[12] She emerged from her seclusion to act, alongside Mary Evelyn ('my cousin Evelyn's wife'[13]), as godmother to the daughter of their glamorous Paris friends, the Wallers.

Margaret Cavendish, young marchioness of Newcastle, was

also in London at this time. She and her husband had run out of money in Antwerp and he'd sent her back to London to 'seek for reliefe'.[14] Like Ann, she insisted she barely went out – except to 'take the aire' in 'Hide Park' or 'to hear Musick' at the Royalist composer Henry Lawes's house. Overwhelmingly she missed her husband, 'with whom I had rather be a poor beggar, than to be Mistriss of the World absented from him'.[15]

Ann would have sympathized. She received just four letters from Richard in this time, 'which made the pain I was in more difficult to bear':[16] he had been right to warn her not to expect anything from him. These letters don't survive but the few letters from their time in Spain in the 1660s give a flavour of what Richard might have said to hearten Ann, addressing her as his 'dearest life' and his 'dearest only love'[17] and calling for God's blessing on them all.

Her replies add another facet to our understanding of her character. I have sometimes wondered how differently I would view Ann if I had access to the scraps of daily life we take for granted today, our unthought-of digital footprint: hastily typed emails, lists of books to read, even data trails through online shops. Barely anything she wrote herself has survived the centuries – both the receipt book and the memoirs were written mostly in other hands – and I'd give anything to see more that she had written spontaneously, perhaps a scrap from the diary she must have kept, however patchily, for her memoirs, a scrawled note to her friend Elizabeth Carteret, a quote from an especially meaningful sermon or a snippet from a poem she loved, even a shopping list.

The other thing I lacked, researching her life, was other people's descriptions of her, those lovingly revealing little details she included about Richard and which make him feel so real to us. Sadly, I found no letters in which she was mentioned, however casually, no real documentation beyond what she left us herself. What we have was written by Ann and polished for posterity; I'd like to have seen something of her living in the moment, unguarded and raw.

Writing to Richard between January and March 1666, Ann addressed him as 'my dear soul', urging him to be cheerful and promising him that 'as thou has always had God and honour before thy eyes, so thou wilt never want his blessing… Dear Lamb,' she added impulsively, 'it is much to be wished thy sudden return'.[18] A Spanish friend has given them a greyhound puppy, she wrote in February, 'so fine a creature I never saw in my life, which I take care of much for thee, but Dick lugs her by the ears and is very fond of her. God's name be praised, he grows a lovely fine boy and all the girls are very well and so am I, but wish thee with me a thousand times'.[19]

Other private letters attest to similarly touching relationships between seventeenth century husbands and wives and the blow they felt being separated. Ralph Josselin, chaplain to an army regiment in 1643, was worried about how 'wondrous sad and discontented'[20] his wife had been in his absence. 'Dear, let me hear often from thee,' wrote Simon Harcourt to his wife, 'for thy loving lines must & ever shall be the most wellcome and acceptable present that can be sent unto thye most faithful and affectionate husband.'[21] Newly married Elizabeth Feilding wrote to her husband, Basil – rebel son of Ann's friend Susan Denbigh, who had faced his father at Edgehill from the Parliamentary side – 'you cannot imagine what I would give to see you again'.[22]

Passion was not restricted to Cavaliers or even to the young: at nearly fifty Elizabeth Cromwell wrote to the austere Oliver, away on campaign in the 1640s, 'Oh my heart, so you were safe I did not care if I were dead... For God's sake write to me and come as soon as you can. Stay not away from your dutiful and obedient wife and humble servant', and in another letter, 'I am in perpetual fear for you. I would rather live with you with bread and water than from you with all the plenty in the world.'[23]

When her baby was due, Ann moved to lodgings in Great Queen Street, near St Paul's, lying-in 'in a very good lodging'[24] to give birth to another girl she named Elizabeth, in memory of the daughter who had died eleven months earlier in Madrid. In London, this little girl had a wider choice of sponsors: her godfather was Sir Oliver Boteler (a connection of Richard's through his sister's first husband) and her godmothers were Richard's sister-in-law, Elizabeth Cokaine, and 'my cousin Young', Anne, a distant cousin and kinswoman through the Boteler and Fanshawe families and a true friend to Ann during these hard times.

Meanwhile, in Scotland the young king had told Richard he needed him to remain by his side. On 5 May, at last, one of Richard's letters to Nicholas got through to The Hague, informing him that the king had asked him to stay with him and enclosing letters for Nicholas and one from the king to be forwarded to Ormonde. Richard's tone was reassuring: 'we are not so merry here as the persons your letters name in Paris [the queen and her party], yet despair not neither'. Charles's kingly activity and judgement were increasing daily and, Richard hoped, the foundations of a 'great person'[25] were being laid.

Nicholas reported to Hatton that 'Mr F the K. keeps by him to help him, whereof all honest men are glad'. Richard's next letter, dated early June, confirmed the reason he was there, describing 'the great influence that those at the Louvre have on His Majesty's resolutions… I pray God it prove not as fatal to him as to his father'.[26] To his patron, Ormonde, he let down his guard, telling him how badly they needed money and confessing that without word from his friend he was groping 'in the dark as well as I might at all I could imagine conducing to serve you':[27] for Richard, serving the king was serving Ormonde.

Worry made the exiles even more desperately homesick. Nicholas wrote to a friend praying to be 'peacefully in England'; Hatton told another friend how he longed 'to be settled at home in peace and quiet'; Hyde, as ever thinking of his stomach, expressed the hope to Richard Browne in Paris that they would survive their hardships to 'eat cherries at Deptford again'.[28]

Charles is crowned King of England and Scotland at Scone Palace on 1 January 1651. He leads an invading army south from Scotland through England that summer, reaching Worcester at the end of August, but Cromwell's victory is conclusive. Charles only just manages to escape capture afterwards, fleeing to France.

After her baby was born in June, Ann went to Ware Park, to her brother-in-law, while her sister returned home to Balls. Their father and his new family had recently moved back in, although, having compounded and with debts of £25,000, it was a scraping existence. Ann was there when she heard news of the Royalist defeat at the Battle of Worcester on 3 September and the young king's disappearance, there as she waited for word of Richard, 'dead or alive, for three days it was inexpressible what affliction I was in. I neither eat nor slept, but trembled at every motion I heard, expecting the fatal news'.[29] At last a news-sheet put her out of her misery: Richard had been taken prisoner.

The Battle of Worcester, the Royalists' last vain hope of defeating Parliament, turned out to be a rout. The Commonwealth's New Model Army, with Oliver Cromwell at its head, was larger, better trained, better prepared and better informed. As the day drew to a disastrous close Charles tried to rally his troops but to no avail, and he fled the town while a last-ditch cavalry charge led by the earl of Cleveland (later he would contribute a receipt to Ann's book) caused a distraction, knights of old bravely storming down the timber-framed high street.

With a small group, Charles fled north-east, towards Boscobel – famously hiding in an oak tree there before making his slow escape to France – while Richard headed south-west, to Newport, perhaps hoping to take ship for Europe. He and the Scottish earl of Lauderdale were arrested there the day after the battle and marched back to London as prisoners along with perhaps ten thousand Royalist soldiers. Thinking quickly, Richard had managed to burn all his papers before he was arrested, 'which saved the lives and estates of many a brave gentleman';[30] as a man of letters, he had not been involved in any fighting. He wrote to Ann telling her that he was safe and 'very civilly used' and asking her to meet him in London: as a great favour his keeper had promised he could stop and meet Ann 'at dinner-time' on an appointed day.

On hearing Richard had been captured, Ann rushed to London hoping to seek out more information. There his messenger found her and, expecting her husband 'with impatience' a few days later, she booked a room in Charing Cross, as he'd asked, and ordered dinner. She and her father and some other friends were waiting when, at about eleven o'clock, the soldiers began filing past, 'both English and Scotch... all naked on foot' and among them Richard, 'very cheerful in appearance', who greeted Ann and his friends with wonderfully Cavalier disregard for his circumstances. 'Pray let us not lose time, for I know not how little I have to spare. This is the chance of war, nothing venture, nothing have; so let us sit down and be merry while we may.' Then he took Ann's hand and tenderly kissed her damp face, saying, 'Cease weeping, no other thing upon earth can move me: remember we are all at God's disposal.'[31]

Instead of complaining about the march, Richard told Ann and their friends how kind his captain had been and how the people they passed on the road had offered them food and money. Passing through Borstal in Buckinghamshire he met a friend, Lady Denham, who tried to give him 'all the money in her house'. Gallantly he told her that 'he had so ill kept his own, that he would not tempt his governor with more' but a shirt and some handkerchiefs would be welcome if she had any to spare. She had no men's linen but she gave him 'two smocks of her own',[32] wishing she had something better to offer him.

All too quickly the precious day passed and guards arrived to take Richard to Whitehall where he was held prisoner 'in a little room yet standing in the bowling green... without the speech of any, so far as they knew'.[33] On 13 September the Council of State committed him to the charge of the sergeant-at-arms, 'who is to take special care of him, that no one speaks with him, and that he does not make his escape, and bring him before the Commission of Examiners this afternoon'. The charge was 'High Treason in adhering to Charles Stuart'.[34]

This document says he was to be kept in the Tower, rather than Whitehall, but since Ann said she visited him secretly every day he was held prisoner – delightedly subverting the stricture that he be held 'without the speech of any' – her testimony must be more accurate. She was lodging with Anne Young, baby Elizabeth's godmother, in Chancery Lane. Every morning before dawn, as the clock struck four, she would take a lantern and walk half an hour down through the dark and silent streets to Whitehall, 'in at the entry that went out of King Street into the bowling-green'. There she would stand under Richard's window and call softly to him; 'after the first time excepted, [he] never failed to put his head out at the first call: thus we talked together, and sometimes I was so wet with the rain, that it went in at my neck and out at my heels'.[35]

The Royalist exiles in Europe were thrown into consternation by news of the defeat and Charles's disappearance. Even if many of them had disapproved of Charles's Scottish adventure, they had hoped that it might succeed. But after Worcester, at last, their long years of struggle seemed to have come to naught. Ormonde wrote to Edward Nicholas saying he had never been 'soe confused in all my facultys'[36] and Lord Hopton, urging Hyde and Nicholas to compound, declared no hope was left. Nicholas, who had spent the year agonizing over his own position, described himself 'in doleful condition'.[37] News 'of ye fatal battail at Worcester' arrived in Paris on 22 September and was quickly disseminated by Sir Richard Browne but it was more than a month later that word of Charles's 'miraculous escape' arrived and 'exceedingly rejoiced us'.[38]

A small group travelled to Monceaux, just outside Paris, to welcome back the returning king. Charles had been on the run, in disguise, for six weeks. He was hungry and dirty and desperate for a clean shirt. La Grande Mademoiselle, Louis XIV's cousin Anne Marie Louise and a great heiress in her own right, who was considering marrying him at this time, admired his thinner, bearded new look: she thought her suitor was 'much better looking than before his departure'.[39] Chivalrously he told her that the loss of the battle had mattered less to him than coming back to France – he wanted so much to dance, he said – but Richard Browne noticed how quiet he was.

The exiles were also gathering news of their comrades, Hyde telling Nicholas on 4 November that he had received a letter from Dick: 'I wish he were at liberty, for upon my word he is a very honest, excellent man'.[40] He can't have been too constrained in his cell, for two weeks later the young duke of York told Nicholas that he had received letters from Fanshawe too.

Although he was managing to write letters, Richard's health was failing. 'The cold and hard marches he had undergone', not to mention the lack of good food, 'and being pent up in a room close and small... brought him almost to death's door':[41] he was suffering from terrible scurvy. Outside his prison, Ann was working tirelessly for his release. In their early-morning talks Richard advised her 'how I should make my addresses', singling out Oliver Cromwell not only as their most important contact (he and Richard were third cousins) but also because he 'had a great respect for your father [Richard], and would have bought him off to his service upon any terms'.[42]

Even while he was in gaol, I imagine Ann was preparing remedies for Richard's scurvy. Since Putney Bridge was not built until the following century, she would have ridden or taken a coach as well as a boat across the river to Roehampton, a rural village six miles south-west of her lodgings in London, to collect the precious pine needles for this antiscorbutic vinegar. Scurvy is caused by a deficiency of vitamin C and its symptoms are horrific, with the connective tissues of the body melting away: intense fatigue followed by pallor, spots, bleeding from mucous membranes, gingivitis and loss of teeth and finally fever, open, suppurating wounds and, ultimately, bleeding to death. Ann's vitamin C- and antioxidant-rich, pine-needle mouthwash was intended to cool and cleanse Richard's agonizingly disintegrating, blackening gums.

Cromwell told Ann to bring a doctor's certificate to the Council of State. She went straight to John Bathurst, handily physician both to Cromwell and to the Fanshawes, 'who gave me one [a letter] very favourable in my husband's behalf'. That afternoon she presented it before the council, where Cromwell himself moved that Richard be released because he was so ill. Sir Harry Vane – one of the most radical of the council members – declared that Richard 'would be as instrumental for aught he knew, to hang them all that sat there, if ever he had the opportunity, but if he had liberty for a time, that he might take the engagement [the new Commonwealth's oath of loyalty] before he went out'. Cromwell then made a joke: 'I never knew the ENGAGEMENT was a medicine for the scorbutic [sufferer from scurvy]'.[43] It was a pun – in Ireland an engagement was an issue, something issuing forth. Surprised by this moment of unaccustomed levity, and taking into account Cromwell's evident sympathy for his cause, the council ordered Richard be given his freedom on bail of £4000.

With Ann on his side, Richard was one of the lucky ones. Charged with treason, his release meant he avoided execution as well as possible death from scurvy. Perhaps as a man of letters he was considered less dangerous to the regime, and had been less obviously damaging to it, than a soldier might have been. Despite his cast-iron loyalty he also had that valuable connection to Cromwell. Then, too, his party had been conclusively defeated: however able Richard might have been, there was very little more the Council of State feared he could do for his king. Eighteen months earlier, still fighting for survival, Parliament had been less merciful, executing Lords Holland and Capel and the earl of Warwick; after Worcester, even the earl of Lauderdale, who had persuaded Charles to join the Scots and led the troops south and was captured with Richard at Newport, avoided execution.

Helped by Richard's elder brother Thomas and his sister Alice Bedell, Ann scraped the £4000 together; her father, who had been so helpful five years earlier, could no longer afford to contribute. Later, Ann would single out Thomas Fanshawe for his kindness 'during the time of the war... by assisting us in our wants, which were as great as his supports'.[44]

On 28 November, after three months in captivity, Richard came to Anne Young's a free man. For once his wife's powers of description faltered: 'He there met many of his good friends and kindred; and my joy was inexpressible, and so was poor Nan's, of whom your father was very fond.'[45]

As ill as Richard was, he and Ann were overjoyed to be reunited after a separation of almost a year. Their seventh child would be born exactly nine months and two days after Richard's release from prison.

For the Scurvy.

A Han +
Scurvy grass of both sorts, Sage of each 4 handfulls: Wormwood, Horse radish roots of each halfe a handfull, pound all together, straine the same and drinke three or foure spoonfulls so long as it lasts.

A Vinegar to wash the Teeth for the Scurvy

A Han +
You are to take 4 good handfulls of the tops of Firre and you are to take a pottle of the best white wine Vinegar you can get You are to boyle the said Vinegar till it comes to ye 3d. part these tops of Firre are not to be had in any place in England but at Roe Hampton neare Putney When you have boyled these together You are to wash your mouth evening & morning but in the day as often as you please.

A Medecine for the Wormes

A Han +
Take Lemmon, mingle it with saffron in powder, to every 3 spoonfulls of ye juice put the weight of 6 pence in Saffron, to a child of a year old you may give 2 spoonfulls at a time 3 Mornings fasting. To one of 7 or 8. or older 3 or 4 spoonfull

A Han
~~This Medecine hath been approved for ye Wormes~~

~~Take Aloe rosatum made up into pills somewhat bigger then the biggest pease. Take them fasting 3 pills every day one. At two houres after you have taken your pill make a Glister of a pint of new milke wth. 2 spoonfulls of honey, set it on ye fire till it be hott & ye honey dissolved stirring it all ye while. And when it is so cold~~

that

One of the pages of scurvy and worms receipts from Ann's book, showing her cross for 'probatus' and an ineffectual remedy crossed out. The top remedy is in her hand, evidently rushed, while the second is in Joseph Avery's immaculate copperplate.

CHAPTER 10

1652
An excellent water to be used constantly all winter for the scorbute

Scurvy-grass bruised three pounds, horse Radish roots cut sliced and [illegible] one pound, 12 oringes cut into thin slices, put these into a glass still, powre in as much sack and white wine as will cover them 3 fingers deepe, stop the glass close, let this stand 24 howers in digestion, the next day distill a water from hence.

Take a wine-glass full at pleasure, sweetened with syrup of elderflower, or oringes, or wood-sorrell, or cloves, gilly-flowers.

Uniquely in Ann's receipt book, the three pages or so of remedies for scurvy are hastily, messily handwritten, sometimes by her, and mostly unattributed, indicating that she collected them herself for immediate use. There was no time for clean copies or seeking out recommendations from friends: these were needed urgently.

Richard was released on 28 November 1651. Within ten days – so on about 7 or 8 December – 'he fell very sick, and the fever settled in his throat and face so violently, that, for many days and nights, he slept no more but as he leaned on my shoulder as

I walked'.[1] The date is important, because Joseph Avery began copying out Ann's receipt book on 11 December of either 1651 or 1657. It's possible it reads 1657 because I think it unlikely that, with her husband desperately ill and newly released from prison just days earlier, she would have embarked on this project. Having said that, all she needed to do was direct Avery what to copy. Perhaps its beginning was a triumph of delegation, the work of an efficient housekeeper at a time when she had great need of remedies.

Regardless of when she began her book, Ann had been preparing for it since her childhood: it was a lifetime's work. An earlier edition was surely a book she had copied out under her mother's loving tutelage as a handwriting exercise, supplemented with scraps of papers given by friends and family over the years. When Sir Walter Raleigh's son sent his father's collection of receipts to Lord Conway in 1652, at Conway's request, they were a ragged 'parcell of papers… I am ashamed off, old, rotten, dirtie, and torn things and such as a person less intelligent than your selfe would hardly understand, but they are all of this kynd (recepts) which I have, that you have not alreaddy seene: they are most of them in my Fathers owne hand, and therefore I thinke approved ones'.[2] Ann's packet of receipts had gone with her on all her travels, from Balls to Oxford and then through England and across Europe and back again: now, with her beloved husband close to death, their moment had come.

What's interesting about Ann's scurvy remedies is that all except one contain vitamin C, the only cure for the disease and one that is completely effective in a matter of weeks. Although scurvy and its cure were not defined by science until the late nineteenth century, folk and experiential remedies using fresh fruits, herbs and vegetables – notably scurvy-grass, a kind of water-cress, but also horseradish and citrus fruits – had been known from the Middle Ages, especially to sailors. Vasco da Gama's men ate citrus fruits on his 1490s expeditions and so did the sailors of Sir John Hawkins's fleet a century later. However, since no one could explain why these remedies worked (and it was difficult to store fresh food on long sea journeys or observe their effects experimentally), they weren't systematically used. Ann's drinks and mouthwashes were distilled, a sophisticated, modern technique she would have believed strengthened their potency but which actually would have weakened their effectiveness, despite the fact that they contained the right ingredients. Elsewhere I've seen remedies that called for the pure juice of scurvy-grass mixed with the pure juice of oranges but, because of the way she made them, Ann's remedies would have worked less well than she would have liked – perhaps this explains why Richard's illness, though relieved by Ann's treatment, would linger for so long.

Interspersed with the remedies for scurvy – mostly drinks but also gargles and pills – are two remedies for worms, one marked with Ann's X for *probatus*, made from lemon juice and saffron, the other crossed out. It seems likely, from their place in her book, that Richard was suffering from worms as well as the high fever caused by late-stage scurvy, one symptom of which is chronic diarrhoea, shot through with yellow mucous, with a characteristic smell. After ten days, and 'all the Doctor and Surgeon could do',[3] Richard's fever broke. Gradually, lovingly nursed by Ann, he began to recover his strength.

Good health meant much the same to the people of the seventeenth century as it does today. The theory of the humours, however outlandish talk of black bile and yellow phlegm may seem to modern ears, was based on balance and moderation.* Ann's brother-in-law Philip Warwick held up Charles I's eating habits as a model of good health: he had a good appetite but preferred plain foods, seldom eating from more than three of the multitude of dishes offered to him and drinking usually one glass of small beer, one glass of wine and, finally, one glass of water. He did not snack between meals and he was very fond of fruit.[4] Ann noted approvingly of her father that he never drank more than six glasses of wine in a day – a glass at that time being about the size of a large thimble. She included several receipts in her book to relieve surfeit, or overconsumption of food and drink.

Exercise was important and corporal health was strongly linked to spiritual health: each fed on the other. Lady Harley, who like Ann kept a receipt book, told her son Ned, when he was at Oxford in the late 1630s, that 'the means to presarufe health, is a good diet and exersise: and, as I hope you are not wanteing in your care for your health, so I hope you are much more carefull for your soule'.[5] The three rules of the medieval poem of health advice, *Regimen Sanitatis Salerni* (also called *The Lily of Medicine* and translated by Thomas Paynell in 1528), to eat a moderate diet, to maintain tranquillity of mind and to live joyfully,[6] are worthy of a Dalai Lama.

* The herbalist Marcos Patchett, who generously discussed Ann's remedies with me, suggests that the ancient theory of the humours is a European version of traditional Chinese medicine or Ayurveda, with equally relevant lessons for contemporary medicine. Based on close observation of the patient, seeking always to support good health and restore balance, except for the fact that it could not combat infectious disease it was a remarkably sophisticated and well thought-out system.

Richard's convalescent regime would thus have included simple, nutritious food and gentle exercise as well as Ann's vitamin C-laced cordials, gargles and vinegars. Her care would have been vital in an age without hospitals. Jane Anger, in her 1589 tract in defence of women, reminded her readers that men 'are comforted by our means: they [are] nourished by the meats we dress [prepare for serving]; their bodies [are] freed from diseases by our cleanliness'.[7]

Keeping clean, as Anger noted, was another essential part of good health. The Fanshawes would have washed daily in a basin of warm water in their room, using Castile soap made from olive oil (well known to be the best) and rubbed themselves down with scented waters, made by Ann (stimulating, antioxidant rosemary was an essential ingredient of waters like these); fresh linen, daily, was an indispensable luxury for anyone of gentle status. Sanitary towels were made from scraps of old linen, rinsed and reused. A full bath in a tub would have been a several times a year event, although London did have bath houses that Pepys recorded his wife liking. Teeth were rubbed with burnt rosemary and mouths rinsed out with vinegar and herb washes, unless you were lucky enough to have one of the newfangled toothbrushes from Paris.

Richard was well enough by early February to receive visitors and go out himself, the great pleasure of returning home after so many years of exile. When he heard news that Ralph Verney had received a magnificent pass from Edward Nicholas, sealed with the Dutch lion rampant, that permitted him to travel back to England the following year after nine years' absence, Roger Burgoyne (a Parliamentarian, but devoted to Verney despite their differing politics) wrote to tell his old friend that 'if I may have the happinesse to see my dearest friend it will make my old legges to Caper'.[8]

John Evelyn, back in London from Paris and fresh from admiring Mrs Lane, 'the Lady who conveied the King at his Escape from Worcester to the Sea-Side',[9] went to see Richard on 3 February and Richard called on him five days later. They had much to discuss, from poetry to politics. Evelyn recorded Richard telling him 'of many considerable affairs':[10] maybe his time in Scotland with the young king, the campaign through England, being held prisoner; his new translation of some verses by Horace; or the remedies used by Ann to bring him back to health, perhaps for the Evelyns' own receipt book.

All through the spring of 1652, according to Evelyn's diary, there was a great drought – a contrast to the rain-sodden years of the 1640s. It broke on 25 June with a tremendous storm 'of haile, raine, wind, Thunder & Lightning, as no man alive had seene the like in this age'. In London the hailstones, several inches in diameter, broke windows. Evelyn recorded some people saying they were shaped like crowns or the order of the garter, 'but these were fancies'.[11]

Just before the great thunderstorm, Evelyn was accosted by highwaymen. He was riding between Tonbridge, where his wife, recently arrived from Paris with her mother, was taking the waters, and Bromley. The weather was very hot and Evelyn had sent his manservant on ahead while he rode 'negligently under favour of the shade'. Hugging the side of the road and the tall trees alongside it, he was idling along when out of the woods jumped two 'cut-throates' with long staves who grabbed his horse, took his sword and pulled him into a 'deepe thickett'.[12]

What they stole provides a useful glance at the everyday wear of a gentleman. Tugging off his fingers two rings, an emerald and an onyx engraved with his coat of arms, and taking his silver shoe buckles set with rubies and diamonds, as well as his sword with its silver hilt, Evelyn's attackers pulled off his boots and tied him up, leaving him hidden in the woods, sweating intolerably and plagued by flies. They left his horse, too, which, being well marked and cropped on both ears, would have been too easily identifiable and therefore not worth trying to sell. It took him two hours to untie himself. Once free he rode straight to the local justice of the peace, a Colonel Blount, who raised the hue and cry. Evelyn had 500 fliers printed the next day with details of what he'd lost. Everything but the sword was returned to him within two days – and the goldsmith who returned one of the rings led him to one of the thieves, who was duly arrested, his accomplice soon afterwards.

Not 'wanting to hang the fellow', since stealing anything worth over several shillings carried the death penalty, Evelyn didn't turn up to see him tried. His accomplice petitioned Evelyn for mercy and was reprieved, but Evelyn 'heard afterwards that had it not been for his companion, a younger man, he would probably have kill'd me. He was afterwards charg'd with some other crime, but refusing to plead, was press'd to death'.[13] Pressing, or more correctly *peine forte et dure*, was a form of punishment in which a criminal who refused to plead guilty was crushed to death by heavier and heavier stones being placed on his chest. Prisons (apart from debtors' prisons) were more commonly used as holding places for those awaiting trial or punishment (at this stage usually branding, whipping or hanging; transportation to the American colonies was just beginning) than as places of punishment.

Highwaymen were one consequence of the end of the wars, when discharged soldiers – often Royalist, and often unpaid – who for one reason or another could not or did not want to go home, embarked on careers as gentlemen of the road: their rapaciousness was reputedly equalled only by their gallantry. In 1652, the most notorious of them, James Hind, was hanged, drawn and quartered – not for robbery but, as a declared Royalist, for treason. Claiming to have robbed John Bradshaw, who had presided over Charles I's trial, and eagerly notching up victims known to be regicides, he was arrested while trying to rob Oliver Cromwell. Before he was killed he declared that nothing troubled him as much as dying before he had seen his master restored to the throne.

The lone highwaywoman of the period has sometimes been identified as Katherine Fanshawe, née Ferrers, Richard's dead brother Simon's ward who'd married one of his nephews four years earlier. During the 1650s Katherine's husband was away from home, either studying at Middle Temple or, briefly, in prison as a malignant. Having apparently been taught the art of highway robbery by a local farmer, the 'Wicked Lady' was said nightly to haunt the roads leading out of London towards Hertfordshire, returning home to act the fine lady during the day. There is, however, no contemporary evidence for this – the story sprang up long after her death in 1660.*

* It's more than likely that the entire story is based on the confusion around the name of Ferrers, which Katherine shared with the eighteenth century

Whatever the truth of her story, Katherine was eighteen in 1652 and Ann, who spent so much time over the years with her in-laws at Ware, knew her well; she was, Ann said, 'a very great fortune, and a most excellent woman'[14] (the two being intertwined). It's quite possible that the Fanshawes' seventh baby, born on 30 July, was named for her. Little Katherine was born at Anne Young's 'on Thursday morning early', baptized by Dr Barrow (later Bishop of St Asaph, who had christened baby Elizabeth the previous year), with the ardent Royalist Sir Humphrey Bennet, Lady Rockingham (a daughter of the earl of Strafford) and 'my cousin Ayloffe'[15] – perhaps the source of Ann's receipt for green-sickness, Margaret Ayloffe, a Fanshawe cousin (see the end of Chapter 1; another argument for the receipt book being written at this time) – her godparents.

After Katherine's birth, Richard went to Bath to take the waters, internally and externally. Despite his illness, he was in a happier situation than his friends in Europe, for whom Charles's defeat at Worcester had spelled further ruin. Resuming his diplomatic overtures to the various courts of Europe, Charles's requests for aid fell on sympathetic but unhelpful ears. His followers were no better off, although because the Louvrian tactic, of collaboration with the Scots, had failed, at last Edward Hyde found his views appreciated and listened to. Patience was what he counselled: when the moderates had been won over, Hyde predicted, Charles would find the route home was clear.

murderer Lord Ferrers, also known as the 'Wicked Earl', who was hanged at Tyburn for killing his valet in 1760.

That conviction did nothing to make the day-to-day life of Royalist exiles any easier; patience was required for them, too. Hyde wrote to Nicholas, his companion in adversity, in the autumn of 1652 that he had 'not had a crown these two months but borrow, that is Edgman [his secretary, William Edgeman] borrows. For so God help me I have no credit, every week two crowns to fetch my letters from the post… and to buy paper and ink, and my wife is in the meantime in as sad a condition as can be imagined'.[16]

Richard and Ann made the difficult decision not to rejoin them. On his return from Bath Richard began negotiating with the young earl of Strafford, the son of his former patron who had been executed at Parliament's behest in 1641 and sister of Anne Rockingham, who had just acted as godmother to the Fanshawes' new baby Katherine, to rent the Old Hall at Tankersley, in Yorkshire, on a long lease of twenty-one years for £60 a year (Ann remembered £120 in her memoirs). After eight years of living out of cases and cloak bags and frequently apart, at the end of 1652 Ann, Richard and their small family could at last look forward to being settled together in a home of their own.

CHAPTER 11

1653
To Make Water of Life

Take Balme [melissa officinalis] Leaves and Stalks, Burnett Leaves & Flowers, Rosemary, Turmenstill [tormentil or potentilla erecta] Leaves and Rootes, Rosa Solis [sundew], Red Roses, Red Fennell Leaves & Rootes and red Mints, of each one handful, putt all these hearbes into a pott well-glased [glazed] and putt thereto as much white wine as will couer the hearbes, Lett them soake therein 8 or 9 daies, then take Cinnamon, Ginger, Cloues, Saffron and Nutmeg of each one ounce, of Anyseeds, Raisins of the Sunne [sun-dried grapes] and Sugar of each one pound, of dates stoned a pound. The hinder parts of an old Rabbet, a good flesht running Capon, the Flesh and Sinews of a Leg of Mutton, 4 Young Pigeons, a dozen of Larks, ye yolkes of 12 eggs, a loafe of white Bread cutt in slices, 3 gallons of Muskadine [Muscat wine] or as much as sufficeth for the distill, all these in a Limbeck [or alembic, two connected vessels used for distilling] at one time, and putt thereto of Mithridase or perfect Treacle 3 ounces. Distill it with a moderate fire, and keep the First Water by it selfe, when there cometh not more water with Stilling take away the Limbeck and putt into the Stuffe more Wine and distill it againe and you shall have another good Water.

Of the First Ingredients of this water you must keepe in a double glasse verily for it is a restorative to all principall Members, and defendeth against all pestilent Diseases, as the Palsie, Dropsie, Spleene, Yellow or Black Jaundices, and for wormes in the Belly, and for all Agues be they hott or Cold, for all manner of Swellings, for Melancholicke and Phlegmatick Persons, & it comeforteth all the Spiritts and Strings of the Braine, Heart, Milt [an archaic word for spleen], Liver and Stomach, by taking thereof 2 or 3 Spoonfulls, at a time, with olye, wine or Beere, putt a little sugar therein, it helpeth digestion, breaketh Wind, stoppeth a loosenesse and bindeth, it easeth the heart burning, it quickeneth the Memory. takeing of this water 3 Spoonfulls a day, one in the morning, one at noone, & one at night.

In March 1653, with their three elder children, Nan, Dick and Betty, Ann and Richard moved into Tankersley, a late medieval hunting lodge remodelled in the Tudor period, set in a large deer park in Yorkshire. Their youngest child, one-year-old Katherine, was at nurse, probably in Hertfordshire. Margaret, Ann's younger sister and companion for so many of the previous ten years, had elected to remain in London where she would soon marry Edmond Turnor, a brother-in-law of Richard's brother-in-law Philip Warwick. At last Ann could unpack her trunks, shake out her bedding, unroll her carpets and hang the family portraits on the walls. She would have known by then that she was expecting another baby, her seventh, and for the first time she could plan for it to be born in her own home.

Here, at this 'very pleasant and good'[1] place, was Ann's chance to become a seventeenth century matron, the great career available to women of her time and background. In Yorkshire, she would be not just wife and mother but mistress of the house, consumed and fulfilled by managing her own household. She could settle into the daily routine for which her mother had raised her: bringing up her children, overseeing their health and education, supervising her servants from a 'waiting gentlewoman' and footmen down to scullery maids and nurses, entertaining and writing to friends and relations, ministering to the local poor, performing the household's daily devotions, managing her own kitchen, dairy, laundry and gardens and working in her own still-room. Almost all the household's clothes would have been made at home, apart from Ann and Richard's finest outfits, and adorned with embroidery by Ann, her maids and, later, when they were old enough, her daughters. Her work in the still-room would produce not only salves, cordials, waters, preserves and wines but also lavender bags for their linen cupboard, scented powder for their gloves and clothes, whitening paste for their hands and faces and burnt rosemary to clean their teeth.

Tankersley, with its 1800 acres, about a week's journey from London and on the edge of the moors, was set in wilder country than gentle, familiar Hertfordshire, but Ann would have hoped to create at her home a similar atmosphere of comfort and refinement to that in the two houses she knew intimately, her father's Balls Park and her brother-in-law's house, Ware, barely two miles across the Lea valley.

An engraving dating to the 1690s depicts Balls Park as it was when inhabited by Ann's father's heir, her half-brother Richard, named for her husband when he was born in 1646. The house was still brashly new, very much the declaration of the self-made Sir John of the mid-1630s. Replete with prosperity and confidence, classically inspired but by no means austere, it was dotted with apt ball finials, emblazoned with an elaborate stone frontispiece surmounted by a pair of unicorns, its corniced windows decorated in a variety of styles and an approach through a wall topped with urns: the latest word in 1630s money-is-no-object architectural fashion. The ceilings were fretted, the steps of the great staircase wainscotted and the hall paved in black and white marble. Even sixty years after it was built, the unicorns looked out over a 'most pleasant and delicious prospect',[2] attractive but still immature gardens and parkland, the trees in twin avenues (probably limes, very popular in the seventeenth century) and its orchard petite and neatly shaped.

Ware (in which Richard's elder brother Thomas and his family lived, after compounding for £1300 in 1648) was more established, the house dating back to the previous century. Richard's father, Sir Henry, had been a patron of the arts as well as a successful crown official, retaining the composer John Ward as part of his household and creating an exquisite garden which his friend Sir Henry Wotton admired in his *Reliquiae Wottoniae*. He'd planted a lime avenue (perhaps the very one imitated by his neighbour John Harrison) and laid out alleys and 'knots', or knot-gardens of herbs and box, and installed a fine fountain and a stream stocked with fat trout. His kitchen garden was 'full of all manner of good things in extraordinary number':[3] quinces and plums which flourished in the English climate but also hothouse fruit like peaches, grapes and melons so good Sir Henry used to send them to James I when he was at nearby Theobalds. Nothing had excelled the fruit, flowers and 'physic herbs' Richard's father grew at Ware, 'in which things he did greatly delight'.[4]

Gardens were one of the great passions of the period, allied to many of its preoccupations: the idea of taming nature, the exotic, medicine, food and drink, philosophy and astrology, the expression of status. Although the mania for Dutch bulbs had faded by this time, the typical Stuart gentleman and his wife had lost none of their enthusiasm for creating their own little paradise around their houses, fleeing (in the words of Andrew Marvell) 'rude society' for the solace of 'sweet and wholesome hours' reckoned 'with herbs and flowers'. Shaken by civil wars, the seventeenth century soul was soothed by 'Annihilating all that's made/To a green thought, in a green shade.' In July 1655 Christopher Hatton wrote to Edward Nicholas thanking 'God I am confined to the low culture of my garden again',[5] and when Ralph Verney returned to England from exile almost his first action was to begin planting: apple, cherry, mulberry, almond and walnut trees, French limes, ashes and elders, along with roses and asparagus.

Thomas Kynvett, staying in London while he petitioned for sequestration of his estates in April 1644, raved to his wife in Norfolk about the glorious garden where he was staying in Petersham. He sent her a pressed anemone flower ('I never saw a rar'er') of which he was promised 'halfe the roote [tuber]' for her. 'Heer is a world of variety of other flowers, prim'roses, beares Eares [auriculas], & what you can think of,'[6] he told her, adding that 'the nightingales doe singe most melodiously'.[7]

Disappointed to find there were no fruit trees at Tankersley, Ann set out to create an orchard. (Later in life she would confess to falling sick with an 'aguish distemper' she attributed to eating too many Frontignac (Muscat) grapes, 'being tempted by their goodness'.)[8] There's a rough sketch in Ann's receipt book (see plate section) which I like to imagine dates to this time in her life. It shows a house surrounded by gardens, with a neat wood laid out beneath it, and the 'London Road' (unfortunately, the only legible words on the plan apart from 'House') on one side. In December she and Richard received permission from their landlord to build walls around part of the garden, a necessary precaution for growing fruit successfully in the north of England.

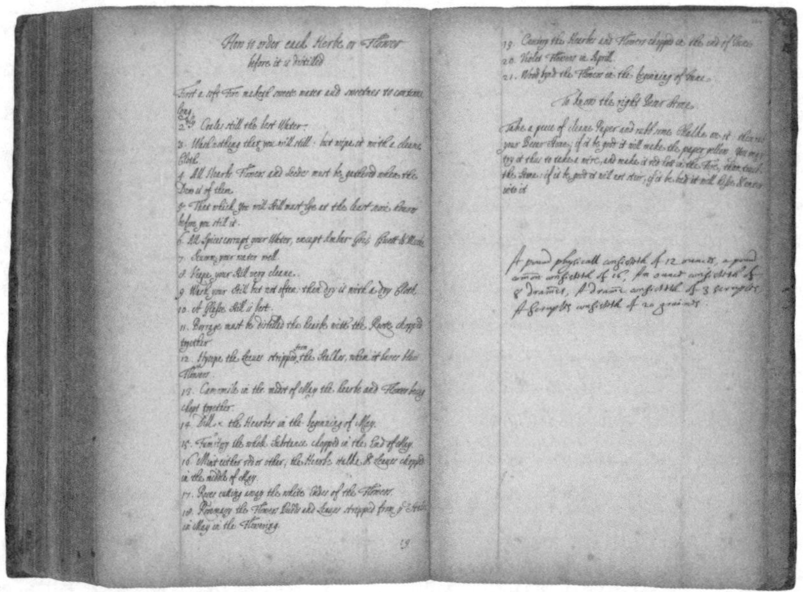

Ann's general instructions for distilling and preparing herbs. The note on the right-hand page is in Ann's handwriting.

She would have planted other plants and herbs, too, for use in her new still-room, perhaps in a preventative drink like this Water of Life: melissa, rosemary, fennel, roses, mint. Tormetil is a wild herb with astringent qualities, used to increase resistance to disease. This receipt, with its large variety of ingredients, required expert preparation over an extended period of time, so perhaps it was one Ann could have made especially well in a still-room of her own, undisturbed by a hostess (however well-meaning) or a landlady. After Richard's illness she would have been eager to store up the health of her family and a richly nutritious, herbal concoction like this, given to her by the wife of a relative of Richard's, was ideal. Richard, coming to terms with having abandoned his master and comrades-in-exile, would have had particular need of its anti-melancholic, spirit-raising qualities.

Even though, by her standards, Ann was living in vastly reduced circumstances, the ingredients she used in both medical and culinary receipts placed her as part of the elite, able to afford expensive sugar and spices from across the known world. At the apothecary's shop, a handful of herbs could be had for a halfpenny, powdered exotic spices like cinnamon and ingredients like ground bezoar stone cost about sixpence for quarter of an ounce, although ground pearls were eighteen pence and the various essential vessels cost several shillings: receipt making was an occupation only for those who could afford it.

As well as rosemary and roses and various other herbs, wild and domestic, that Ann would have gathered at Tankersley, this receipt for Water of Life calls for Muscat wine from France, sugar from Portuguese Brazil and cinnamon, cloves, nutmeg and ginger from Indonesia, sourced by Portuguese, Dutch and British traders. Other remedies included precious ambergris, the scented secretion from sperm whales; frankincense, an aromatic resin from the Boswellia tree traded through Arabia (the best quality frankincense came from Somalia); and sassafras, the leaves and bark from a North American tree introduced to Europe in the sixteenth century and used to combat a multitude of ailments from arthritis and gout to impotence and indigestion.

A global network was coming into place to make receipts like Ann's possible. The academic Kim Hall has suggested that not only did the habits of the English housewife shape social order but also her demand for ingredients stimulated colonial expansion: profit-seeking English traders spanned the globe to bring home rare ingredients to adorn English tables and be used in still-rooms.[9] Diplomatic crises reverberated through the kitchens of the seventeenth century: when England was at war with Spain there was no marmalade, for instance, because Spain was its sole source of Seville oranges (China, or sweet, oranges, had not yet been introduced to England).

Oliver Cromwell consolidates his grip on power throughout 1652 and 1653, in April forcing the radical Rump Parliament to dissolve against its wishes and replacing it with a selected, rather than elected, Parliament. This body, the Nominated Assembly, surrenders its authority to Cromwell and declares him Lord Protector in December 1653.

Ann, painted at about the time of her wedding in 1644 by Cornelius Johnson, one of the most celebrated portraitists of the day. At nineteen she was (according to one of her contemporaries) already past the peak of youthful beauty: 'After eighteen… there is noe face but decays apparently'.

Richard in 1643 by the court painter William Dobson, painted in his wartime studio at St John's College, Oxford. The letter and classical mask represent Richard's literary interests while the graceful hound at his knee is a symbol of loyalty – both to his doomed king and to his spirited wife.

Balls Park just outside Hertford, built by Ann's father Sir John Harrison in the late 1630s as the lavish expression of the wealth and status he had acquired as a customs officer in the service of Charles I. Note the unicorn finials above the front door – the height of seventeenth-century fabulousness.

This undated and almost illegible sketch from Ann's receipt book appears to show a house set in its garden, with the 'London Road' running alongside it and a small, neat orchard. I like to imagine it was her plan for Tankersley, the house she and Richard rented in Yorkshire in 1653 and where they planted fruit trees watered with their hopes for a peaceful future there.

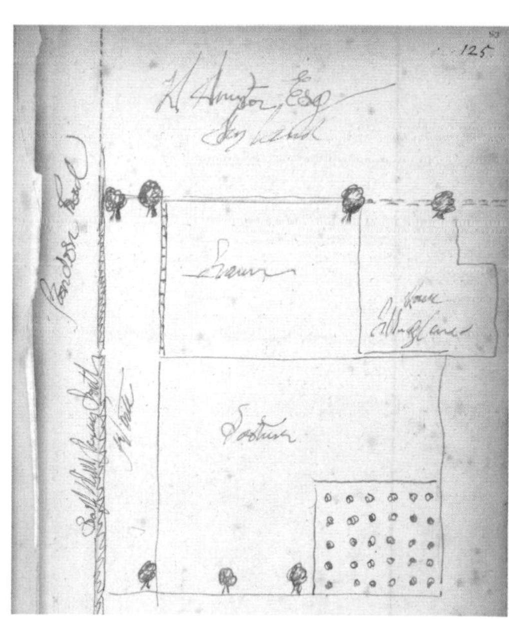

Dick, the Fanshawes' eldest son, who would die of smallpox aged eleven. Ann's grief caused her to have a miscarriage. He was buried in the Protestant churchyard in Paris; of the nine Fanshawe children to die young, all but two lay in different places.

Margaret, by the circle of Theodore Russel in the mid-1660s, who had smallpox at the same time as Dick but survived. Her brown eyes are the same as her mother's while her sister Ann (*above right*), painted at the same time, has Richard's grey eyes.

Ann also survived smallpox in 1659, aged five. She was probably nine or ten in this portrait and wears the same jewellery, with the same elaborate hairstyle, as her elder sister Margaret (*below left*).

A Restoration beauty: Ann as a young woman, perhaps ten years later, in the style of Sir Peter Lely who painted her parents as well as the 'Windsor Beauties', the feted ladies of Charles II's court, who now hang at Hampton Court.

An English seventeenth-century glass mortar and pestle – too fragile to be a part of Ann's luggage but perfect for a trophy still-room. It would have been used for preparing roots, resins and other ingredients for distilling.

A tin-glazed earthenware jar used for Poppy Conserve. (England, 1670–1740.) Ann's receipt book includes an early recipe for laudanum, the gum of opium poppies diluted in alcohol.

A posset pot like this one, of tin-glazed earthenware with its monogram and date, would have commemorated a specific occasion like a wedding or a christening. Although more valuable, silver couldn't be used as it conducts heat and possets were served warm. (England, 1651.)

Simple earthenware pharmacy jars, such as this one with blue 'Delft' glazing, were used for storing ointments and salves. (England, 1601–51.)

A travelling pharmacy cabinet of wood, silver and glass of the kind Ann might have used to transport her medicaments. (Switzerland, seventeenth century.)

The gold-tooled cover of Ann's receipt book. Note the marks at the middle of the right-hand side, where a clasp was once fitted.

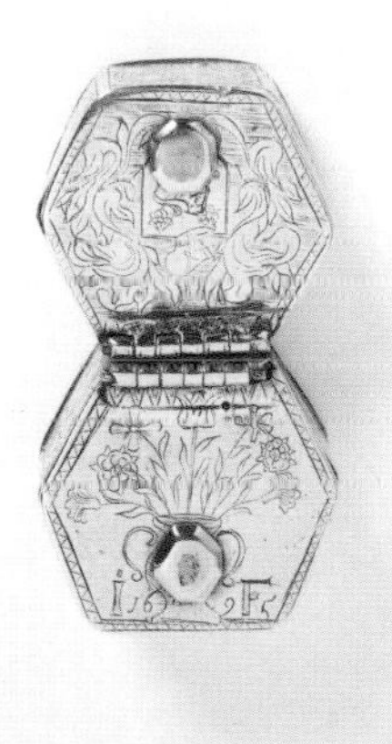

A brass spice pot from a travelling set. (England, 1695.)

An oak spice cupboard made in Yorkshire (1650–1660). It is tempting to picture Ann storing her still-room ingredients in something similar during her time at Tankersley.

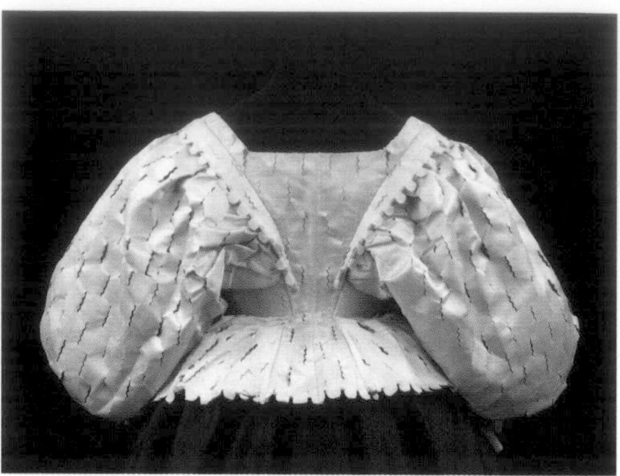

The nipped-in, puffed-sleeve bodice of a woman of fashion, hand-sewn in England in the 1630s from silk, canvas, buckram and whalebone. Seventeenth-century clothes invested their wearers with not just status but structure.

Daily laundered and starched, cotton and lace smocks like these were the everyday underwear of people such as Ann and her family. Fresh linen was an essential mark of gentility as well as cleanliness. (England, 1620–1640)

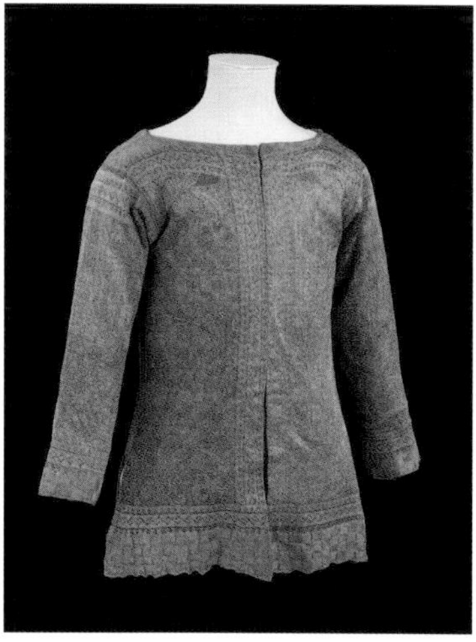

This Italian waistcoat is one of the few pieces of informal wear from the seventeenth century that have survived to the present day. Although it was intended for private moments it is a luxury item, knitted in silk and gilt thread and lined with linen – just the sort of souvenir exiled Royalists might have brought back to England from their European travels when Charles II was restored to the throne.

An English-made shoe of the period immediately following Charles II's restoration in 1660.

While Ann and her small brood of children were enjoying their 'harmless country life, minding only the country sports and country affairs',[10] Richard's new existence was more limited. Bound by his engagement, or oath of loyalty to the Commonwealth, as well as the £4000 bond Ann, his brother and his sister had paid two years earlier to guarantee his docility, Richard was not allowed to travel further than five miles from Tankersley without official permission. As a delinquent, he was also banned from taking part in local politics or government – the gentleman's natural role in society – and subject to extra fines and taxes. Added to these physical and financial constraints was the knowledge, surely shameful, that many of his friends and colleagues remained abroad in the service of their master, enduringly loyal despite the in-fighting, despondency and hardship from which he was now free.

Richard buried himself in poetry, translating Luís de Camões's 1572 *Os Lusíadas* from the Portuguese (probably helped by a Spanish translation as he seems not to have spoken fluent Portuguese). But even when he was escaping reality in verse, his work betrayed his true concerns. The original text, an epic tale of the adventurous group of men led by Vasco da Gama who opened up the Far East to Portugal, is dedicated to the inexperienced, eighteen-year-old King Sebastian of Portugal. It celebrates the achievements of his proudly developing seafaring nation as traditional values of courage, faith and loyalty clashed with modern mercantilism and its attendant evils, exploitation and social upheaval.

The poem's final stanzas might as well have been directly addressed to Charles, only five years older than Sebastian, the poem's dedicatee, whose loyal subjects are prepared 'to doe and suffer All for You':

And to obey in the remotest Land
(Though n'er so bitter and though n'er so hard,
Without Reply, or stop) what you Command
With You they'll charge the Devill and his Guard
Ev'n to the Gates of Hell, did You but stand
    A meer Spectator by: and never feare
    But they will make You too Victorious there.

Then warm and glade [gladden] them with Your
    present Rayes,
Sweetly majestick, and severely kind:
Their shoulders of their heavie Taxes ease:
Thus, thus, the path of Honour You shall find.

As in his 1646 translation of *The Loyal Shepherd*, Richard urged his prince, for whom his followers had suffered so much without complaint, to reward them with good governance, by choosing 'men rightly qualifi'd thereto' as his counsellors. It is not hard to imagine who he had in mind.

Even the poem's introduction, when it came out in 1655, was overtly political. Richard dedicated his *Lusiads* to his landlord at Tankersley, the young earl of Strafford, the son of his old friend and colleague. His Camões translation, he added pointedly, was truly a native of Yorkshire because he had not once slept outside Tankersley's walls while writing it: the subtext is that, living virtually under house arrest, he could not have slept beyond its walls. Later, writing to his old friend Edward Nicholas, he would refer to this period as his 'captivitie'.[11]

Much of the literature of the time, like Richard's poetry, can be read on several levels: less retreat from the world than a celebration of a lost ideal, keeping the embers alive so that one day a fire could be relit; less nostalgia than a quiet call to arms, reminding Royalists to keep the faith and remember. This kind of communication needed to be coded because for the moment the Royalists were not in a position to do any more than, in the words of another Cavalier poet, Mildmay Fane,

> ... settle to a Country life;
> And in a sweet retirement there,
> Cherish all Hopes, but banish fear.[12]

After the Rump was expelled from Parliament, the month after the Fanshawes arrived at Tankersley, a Royalist letter that found its way into the council's files (as the historian David Underdown observes, 'with ominous speed') observed that patience was the best way forward. However much people 'would have [liked to see] the king in action, I think it fit for him to lye still, and expect [wait for] further events'.[13]

It was not just poetry that contained double meanings embedded to sustain unhappy Royalists as they struggled to accommodate themselves to Cromwell's new regime, but music and popular literature from romances to receipt books, too. Cavalier soldiers had sung rowdier, less coded tunes – these were the songs that rang out in the army camps of the 1640s – like 'When the King Comes Home in Peace Again'. Though cobwebs might hang on Whitehall's walls for the moment, the lusty singers looked forward to the sweet day of Charles's return when maids would enjoy their mates again and honest men their lost estates. After Charles I's death and the defeat at Worcester, the mood changed. The lyrics of composer Henry Lawes, formerly Gentleman of the Chapel Royal, which date to this period, articulate unswerving loyalty within the context 'of a harmless private pastime'.[14]

Female poets were as engaged in politics as their male counterparts, although their verse lacks the sense infusing Richard's and others' that polemical poetry could act as a substitute for service. Instead, their role was to celebrate and mourn Charles I. 'To pray and weep for him I am resolv'd,' wrote Hester Pulter. In so doing she would comfort and heal his followers, her tears acting as 'a Cordiall to my friends'.[15] Katherine Philips – 'the matchless Orinda', whose circle included the marquess and marchioness of Ormonde, the Boyle family, Henry Lawes, Mary Evelyn and Dorothy Osborne, one step away from Ann and Richard – figured friendship as a metaphor for political loyalty in various poems written for absent friends:

> Here let us sit, and blesse our Starres
> Who did such happy quiet give,
> As that remov'd from noise of warres
> In one another's hearts we live.[16]

The first edition of Isaak Walton's *The Compleat Angler*, published in 1653, exemplifies the way a book ostensibly about retreat and contemplation could be a celebration of Cavalier identity. Although the title suggests a fishing manual and, especially in later editions, contains plenty of angling advice, *The Compleat Angler* is a prose pastoral, as romantic in its own way as Christopher Marlowe's 'The Passionate Shepherd to His Love', sung by the shepherdesses Walton's heroes encounter. At the book's end Walton's fishermen bid each other farewell and Walton extends their good wishes out to his readers, pointedly bestowing blessings 'upon you all that hate contentions, and love quietnesse, and vertue, and Angling'.[17]

Implicit in Walton's writing is the sense that traditional knowledge passed down from one generation to another, faithfulness to the English church and being in tune with the seasons and the countryside will restore the ailing nation. Hospitality and civility are linked to good governance; personal and national well-being are intimately connected. It was no accident that, in her memoirs, Ann praised Richard for his generosity: 'he loved hospitality'[18] was code for 'he loved Royalism'.

An important receipt book was also published in 1653, attributed to the learned and pious Elizabeth Grey, countess of Kent, who had died two years earlier. *A Choice Manuall of Rare and Select Secrets of Physick and Chyrugery* was a collection of receipts much like Ann's handwritten manuscript. Its significance lies in the fact that it was the first such book published by a woman (even if after her death) and the first of a series of receipt books by known Royalists. 'Our Stationers Shops have lately swarmd with bookes of Cookery,'[19] observed a literary clergyman and friend of Evelyn's, John Beale, in 1659.

Of the ten receipt books published between 1653 and 1658 – exactly the period in which Ann was compiling her book – eight were directly connected to prominent Royalists. In these books 'good household management', writes the historian Madeleine Bassnett, was linked to monarchical rule and the restoration of social order, making the implicit claim that 'royalty and Royalists could and should heal, order and feed the nation'.[20] I'm reminded of the poet Hester Pulter's cordial for her friends, made from the tears she shed mourning Charles I.

As with Ann's book, *A Choice Manuall* celebrates networks of Royalist women, collecting and exchanging receipts that would nourish and heal their families, a process that would begin the nourishment and healing of the divided English household. The domestic and public spheres were here interconnected: national restoration and recovery would begin at home.

Another 1653 publication, *The Card of Courtship*, was a manual for lovers, addressed to the constant suitor dreaming of his ideal mistress – a metaphor for the loyal Royalist waiting and hoping for his king's return. It also acted as a conduct book, in the aftermath of civil disarray, teaching people how to behave: how to thank a friend for a kindness or remind him of something; how to address and close letters as well as how to court a lover in verse or epigram. 'Yours to my latest gasp', or 'Yours living and dying', it suggests; or, 'To his loving master'. One sample letter, written 'from a gentleman in the country to his sweetheart in the city', has clear Royalist overtones. 'When I am abroad [in the country], my actions shall testifie that you are always in my heart. And if I can be so happie to keep a room in your thoughts and memory, it will be my greatest comfort in my loneliness, and my chief joy'.[21] Constancy, chivalry, gallantry and hope overcoming despair were the faithful suitor's watchwords, just as they were the Cavalier's.

Though she never mentioned light reading, it is safe to assume that Ann had access to novels like Madeleine de Scudéry's wildly popular *Artamène* – French romances were after all the staple reading diet of Henrietta Maria's court, even though Samuel Pepys disapproved of his wife reading them – and, as the wife of a poet and linguist, to the most modern verse as well as cutting edge foreign works including Cervantes's *Don Quixote* and Montaigne's *Essays*. Shakespeare was universally known and dramatic metaphors recur in Ann's writing. Her memoirs may not have the literary breadth of *The Compleat Angler*, which quoted from or alluded to a variety of sources from books of devotion, ballads, broadsheets and plays as well as classics like Pliny and contemporary poets like George Herbert and Edmund Waller, but it is hard to imagine that as a writer, she was not also a reader. 'In writing of it [this book],' observed Walton, 'I have made a recreation, of a recreation.'[22]

When Lady Anne Clifford (also a diarist) commissioned a self-portrait, as an independent woman in her fifties, she designed a triptych with her parents and elder brothers, both of whom died as children, in the centre panel, flanked by portraits of herself as a girl and as she really was in 1646. The figures in both images of her are surrounded by books: as well as books of music, Castiglione's *The Courtier*, Gerard's *Herbal*, Chaucer's *Canterbury Tales*, Edmund Spenser's *The Faerie Queen*, two atlases, Philip Sidney, *Don Quixote*, Thomas More, Montaigne's *Essays*, John Donne's *Poems and Sermons*, George Herbert, the Psalms, Ben Jonson, Plutarch, Ovid's *Metamorphoses*, St Augustine's *City of God* and more, a catholic mixture of devotional reading, entertainment and scholarship.

The book on which the adult Lady Anne's hand lies is the Bible. It was a given that everyone knew the Bible inside out, the familiar stories illustrating so many aspects of daily life, but the stories of its women had special meaning for female readers.

Strong Biblical heroines like Judith, Esther and Susanna were favourite subjects for needlework samplers. They were turned to again and again in paintings by one of the most prominent women of the seventeenth century, the artist Artemisia Gentileschi, who was in London helping her father, Orazio, paint the ceiling of the Queen's House in Greenwich in the late 1630s. During this time she painted a 'Self-Portrait as the Allegory of Painting' for Charles (he collected self-portraits and also commissioned them from Van Dyck, Rubens and Mytens) in which she fills the canvas, a powerful presence, absorbed in her work – an effort, art historians have speculated, to show that she was capable of large-scale fresco work instead of being, as a woman, nothing but a small-scale easel-painter. 'You will find that I have the soul of a Caesar in a woman's heart,' she said. [23]

Collecting and commissioning paintings and sculpture required not just money but space. By contrast, in the more constrained 1650s, relatively affordable and easily transportable antique medals, seals and intaglios were the desirable accessory of the mid-century, appealing as much to society ladies as to scholars like Edward Hyde and souvenir-hunters like Ralph Verney. John Evelyn remembered Richard telling him that as children he and his siblings had played with their father's collection of antique seals like counters and together they marvelled at a great collection of 'achates, onyxes, and intaglios... collected by a conceited old hatt-maker in Black Friers'.[24] In her will, Ann left her eldest son all her seals, among them perhaps some of those Richard had played with as a boy, including a gold ring with an engraved onyx, and her purse of medals (as distinct from her jewels, which she left to one of her daughters).

In early 1653, Dorothy Osborne admired a seal William Temple had used on a letter showing Neptune riding a dolphin and told him she had sent off for some from Italy. 'Seal's are much in fashion, and by showeing me some that she has, [Diana Rich] has sett mee a longing for some too, such as are the oldest, and the oddest, are most prized'. Another friend, Doll Sunderland – whose brave husband had died at Newbury in 1643, but was now remarried to a Mr Smyth – 'wear's twenty strung upon a riban like the nutts boy's play withall... and Mr Howard presented his Mistresse but a dosen such seals as are not to bee vallewed as times now goe'.[25]

That September, Dorothy told William that Lady Ormonde, Ann's friend, was 'wayting for a passage [to France] and [with] divers others, but this winde (if I am not mistaken) is not good for them; In earnest 'tis a most sad thing that a person of her quality should bee reduced to such a fortune as she has lived upon these late years'.[26] London was 'very empty in all respects', wrote the dowager countess of Devonshire to her nephew, Lord Bruce, a month later, reporting that Lady Ormonde had embarked the week before. Her newsy letters were full of aristocratic politics and the progression of her efforts to obtain preferment for her son and nephew. 'Much of our discourse is of ladies come from France. My Lady Isabella [Thynne] and her husband are agreed to part [separate]'.[27]

By November, though, the pace of life in London had picked up and the countess was writing excitedly to Bruce, 'All I can tell you is that suppers and balls are much in request, there are those of your society whose mirth far exceeds their cares, you must begin to reclaim your high flying hawk and your swift tiring fox, that you may be received to the nobler society. Tell my niece,' she continued, 'the garb in town is ladies all in scarlet, shining and glittering as bright as an "anty maske [at court]." You would wonder to see such stars in these our cloudy days.'[28]

It was at about this time that John Evelyn 'observed how the women began to paint them selves, formerly a most ignominious thing and us'd only by prostitutes'.[29] One senses the almost imperceptible stirrings of a Restoration spirit. ''Tis strange to see the folly that possesses the young People of this Age, and the Libertys they take to themselves,' Dorothy Osborne noted to her fiancé of Lady Devonshire, Lord Rich and a scandal over an unwise marriage, with all the wisdom of twenty-seven. 'I have the charity to believe they apear very much worse than they are, and that the want of a Court to govern themselv's by is in great part the cause of there Ruine. Though that was noe so perfect schole of vertue yet vice there wore her maske.'[30]

But the court was about to be reinstated, albeit in a different guise. Oliver Cromwell was invested as Lord Protector in December 1653, moving his family into the former royal palace at Whitehall and living there, according to disapproving commentators, most splendidly. The news of his new title and residence must have seemed as far from Tankersley as crimson dresses and society gossip. In October Ann and Richard's eighth baby, Margaret, was born on a Saturday afternoon and christened by the local vicar, with Lady Rookeby and 'my cousin Bothwell' her godmothers and Mr Edmonds her godfather.

The churches wouldn't have been open at Christmas as it fell on a weekday but, like their cousin Evelyn two years earlier, the Fanshawes and their children would have 'observ'd it at home',[31] perhaps with discreet wreaths of greenery and family-only carol-singing, safely together 'with great content'.[32] Looking out over the deer in the park feeding on hay they'd provided for them and the delicate trunks of the saplings they'd planted in their orchard, ringed with freshly built walls, they must have prayed that their fragile new happiness might last.

CHAPTER 12

1654
The Lady Allen's Water for the Stomacke Small pox or Surfett

Take of Sage, Sallandina [celandine], Rosemary, Rue, Woormwood, mugwort, Pympernell, dragons [arisaema], Scabious, Egremony [agrimony], Balme, [illegible, illegible], Cardus benedictus [holy thistle], [illegible], Rosasolis, of each a good Handfull, Angelica Rootes, henbane rootes, turmenstyle, [illegible], liquorish, of each halfe an ounce, slice the rootes and wash the hearbes, & shake them and dry them in a cloth and shred them, put them altogether in a gallon of white wine and steep them in it 2 dayes & 2 nights close cover'd, and then put it into an ordinary Still, & so still it, and when you take it let it be like [illegible] and put some Sugar in it 2 or 3 or 4 spoonfulls to a child of the strongest and 6 of the smaller, & to an elder more.

Ann miscarried a tiny son in February. 'Falls, Blows, Anger, Fear, Sorrow, Running, Leaping, Lifting, immoderate Exercise &c'[1] were all possible causes of miscarriage; perhaps Ann's new life in the country had proved too active. She can't have been more than four months pregnant, but it is a mark of her maternal devotion that Ann recorded all her miscarriages in her memoirs, unusual in all but the most thorough of seventeenth century accounts. This was her second miscarriage, after the loss of a baby in Ireland four years earlier, and it must have been cause for some concern because it was understood that if a woman had one miscarriage she was more likely to have another.

But she was too busy with her growing family and their new country life to worry for long. She was pregnant again by May and her children were growing up, becoming young people rather than mere infants. Margaret, named for Ann's mother, was at nurse, probably nearby or even at Tankersley, still in swaddling clothes. Katherine, at two, would have been teething: chewing on a piece of coral and possibly wearing a wolf's tooth around her neck, a traditional remedy for aching gums. Perhaps she was considered old enough to leave her wet nurse and join her parents and siblings in Yorkshire, sitting on a pillow in front of a trusted servant as he rode north, well wrapped up in a rug.[2]

At three, Betty was the right age to put on whalebone stays for the first time, since seventeenth century children wore the same stiff clothing as their parents once they had been weaned. Anne Clifford recorded in her diary the sequence of events when she first put her daughter into stays, aged two and three-quarters. First came the corset, then two days later Anne cut the leading strings from her coats so that the little girl could walk independently and the following day she put on a new coat of red baize, her first decorated with lace. As a record of this milestone Anne sent a lock of her daughter's hair to her sister-in-law.

For boys, the important moment of initiation was being breeched, usually at about six – Dick's age – when they stopped wearing the petticoats of infancy and began wearing miniature versions of their fathers' clothes. 'You cannot beleeve the great concerne that was in the whole family here last Wednesday, it being the day that the taylor was to helpe to dress little Ffrank in his breeches,' wrote a proud mother to her absent husband, after their son's breeching. She continued proudly that he had given her his 'first salute, but he sayd that if old Lane [perhaps his wet nurse?] had been here she should' have had the honour. His new clothes fitted him very well 'and he looks taler and prettyer than in his old coats'.[3] The Fanshawe children's clothes, like those of the young Margaret Cavendish and her sisters, would have been 'neat and cleanly, fine and gay, but rich and costly; maintaining us to the heighth of her [their parents'] Estate, but not beyond it'.[4]

Dick and Nan, nearly eight in the spring of 1654, would have progressed beyond learning their letters from a hornbook, a printed alphabet glued to a wooden board with a handle, moving up to the Lord's Prayer when they began reading properly. Most families didn't bother teaching their daughters Latin, though perhaps Richard, as a Latinist, let clever Nan join her brother while he taught him his first conjugations and declensions. When Ralph Verney's ten-year-old niece and goddaughter confessed her hopes of 'outreaching' her godfather and male cousins in Hebrew, Greek and Latin, he squashed her with finality. 'Good sweet hart bee not soe covitous; beleeve me a Bible (with ye Common prayer) and a good plaine cattichisme in your Mother Tongue being well read and practised, is well worth all the rest and much more suitable to your sex; I know your Father thinks this false doctrine, but bee confident your husband will bee of my opinion.'[5]

The Fanshawe children would have learned French and perhaps

Italian, because Richard at least was fluent in both. They would have learned to play a musical instrument, if possible, the guitar, lute or theorbo, a large lute, and to sing as well; if there was a dancing instructor in remote Yorkshire he would have been employed to teach the children not just how to dance but how to bow or curtsey with elegance and how to move gracefully, as befitted their gentle status. Some girls were taught to draw; Mary Evelyn was an accomplished amateur artist. Handwriting, recall and piety were improved by copying out sermons from memory and immaculate embroidery was considered an essential feminine skill. Perhaps Nan kept a little account book for her pocket money.

Ann would have made her copy out recipes and remedies into her receipt book, as she had copied out her mother's. At least four other hands feature in Ann's book beside Joseph Avery's immaculate script and Ann's own impatient, sometimes unreadable scrawl as receipts were added, tested, crossed out or replaced. In her will, leaving the book to her oldest surviving daughter, Ann named all her daughters as copyists.

Urging his niece to practise her French, 'for you cannot be too cunning for that language', Ralph Verney recommended the French works that would complete her education: the 'many admirable books fit for you as Romances, Plays, Poetry, Stories of illustrious (not learned) Woemen, receipts for preserving, makinge creames and all sorts of cookeryes, ordring your gardens and in Breif all manner of good housewifery'.[6] After the age of about eight, children were quite often sent either to a boarding school or to live with relations to be educated. A charming account-sheet exists for a girl's expenses at school: faggots for her fire (the biggest expenditure she made), soap and starch to ensure her linen was clean, 3 shillings sixpence for a sampler and thread, several entries for sixpenny-worth of liquorice and sugar. She wrote to her parents – sixpence went on 'carrying letters' – and she treated herself to a necklace.[7] When Sir Edward Molineux sent his daughters to his cousin's house he expected them to be brought up 'in virtue, good manners and learning, to play the gentlewoman and good housewife, to dress meat and oversee their households'.[8]

The phrase 'spare the rod and spoil the child' is a seventeenth century one (it comes from Samuel Butler's mock-heroic poem *Hudibras*, written in the 1660s) and discipline was considered an essential element in a child's education. Parents who indulged children for 'their present pleasure, instead of discharging faithfully their great trust for their immortal souls' were seen as wickedly negligent. They were warned to guard against being 'inordinately fond of children in minority... [and] vainly inconsiderate in the schooling of them'.[9]

Seventeenth century parents may have been strict but they were also loving – the fact that they needed to be warned against being inordinately fond demonstrates how often they were. A French textbook describes a doting mother chatting to her baby and his nurse in the nursery in words that a mother of any era might have uttered: 'O my little hart! God blesse thee... His little cheekes are wet, I believe you did leave him alone to crye and weepe... What a faire neck he hath! Pull off his shirt, thou art pretty [and] fat my little darling, wash his armepits... How he spreadeth his small fingers!'[10]

In an essay on married life, the writer and theologian Jeremy Taylor movingly described the delights of parenthood. 'No man can tell but he that loves his children, how many delicious accents make a man's heart dance in the pretty conversation of those dear pledges, their childishness, their stammering, their little angers, their innocence, their imperfections, their necessities, are so many little emanations of joy and comfort to him that delights in their persons and society.'[11]

Many parents doubted that punishment was the best way to steer their children, one writing to his son's tutor that he had 'ever observed… that persuasion works more on him than any other way'.[12] When three-year-old Edmund Verney, or Mun, moved from his great-grandmother's house to his parents', his great-grandmother wrote to tell them he was 'of a gentel sweet nature, sone [soon] corrected' and reminded them that he was too young to be 'strudgeled in any forsing waye'.[13] Mun's brother Jack was affectionately described at thirteen as rising 'in the morning by 6 a clake of his own accord, and sings and danceth without cease'.[14]

The First Protectorate Parliament assembles in September 1654. The following month three colonels formally protest that Cromwell has been given greater powers than a king. Cromwell dissolves the First Protectorate Parliament in January 1655.

In the summer of 1654, after just over a year at Tankersley, Richard and Ann's happy new existence was shattered. Nan, their adored eldest child, fell ill aged eight years. At first it would have looked like a bad fever, with a high temperature, headache and aching muscles, and nausea. Then the characteristic pustules, hard but leaking fluid, would have covered her body, appearing especially thickly on her beloved face and the tender palms of her hands and soles of her feet. Her death, at three o'clock on a July afternoon, after five days' illness, probably occurred from heart failure. Although she was their fourth child to die, the others had been either new babies (Harrison and the first Elizabeth) or still at nurse (Henry, aged two). For seven years (since Ann retrieved her from her wet nurse in Jersey in 1647) Nan had been, as Ann said, 'the dear companion of my travels and sorrows'.[15] Her loss was a catastrophe.

Even today, although smallpox is practically unknown because of vaccination, there is no cure for the disease. About a third of cases are fatal and survivors are usually scarred – black beauty spots were invented to hide the indentations left behind by the disease.* Despite all Ann's care and skill as a nurse poor Nan could not be saved. This Water is marked with the cross Ann used to indicate she had found a remedy successful, and was full of powerfully medicinal plants. These included henbane (as well as being psychoactive, henbane, or stinking nightshade, has narcotic and painkilling properties), celandine (traditionally used as a painkiller and antispasmodic), and wound herbs like scabious and tormentil, which helps increase resistance to disease and acts as a diaphoretic,

* Just as Dorothy Osborne and William Temple were formally betrothed, in late 1654 after seven years' courtship, she fell dangerously ill with smallpox. She recovered but she was dreadfully disfigured; where some men might have cried off, William didn't care. Her beauty was the least of her charms. Wed at last on Christmas Day 1654, they would celebrate forty happy years of marriage the year Dorothy died.

sweating the fever through Nan's agonizingly hot little body. Nevertheless, it would have had no curative effect except to make Ann feel she was doing something as she watched her daughter suffer. 'We both wished to have gone into the grave with her,' Ann wrote: her darling girl, whose 'beauty and wit exceeded all that I ever saw of her age',[16] was irreplaceable.

From 1644, the Directory for Public Worship had decreed that corpses should be 'immediately interred, without any ceremony'; in the Commonwealth, a minister was no longer required for burial. Rituals like singing, readings, bell ringing, kneeling to pray and prayers for the dead were 'in no way beneficial to the dead, and have proved many ways hurtful to the living'.[17] I feel sure, though, that Ann would not have permitted Nan to be buried in this manner.

For her the traditional ways were best. Nan would have been buried in white, the colour used for children, young men and women, and mothers dying in childbirth – people taken before their time. Ann and Richard and Nan's brother and sisters would have worn black for many months and carried sprigs of rosemary or bay, their heavy scent masking the odour of death, symbols (respectively) of remembrance and victory over death; when Ann died she hoped her children would wear mourning 'with plain linen'[18] (without lace) for three years, unless one of them were to marry. Friends and family would have been sent black hatbands and gloves and mourning rings, ghostly reflections of the joyfully coloured tokens given out at weddings.

Most children who died in the seventeenth century died younger than Nan and three-quarters of children who reached the age of ten survived to adulthood. Her parents must have felt that Nan, at eight, was almost through the high-risk years of early childhood and that they were free to love her without fear of losing her. When a friend lost a one-year-old, Ralph Verney reproached him for his grief: ''twas not the custom heretofore to mourn for such little children'.[19] (One of the arguments against breast-feeding was that a mother who had suckled her child would love it more and its death would be harder to bear.) But Ralph's wife Mary was reported to be barely lucid for days after their eight-year-old daughter Peg's death and even Ralph admitted, months later, that 'till now I never knew what a grief it was to part with a child'.[20]

The death of a child or children was tragically commonplace, something seventeenth century parents had to be hardened to. That did not make it any easier. Lady Isabella Twysden, each of whose six children lived to adulthood, was exceptional, but so was Elizabeth Walker, whose eleven children all predeceased her. Grieving parents were urged to submit to God's will, remembering that their child had gone to heaven where one day they would be reunited. Excessive grief was seen as unseemly – sorrow should be 'discrete'[21] – but only a few parents were pious enough to say, like the vicar Ralph Josselin when his eight-year-old daughter Mary died, 'Lord, I rejoice that I had such a present for thee'. (Twenty-three years later he would write, 'God hath taken 5 of 10 [children]. lord lett it be enough'.)[22] When his five year old son died in 1648, Evelyn confessed to his diary that 'the joy of my life' was ended. For little Richard's sake he would 'go even mourning to the grave'.[23]

Many questioned their faith when faced with the loss of a child. In 1657 Mary Carey gave birth to a stillborn baby. She recognized that while her 'dead formless babe' taught her to prize her living children she couldn't help asking God why he had taken up his rod to strike her such a blow,

> What He doth spy; what is the thing amiss
> I fain would learn, whilst I the rod do kiss?[24]

Every year, on the anniversary of her son's death, the countess of Warwick (born Lady Mary Boyle, Katherine Ranelagh's sister), noted the date in her diary and added assurances she had received that he was in heaven and a reckoning of the sins which had caused him to be taken from her;[25] as she saw it, his death was her punishment. 'Unfit thoughts' haunted Lady Russell when her son was ill: she knew 'a quiet submission [was] required' but confessed, 'I do secretly repine'.[26]

'Let me not fall to wish I had never borne it, rather than to part with it,' wrote Elizabeth Bridgewater, née Cavendish, of one lost child, chastising herself for her 'heathenish'[27] impulses. When her two-year-old daughter Kate died she affirmed her right to grieve ('let none wonder that I should lament my losse'[28]) and relived Kate's last moments as she kissed her dying girl. 'I do not doubt her happynesse, but yet greeve for my own losse, and know it was god's punishment for my sinnes, to separate so soone that deare body and soule of my sweet Babe, though her soule is singing Allelujahs, yet is her sweet body here, seized on by Wormes, and turned to dust'.[29]

Although no elegy written by Richard for any of his dead children survives, many grieving parents found solace in verse. Ben Jonson's eldest son died in 1603:

Farewell, thou child of my right hand, and joy;
My sin was too much hope of thee, lov'd boy.
Seven years tho' wert lent to me, and I thee pay,
Exacted by thy fate, on the just day.

Perhaps Lady Hester Pulter, who had fifteen children, all but two of whom died before her, came closest to Ann's feelings on Nan's death when her twenty-year-old daughter Jane died of smallpox. Not until two years later was she able to write Jane's elegy, describing the red pocks on her daughter's skin as being 'like Lilly leaves, sprinkled with Damask Rose... like drops of blood upon unsullied snow'.[30]

But what a heart I had, when I did stand
Holding her forehead with my Trembling hand
My Heart to Heaven with her bright spirit flyes
Whilst shee (ah mee) closed up her lovely eyes.

With death so near, the seventeenth century was a time of extravagant funerary monuments. Bereaved parents and spouses poured their grief into designing and commissioning marble effigies and epitaphs of their loved ones that would ensure their treasured memories were not forgotten. As the antiquarian William Camden said, epitaphs (and memorials) served several vital purposes. They demonstrated love to the deceased, they commemorated his or her life for posterity, they comforted mourning friends and reminded later readers or viewers of the fragility of human life. Although she did not celebrate Nan in this way, after Richard died (when she had more time to devote to it) Ann spent a great deal of energy and

£200 making sure his handsome marble monument in St Mary's Church, Ware, in which she would lie too, was a perfect reflection of his life. It outlined his career and loyal service to Charles II, in the Latin of which he was a master, and commemorated his children, both living and dead.

Devastated by Nan's death in that summer of 1654, Ann and Richard packed their bags and within weeks had left Tankersley forever, fleeing 'that fatal place to us' where they had once been so happy and hopeful.

They spent the next few months with Richard's sister Alice Bedell at Hamerton, near Ware, mourning Nan.

It's a measure of Ann's enduring grief that, in her memoirs, she summed up the two years following Nan's death in a single paragraph. The High Court of Justice summoned Richard to London later in the year – in his diary John Evelyn recorded that he'd visited him there towards the end of October – and ordered him to remain there, within a five-mile radius, reporting to the court once a month; they stayed once again with Ann's cousin Anne Young in Chancery Lane. By Christmas Richard had received permission to go as far as Kent, to his sister Joan and her second husband Philip Warwick at Frogpool.

In the seventeenth century, writes the historian Mary Beth Rose, 'a newly defined private sphere emerges as an arena for human heroism'.[31] The capacity to endure suffering, to resist with fortitude, had become a Royalist trope by the 1650s and, for once, it was an arena in which women had greater powers and experience than men. When Royalists could no longer fight and die for their king they had to learn to wait for times to change, just as grieving parents had to learn to accept the loss of their dead children. Passivity was required and it took no less heart and spirit than action.

CHAPTER 13

1655
For Melancholy and heaveness of spiretts

Take Siena of Alexandria [the herb Alexander, also known as horse parsley], 4 ounces, of Salsaparilla 3 ounces, of Raisins of the Sunne the Stones being taken out one pound, of Epithamum [cuscuta epithymum, or dodder], of double Camomill Flowers, Stecados [probably a corruption of Lavandula stoechas, or French lavender], of Hermodactylis [iris bulbs] of each ½ an ounce, of Liquorice 2 ounces and 2 drammes, of Anyseeds 2 ounces, Lett the Salsaparilla, Liquorice and Anyseeds each of them be putt by themselves. Then take sixe Quarts of white Wine and putt these together except the Liquorice, Anyseeds and Camomill Flowers into the wine and stop the Vessell and let them steepe one night, then take a great Kettle & fill with Water, and into that Water putt the Vessell wherein the Simples are and being stopt very close when the Water boyleth, Let it boyle so one houre and a halfe then putt in your other Things before reservd and so lett it boyle one houre and a halfe more, then take it of, and straine it thorough an indifferent fine Cloth, and putt that Liquor by it Self, then putt to ye Substance remaining in the strainer Sixe Quarts of small Ale, & lett it be stopt and boile three hours, then take it of & straine it. The first drinke must be used 3 or 4 times a day, and 4 or 5 Spoonfulls at a time, the Second drinke must be used at all times when the Patient is thirsty without drinking any other drinke while it lasteth.

Ann and her diminished family (now numbering just four children; Dick, Betty and Katherine would have been with her while two-year-old Margaret was probably still at nurse) were staying with Joan and Philip Warwick in Kent as 1655 began, while Ann prepared herself for the birth of her ninth baby in February. They named her Ann, 'to keep in remembrance her dear sister, whom we had newly lost'.[1] Still in mourning, they turned to immediate family for godparents: Joan Warwick, Richard's third sister, whom Ann always referred to as 'my sister Boteler', Sir William Boteler, who must have been Joan and her first husband's son and therefore aged about twenty, and 'my sister Newce', Richard's second sister Mary, not as close to Ann as Joan and Alice Bedell, Richard's other sisters, but still a regular name from the memoirs and receipt book.

It was not unusual to name children after elder siblings they would never know – even Charles II had been called for an elder brother who'd died – but the Fanshawes were particularly prone to it. They never named a child Harrison after their first born but, by the time Richard died, when Ann was forty-one, they would have had two Anns, two Henrys, three Richards and three Elizabeths. The only reason presumably that Katherine, Margaret and Mary (not yet born at this point in the narrative) kept their names for themselves alone was that they did not die young. I'm interested, too, in the fact that they never chose a Stuart name for one of their boys – no James, especially no Charles; perhaps familiarity had bred contempt, despite their loyalty to the cause – and, except Harrison, never named a later boy for Ann's father John.

After little Ann's birth and baptism at Chislehurst Church they returned to London, staying again in Chancery Lane, 'where my husband was forced to attend [report to Parliament] till Christmas 1655'.[2] With those few lines in her memoirs Ann disposed of the dreadful year of accustoming herself to Nan's absence. Reading between the lines, there's more evidence of their shared 'heaveness of spiretts' and the long-term effects of Richard's scurvy three years earlier: although Ann and Richard were living together it took her nine months to get pregnant again after their new Ann was born, for them an unprecedented gap.

This drink comes from the opening page of Ann's receipt book. *Cuscuta epithymum*, written here as epithamum, is still used by herbalists today against melancholy; soothing camomile and restorative liquorice would also have helped Ann while she healed. Although this remedy for melancholy came from Ann's mother, it was a poor substitute for what Ann really needed as she grieved: her mother's love, support and consolation.

Many receipt books of the times included remedies for low spirits, which were known to have a negative impact on physical health. Brilliana Harley's Melancholy Water distilled great handfuls of flowers – roses, wallflowers, violets, cowslips, marigolds[3] – and Henrietta Maria's book (see p. 244) included a receipt entitled 'To comfort the Heart and Spirits, and to suppress Melancholy' distilled from apple juice, saffron and borage as well as 'A pretious water to revive the Spirits'. John Finch, writing in 1652 to his sister, who suffered from terrible migraines and depression, had some practical (and surprisingly modern) advice. Be 'a little merry', he told her, 'and if you cannot be so, force a mirth, for I have known some men that have from counterfeiting good actions have at last come to a habitt of being really good; so from forcing a mirth upon you you will come to have a reall mirth, which is a relaxation and a great improvement to your health'.[4]

In grief, as in love, years – even centuries – can disappear: the barriers of time fade away in the face of such intense emotion. Ann's bravely terse account of her beloved daughter's death, her obvious unwillingness to relive those miserable months, rings painfully true. I'm reminded of Adam Nicolson's account in *The Mighty Dead* of using the stars as his guide while he sails at night, which makes him feel as if the distance between him and Odysseus, about whom he's writing, has vanished. 'There is no history here,'[5] he writes of this lightning-flash of intimacy with the past. Here suddenly, in her sorrow or in her joy, we understand a real person lived and breathed and dreamed and suffered, just as we do.

Richard was not alone in chafing under the restrictions imposed upon him by the new regime. From November 1653, just as the Fanshawes were moving to Yorkshire, a secret coalition of Royalists was forming in England that would become known as the Sealed Knot. With the belief at its core that only an English resolution (rather than an invasion supported by foreign powers)

would see Charles securely back to his throne, this new approach was what Edward Hyde had argued for for years.

Charles's instructions to the Sealed Knot were simple: it was to have sole authority over any Royalist plots to overthrow Cromwell, it was to discourage 'impossible undertakings',[6] and it was to prepare for a general rising, when the time was right, by appointing local commanders and raising money. The Sealed Knot was also authorized to make approaches to former enemies if it thought they would be 'well-disposed' to Charles's cause. Although in reality it was rather a haphazard group, particularly when faced with Cromwell's formidable secret police, it allowed individuals like Richard and many other returned exiles, whose consciences had permitted them to take oaths of loyalty to the Protectorate while their allegiance was to the absent king, at last to envision an honourable route forward. While Richard, for the moment under close surveillance in London, was unable to play any part in their struggles, his sympathies lay with this new association and his brothers, nephews and cousins would all join with it.

In March 1655 the Sealed Knot begins to move. Risings are planned across the country but in the end only in York and the West Country do the rebels actually take up arms. The uprising in York is suppressed easily and, although Colonel Penruddock and his troop of three or four hundred men take Salisbury and march west in hopes of attracting more soldiers to their banner, they are defeated by the New Model Army in a single battle at South Molton in Devon. In response, Cromwell appoints ten

Major-Generals to govern the regions of England under military rule and institutes a punishing new fine, the Decimation Tax, a ten per cent income tax levied on known Royalists and justified as a levy that their disloyalty to his regime made necessary.

Across the Channel, scraping a living on paltry and irregularly paid pensions from France or Spain, Charles is moving between European cities ahead of his creditors, accompanied by a skeleton court of perhaps a hundred and sometimes by his widowed sister, Mary of Orange. He is reported to be too poor to eat meat for ten days in the summer of 1655 and in December the gift of a pack of hounds causes terrible embarrassment because he can neither give them back nor afford to keep them.

That summer, with the rising's ringleaders swiftly executed and most of its foot soldiers pardoned or transported, Cromwell set about neutralizing possible supporters of any similar future movement. John Thurloe, head of intelligence from 1653 and Postmaster General from 1655, was a ruthlessly efficient interceptor of Royalist correspondence in England and on the Continent. It was Thurloe who in 1656 recruited as a double agent one of the three founding members of the Sealed Knot, the former Cavalier colonel Sir Richard Willys (under whom Richard's brother Simon had served in the mid-1640s), who was not exposed as a spy until 1659.

The new Major-Generals were expected to clamp down on any Royalist activity, issuing bonds for good behaviour, searching potentially treacherous households, enforcing payment of fines and taxes, banning suspected men from travel and even from meeting in groups. Though Royalists protested bitterly about not being allowed to gather to go hunting, racing, bear-baiting or cockfighting, for Cromwell's government these rules were sensible. In the autumn of 1650 a fencing school had opened in Downham Market in Norfolk as cover for a group of conspirators planning a rising; they had also organized hunting parties attended by large numbers of heavily armed men.

Ralph Verney was one of the discontented gentlemen arrested in the aftermath of the Penruddock rising. He had returned to England in 1653, having lost his wife and two of his children during his ten-year exile, but found it changed. 'I confess I love Old England very well, but as things are carried heere the gentry cannot joy much to bee in it,' he wrote. With views like that it was hardly surprising he was accused of being a malignant in June and held under house arrest in London for four months. Eventually released on payment of a bond of £2000 – a bond that, like Richard's, he would forfeit if he broke his oaths of good behaviour – he was obliged to sign a paper 'soe full of Barbarous conditions that I am ashamed to insert them here'.[7]

Some sought to make their peace with Oliver Cromwell. Ann and Richard's old friend, the poet Edmund Waller, published in 1655 an embarrassingly fulsome panegyric 'To my Lord Protector, Of the Present Greatness, and the Joint Interest of His Highness and this Nation', placing him alongside the greatest English kings of the past and praising his 'matchless worth':

> Your never failing sword made war to cease,
> And now you heal us with the arts of peace.

(Later he would praise Charles II in not dissimilar tones, though without the reference to the sword. When Charles asked why the poem he wrote for Cromwell was better than the one he wrote for him, Waller is said to have replied, 'Sir, we poets never succeed so well in writing truth as fiction.')

Closely watched, his supporters in England tried to behave themselves for the Major-Generals while they expressed their frustration and desire for change through ostensibly harmless channels. Richard's *Lusiads* was published in May, with its political theme and dedication, while other Royalist poets dedicated verses to one another and contributed poems to each other's collections celebrating the twin joys of retirement and loyalty.

The second edition of *The Compleat Angler* came out, with a commendatory poem by Alexander Brome, a noted composer of Cavalier drinking songs, composed and sung in deliberate contravention of the ban on toasting the absent Charles:

> Come, pass about the bowl to me,
> A health to our distressèd king!
> Though we're in hold, lets cups go free
> Birds in a cage may freely sing...
> We do not suffer here alone,
> Though we are beggar'd, so's the king,
> 'Tis sin t'have wealth when he has none
> Tush! poverty's a royal thing!

Perhaps the most important publication of 1655 was *The Queen's Closet Open'd*, a receipt book purporting to be by Henrietta Maria (still living in Paris) but probably edited and released by her friend, the Catholic priest, courtier and sometime Royalist spy Walter Montagu, signing himself W.M. Like the network of Cavalier poets, it revealed a web of Royalist ladies (and men), starting with the queen herself, whose medicinal and culinary skills could heal and nourish the ailing nation. Henrietta Maria was retrospectively recast not as a French princess with dreams of ruling England through her subservient husband but a capable English housewife, respected and autonomous partner of her husband.

While *The King's Cabinet*, published when Charles I and Henrietta Maria's private letters were seized by Parliament after Naseby in 1645, had been edited to make the queen appear foreign, interfering and imperious, *The Queen's Closet Open'd* was designed to show her as a beloved source of good health and hospitality, fully integrated into English society. Nothing in the book revealed her personal tastes – unlike her friend Sir Kenelm Digby's more gossipy volumes, which included Henrietta Maria's recipe for Barley Cream and his method for making weak hydromel, a kind of honey mead, the way she liked it – but the receipts, many of which were unattributed, contained useful advice along with the odd unattainably expensive or exotic ingredient to make readers feel they had a real insight into palace life. It also carefully mentioned a group of Englishwomen celebrated as much for their virtue as for their medical knowledge, like Lady Margaret Hoby and Lady Grace Mildmay, alongside famously learned men, like Sir Walter Raleigh and Kenelm Digby. Propaganda it may have been, an effort to restore Henrietta Maria's reputation, but it does have the ring of authenticity.

It was priced accessibly, at 2 shillings sixpence, which indicates it was not written for an aristocratic audience – those women, like Ann, would have had their own books. Combining habits of self-sufficiency and good housekeeping with the tantalizing revelation of 'secrets' of the royal household, it was designed to offer practical advice alongside a glimpse into 'the status competitions and consumption patterns'[8] – distilling and confectionery-making were the preserves of rich and leisured women – its upwardly mobile readers hoped to emulate.

The idea of healing the disordered body politic had been central to the last masque performed at Charles and Henrietta Maria's court in 1640, *Salmacida Spolia*, in which the queen's beauty, as a metaphor for virtue, civility and harmony, restored the ailing nation to health. It is tempting to see *The Queen's Closet Open'd* as a reference back to that play, providing literal receipts for health and beauty that would effect metaphorical changes on the nation: 'to make hair grow thick', 'Queen Elizabeth's perfume', 'To make the face fair, and for a stinking of breath' and 'a posset drink for one that is heart-sick'.

W.M. gave as his reason for publishing these personal items of the queen without her permission the fact that he had seen other copies made of them, so they were already in the public domain. The receipts, according to the title page, had been transcribed from Henrietta Maria's own receipt books which she had lost in the upheavals of the previous decade, underlining how common it was for literate women to keep books like these and suggesting that, with her inside knowledge of court, Ann might have known of them or even seen copies. Her receipt for Water of Life, which she attributed to her mother, is almost identical to Henrietta

Maria's, indicating a wide exchange and knowledge of receipts in this circle of elite and usually Royalist women, the ripples spreading out ever wider through society as prosperity and literacy rates increased.

The Queen's Closet Open'd, the countess of Kent's receipt book and her sister, the countess of Arundel's, published respectively in 1653 and 1655, were the fruit of an established line of elite women skilled in medicine, and were published to appeal to the aspirational women of a newly literate, increasingly prosperous population. This development converged in the 1650s with the flourishing of another, more populist tradition. Several books of medical advice (as opposed to grand housekeeping books which included medical remedies) were published in this decade, aimed at ordinary women. Underlining their mass appeal and the democratizing intentions of their authors, these books were in plain English rather than in Latin – with the penis referred to as the yard, the word in common currency at the time, for example – and provided clear anatomical information.

The doctor and herbalist Nicholas Culpeper published his *Directory for Midwives* in 1651. In 1652, Leonard Sowerby's *Ladies Dispensatory* claimed to be the first general medical book published in English specifically for women. It contained 'the natures, vertues, and qualities of all herbs... usefull in physick, reduced into a methodicall order, for their more ready use in any sicknesse'. Five years later *De morbis foemineis... or, The feminine physitian* came out, advertising its 'modest' treatment 'of such occult accidents, and secret diseases, as are incident to that sex, which their too much modesty, too often to their sorrow, causes them to conceal from others, for a remedy whereof, they are here taught to be their own helpers; especially in these particulars: of barrenness and abortion: of natural, and unnatural births: of the suppression of the termes, the immoderate flux thereof, and other infirmities'. Its expanded second edition was produced four years later for readers of 'what sex or condition whatever; whether you apply it to private use or publick practise'.[9] These books were relatively cheap and usually small enough to slip into a pocket; surviving copies are bashed and battered, well used and relied upon.

Stimulated by these books and liberated by the examples of the former queen and two countesses' receipt books, respectable women of the middling sort began to contribute to this field, writing explicitly for other women like themselves. In 1658, Sarah Jinner brought out her first almanac for ladies; it included not just medical advice but also astrological observations and forecasts, planting schedules for the garden and reading recommendations. Her last known edition, in 1664, ran to 8000 copies. Thirteen years later the first English book by a midwife for midwives was published by Jane Sharp, who combined thirty years' experience with direct and simple language, describing the neck of the womb, for instance, as opening and shutting 'like a purse'.[10]

1655 was the year, too, when the Royalist theologian Jeremy Taylor, who as a young clergyman in the 1630s had been taken up by Archbishop Laud and served as one of Charles I's chaplains, published *The Golden Grove, Or, A Manuall of Daily Prayers and Letanies, fitted to the dayes of the Week... Also Festival Hymns, According to the manner of the Ancient Church*. It was a manifesto:

'We must now take care that the young men who were born in the Captivity, may be taught how to worship the God of Israel after the manner of their fore-fathers, till it shall please God that Religion shall return into the Land'.[11]

Taylor was an influential thinker in Royalist circles; Dorothy Osborne described herself as his devotee and the poet Katherine Philips was a close friend. John Evelyn was another fan, writing to Taylor in March 1655 to tell him how he had learned, through his teachings, 'to adore the inscrutable pathes of the Most High; God and his Truth are still the same though the foundations of the world are shaken'. Taylor reminded his readers that 'he [he-who-could-not-be-named] cannot hinder our private intercourses and devotions, where the Breast is the Chapell and our Heart is the Altar'. Evelyn begged Taylor for practical advice as he and his friends waited for the 'Captivity' to end: 'Where shall we now receive the Viaticum with safety? How shall we be baptiz'd? For to this passe it is come, Sir.'[12]

Evelyn had to wait for his reply, for as he sent his letter off to Taylor, Taylor was being arrested on charges unknown, but surely connected to the defiantly campaigning tone of his book. Cromwell's regime may not have actively persecuted dissidents or burned their books but it did make life uncomfortable for them. Taylor was released in the autumn when at last he was able to write to Evelyn, who would become a friend.

While Taylor's prayers were published with the specific aim of sustaining Royalists through the Protectorate with reassurances that one day their king and religion would be restored, private meditations could be even more political. This 1654 prayer written by Anne Sadleir was knowingly treasonous but, written in the privacy of her closet, served as a vital clandestine release. 'Lord, thou knowest this armie is more Tyranical, more blouddy, more sacraligious, more prophaine, more rebellious than ever they were… set such a fire of dissension among them, that they may destroy each other, then bring him this King in peace, than this almost destroyed church may once more be restored to its former glorie, and this Kingdome to its former happines'.[13]

Though only one example of her devotional writing survives, the piety of Ann's memoirs suggests that, like so many of her contemporaries, she kept a record of her meditations. Perhaps she found consolation for Nan's loss and living as a political outcast in reading books like Taylor's and in writing prayers like Sadleir's, or one of the mourning prayers from Chapter 12.

CHAPTER 14

1656
The red powder good for miscarrying

Take of Dragons blood one dram, powder of red corall one dram, amber greece [ambergris] the weight of 3 barly cornes, bezoar stone the weight of 2 barly cornes. Make all these into powder and in a little burnt Claret wine give as much of this powder as will lie upon a pennie, at morning and night first and last 3 or 4 times will serve. Make some broth with plantaine rootes and shepheards purse and knotted grasse burnett and bryer leaves and drinke this at pleasure

[AF's writing from here] Put into the broth just as you drinke it the [illegible] of 9 eggs.

I have found good experementalley of this medicin.

The year 1656 did not begin well. 'Upon New Year's Day my husband fell very sick, and the scorbutic again prevailed, so much that it drew his upper lip awry, upon which we that day came to London'. Richard's body was literally being eaten away by the scurvy, the broken-down tissues of his body blackening and putrefying from the inside out and Ann's lovingly distilled remedies weren't working.

This time they found lodgings of their own, rather than staying with Ann's cousin. For two months Richard was treated by Dr Bathurst (also Cromwell's doctor, who had treated him successfully in 1652) and Dr Ridgeley until, 'God be praised! He perfectly recovered his sickness, and his lip was as well as ever'.[1] Once again, Ann would have had urgent need of her receipt book – although perhaps Dr Bathurst recommended fresh juices as well as cordials.

They stayed in London until September, with Richard still regularly reporting his whereabouts to the authorities. It was in this house, as Ann wrote, that their daughter Mary was born – her godparents were Richard's cousin Sir Thomas Fanshawe of Jenkins (as opposed to his brother Sir Thomas Fanshawe of Ware, who would later be Viscount Dromore), his future wife Margaret Heath, and Ann's niece Mrs Compton. It was in this house, too, and about the same time as Mary's birth, that they heard the news of five-year-old Elizabeth's death. Ann had left the ailing Betty at Frogpool with her sister-in-law Joan Warwick, hoping the country 'air would recover her; but she died of a hectic [high] fever, and lies buried in the church at Foots Cray'.[2]

Two of the three children they had taken to Tankersley with such hopes two years earlier now lay in the ground; Ann had borne ten children in twelve years and watched five of them die. At this moment of fresh grief what sustained Ann and Richard was each other. Only through love could their hearts, shrivelled by loss (to paraphrase George Herbert's poem of spiritual renewal, 'The Flower'), recover 'greennesse'. Their happy marriage, the respect they had for each other and the delight they found in one another despite the upheavals they were living through, is the great theme of Ann's memoirs and, indeed, of her life. Richard was her glory and her guide, 'all my comfort in this life'.[3]

The historian Sara Mendelson has scrutinized the records of female diarists of the Stuart age to discover more about their experiences of marriage. Of the twenty-one marriages she examined (she also looked at the lives of two contented spinsters) she found fifteen were loving and six unsatisfactory. Of the thirteen whose arrangements we know about, eight were happy (two love matches where the parents eventually consented, three of free choice, two arranged with the bride's consent and one arranged when the bride was thirteen) and five unhappy (two forced marriages, one arranged, one a love match and one an elopement).[4]

If you compare these numbers to a 2009 poll of 35,000 women for *Women's Day* magazine, contentment rates were rather higher (71 per cent) during the seventeenth century than nowadays (64 per cent). The correspondence of numerous couples from this period, however they were brought together, demonstrate shared interests, a deep involvement in each other's lives and intense emotional connections. Particularly during the civil wars and Commonwealth but also in the seventeenth century more generally, couples endured long separations and frequent bereavement with constancy and devotion. Conjugal happiness was not incompatible with a patriarchal system, although conversely an unhappy union was almost impossible to get out of. Spouses may not have been equal in a modern sense and double standards were accepted without question but marriages could still be respectful, stimulating, enriching and loving.

Happiness, of course, is never guaranteed but still parents strove to help their children achieve it. When his daughter Bridget married against his wishes in 1649 ('she was resolved to have him whatsoever became of her'), in his journal John Oglander darkly begged 'God to bless them and to make them happy, which I much doubt'.[5] Expectations were different; faith and a sense of duty were powerful centripetal forces. It was perhaps more important to find contentment in a mediocre union, as well, when being unmarried (particularly for women) meant not fully being a member of society.

While Ann's memoirs reveal the joy she took in her union, diaries and prayers could also serve as solace for an unhappy marriage. Alice Thornton's journal, written over decades, is the story of social and economic decline alongside disappointment, depression, physical hardship (mostly related to repeated pregnancy and childbirth) and illness – but also of faith, determination and endurance. We know Anne Sadleir sought escape from her unsatisfactory marriage (she used her maiden name on the memorial tablet she commissioned after sixty years of marriage) in reading and writing because her letters, commonplace books and reading lists survive. Mary Rich, Katherine Ranelagh's sister, wrote a journal throughout the 1660s detailing her devotions (she was a devout Puritan) alongside her arguments with her husband, the earl of Warwick, whom she had defied her father to marry at sixteen but bitterly regretted afterwards.

Women's capacity to survive hardship and sustain their families was newly valued in this period. The stress on retreat and endurance that characterized the years of Royalist defeat was an important means of defying the values of the Commonwealth and Protectorate – paradoxically, withdrawal became a public, political stance. Feminine skills and creativity were central to this alternative vision. Women 'thus had remarkable agency within defeated royalism', explains the historian Ann Hughes. Households like

Ann's, 'preserved by staunch women, fostering friendship, loyalty and innocent revelry at Christmas and other festivals, represented an alternative to the republican status quo'.[6]

The feminine sphere of the household – with its 'little language unknown to men', as Virginia Woolf would put it – was central to Royalist life in the 1650s. Behind its 'institutional powerlessness',[7] its inaccessibility to the male world, lay rules, codes and habits organized around kinship and intimate friendships that would sustain their world in this time of opposition and ready it, one day, for its return to a central role in English life. This is why Ann laid so much emphasis on godparents for her children, why she scrupulously recorded who gave her which receipt for her book, why she fought so hard to remain by Richard's side throughout the adversity they faced and why she described their life together for their son: she was constructing a world for herself and her family that would both recall the one she grew up in and survive to be the foundation of the new society she hoped their resilience would one day bring about.

Ann became pregnant very soon after Mary's birth but lost the baby in a miscarriage that summer. I am not sure whether this powder, 'the red powder good for miscarrying' of which Ann said she had 'found good experementalley', was considered *probatus* only for averting a miscarriage or also for helping ease the pain, bleeding and heartbreaking delivery. This was her third miscarriage and her second in two years.

Dragons' blood sounds wonderfully arcane but in fact it was the garnet-coloured resin of the dragon tree which, when used in medicine, lowered fever and acted as a coagulant and antiviral. Powdered red coral, with its high iron content, was good for someone losing blood rapidly; it restores calcium levels and is also effective against problems in the urinary tract. The bezoar stone, seen at the time as an almost magical cure-all and an antidote to any poison (remember Ann giving one to her friend in Ireland), more valuable by weight than gold, probably did nothing: they were lumps formed of hardened material trapped in an animal's digestive system. These ingredients were all expensive and hard to come by, indicating that this remedy was created by a doctor with modern, 'advanced' ideas rather than a wise woman who would have used the traditional herbal remedy for miscarriage, lady's mantle.

Her broth would have been equally healing. Plantain roots, shepherd's purse, knot grass and burnet were traditionally used to stop haemorrhaging and blood loss: burnet's Latin name, *Sanguisorba officinalis*, actually means staunch blood, shepherd's purse has additional medicinal value against bladder and uterine problems, and several of these herbs are astringent too. The egg yolks – I am assuming Ann added egg yolks although the word is illegible – would have strengthened and nourished the patient as well.

Ann's powder, like so many of the receipts in her book, sounds as if it might actually have been beneficial and aided recovery. In *The Queen's Closet Open'd*, on the other hand, one remedy suggested for a miscarriage sounds as messy as it would have been ineffectual: taking roast beef straight from the fire, drenching it in a spiced wine sauce, cutting it in half and binding it to the woman's belly and lower back 'as hot as may be suffered',[8] for a day or longer if need be.

In April 1656 Charles signs an alliance with Spain. The following month Sir Henry Vane, a former political ally of Cromwell's, issues a pamphlet criticizing the powers Cromwell has assumed as Lord Protector and is arrested and imprisoned.

In September, 'weary of the town and being advised to go into the country for his health',[9] Richard received permission to take his family to Bengeo (Ann spelled it Bengy, as she would have pronounced it) in Hertfordshire, to a small house lent them by his brother. Bengeo is just outside Hertford and thus within a few miles of both Ware and Balls: in a way, they were coming home.

They visited John Evelyn in October at Sayes Court, the house in Deptford belonging to his wife's family, the Brownes, into which he and Mary moved in 1651. Three years earlier he'd begun laying out the gardens for which Sayes would become famous. Ann and Richard could wander through his newly wooded grove, admire his beehives, his kitchen gardens and his box parterre, his orchards and avenues of saplings and his ornamental lake and summer house: a poignant reminder of what they had hoped to create at Tankersley.

It's unsurprising to find Evelyn in his diary noting the 'confus'd election of Parliament cal'd by ye Usurper' in August and, the following month, observing 'the pretended Protector fortifying himselfe exceedingly and sending many to prison'.[10] Richard and Ann, keeping their heads down in Bengeo, would surely have agreed with his sentiments and tone. But Lucy Hutchinson, the ardently Puritan wife of a Parliamentary colonel and member of the Commonwealth's Council of State until 1651, who might have been expected to disagree with Evelyn, records in her memoirs that 'during Oliver's reign... both the victors and vanquished were equal slaves under the new usurpers'.[11] By the mid-1650s even Cromwell's natural supporters were beginning to chafe beneath his rule.

If Richard's old friends, the two long-suffering Edwards on the Continent, Hyde and Nicholas, could have heard Lucy Hutchinson's views they would have sent up a cheer: this gradual disenchantment with Cromwell and the Protectorate was what they were relying upon to bring their master home. It wouldn't have made their daily lives any easier, though. When Nicholas's mother died in 1656 he could afford a mourning suit for himself, 'and such a cloak as I could make',[12] but nothing for his wife and sons. The Venetian agent reported that Nicholas and Hyde were 'so heavily burdened and their fortunes are so dilapidated that without money, leaders or support they are better able to grumble than to vindicate themselves'.[13]

In November came yet another blow. Ann was six months pregnant* when she fell ill with what she called a 'quartan ague', which seems to have been a form of malaria: 'a very ill kind of fever, of which many died and it ran generally through all families'.[14] She delivered her son, whom she named Henry, ten weeks before time;

* Her dates in the memoir can't be right, because Ann says she had Mary in July, then had a miscarriage, then had Henry ten weeks early in November. The second Ann was born in February 1655, so Ann could have been pregnant with Mary any time after March or April and had her in the spring of 1656, giving her time to get pregnant and miscarry before conceiving Henry in about May.

he probably weighed less than three pounds. Terribly premature and with a mother close to death, little Henry's chances of survival were minuscule. He was baptized by the local vicar, Mr Carey, who served as godfather, too, along with a Mr Jones and his wife, Mrs Carey, and when he died on 2 December Mr Carey buried him in Bengeo churchyard. His coffin must have been very small.

No one thought Ann would survive. She was in bed for the next seven months, unable to eat meat, fish or bread and subsisting on sage posset supplemented with the occasional egg, turnip or carrot. 'I was like an anatomy,' she wrote, meaning a cadaver dissected by medical students. Twice daily she had a fit – ague means shaking or shivering with fever. Richard was also near death. For the first time neither of them could sustain the other. He managed to get up during the day but he 'had such a greediness upon him, that he would eat and drink more than ordinary persons that eat most, and in perpetual sweats, and that so violent that it ran down day and night like water'.[15]

I wonder whether these illnesses can be put down to the travails of the civil wars and living under the Protectorate. Did Ann suffer especially badly because of the stress under which she and Richard had been living or was it merely the way things were in the seventeenth century? Richard's illness definitely dated back to his time in captivity but they had been lucky not to live through a period of plague: there was a bad year in 1625, the year Ann was born, and then again in 1665, but the closest they seem to have got to it was Ireland in 1650, picking their way through the 'dung, dirt, and rags' of plague-ravaged Galway. I don't think they lost more children than average when they lived like gypsies – Ann seems rather to have thrived on their adventurous lifestyle – but back in England, beneath a regime they despised, with no hopes for employment for Richard and no home of their own, they did not flourish.

The body politic was ailing and perhaps that imperceptibly infected the population. Did opponents of Cromwell's regime suffer some kind of malaise of impotence, of disappointment, a bit like girls waiting to get married drooping into green-sickness? Could the body politic somehow be healed, as the religious writer and prophetess Mary Cary suggested in her 1647 pamphlet, subtitled 'A precious Cordiall for a distempered kingdom', perhaps using the poet Hester Pulter's cordial of tears? Sir John Oglander included in his receipt book (just before the section on veterinary medicines) a 'Recipe for Good Government': 'Boldness, backed by truth and honesty, is the best physic for thy civil government'.[16] At the end of 1656, confined to her sickbed as the weeks turned into months, all Ann would have known was that she needed a remedy as much as her nation did.

AVTVMNE,

Autum doth like a pittying Widdow looke | And mournes to behold the faynting Sunn
Vayled in black to see her fruite downe shoake | Forsake her when the Spring and Sumer's done

3

CHAPTER 15

1657
To make the water calld Aqua Mirabilis

Take the Seeds of Cardamum, Cubebes [a Javanese berry a bit like pepper], Galingall, Melilott Flowers, Cloves, Maie, Nutmegs and Gingers of each a Draihme, being made into powder, putt them into 3 pints of white Wine & one pint of Aqua vitae & one pint of the juice of Salendine [celandine]. Putt all these into a Glasse Still and so let them incorporate all Night, and in ye morning distill it with a soft Fire in Water, let it drop on Sugar Candy, Putt into the Glasse a little Amber Greece & of this Quantity there will be 2 Quarts, keepe one Quart by it selfe for it is strong, When you use it you may mingle it stronger or smaller as you please. You may make it in the Winter with the juice of the Rootes. You may take it when you please. The usuall takeing is halfe an houre before dinner or supper, or before you goe to bed one Spoonfull or 2 at a time.

'Tis of a secret Nature, it disolueth the imposthumation of ye Lungs, without any grieuance, it openeth Melancholy, it expelleth ye stopping of ye Urine, profiteth ye Stomach very much, it also conserveth Youth and preserueth the Memory, it destroys ye Palsie & giue one Spoonfull to a Person labouring for Life & it relieueth & reuiueth very

much. Of all artificial Waters there is none better than this. In Summer use one Spoonfull fasting in Winter 2.

Ann had need of a miracle throughout 1657. All through the early part of the year she was ill in bed. By the summer she was up but still very weak and often shaken by fits. The mysterious, probably malarial illness from which she was suffering was rampant in 1657, sweeping across the country. The Verneys called it the 'New Disease';[1] it reached them in Buckinghamshire towards the end of the summer. Lady Devonshire reported to her nephew that Bedfordshire, the neighbouring county to Hertfordshire, was 'still very much infected with this new disease' in September although by November she was writing to congratulate him on his family being out of danger. The illness had made everyone frugal, she reported: 'no clothes are quite out of fashion. We have nobler things to think of'.[2] This remedy of Margaret Harrison's, a spoonful of which she recommended for 'a Person labouring for Life', must have been one of several Ann tried as she struggled to recover her health and spirits.

In August, Richard and Ann received permission to go to Bath where, 'God be praised!', at last they shed their persistent ailments. Returning to Hertfordshire they rented the medieval former friary, confusingly called Ware Priory, at the edge of town by the river, where they lived quietly, recovering their contentment as well as their health, immersed in their domestic life. For the moment, theirs was a house full of children, a bright spark of consolation for their physical and political worries: Dick, the eldest, was nine; Katherine five, Margaret four, little Nan two and

Mary one. Richard worked on his translation of the Spanish court play from the 1630s, *Querer por solo querer* (*To Love for Love's Sake*), and Ann turned to her receipt book, at once an act of nostalgia and a demonstration of faith in the future.

Perhaps it was Richard's example that inspired Ann to write, just as his friend John Evelyn encouraged his wife to study. Theirs was a literary household. 'You may read your father's demeanour of himself in this affair,' Ann told her son after her description of his time in Scotland and in prison in 1651, 'wrote by his own hand, in a book by itself amongst your books, and it is a great masterpiece'.[3] Many of Richard's diplomatic papers from the 1660s were preserved, but this account has not survived. Perhaps, like other potentially incriminating civil war documents of Richard's that he burned so that they should not fall into the wrong hands, it was deliberately destroyed. Either way this reference indicates that not just Ann but Richard, too, wrote descriptions of their experiences that they hoped their children would read in years to come. Ann's memoirs, particularly when she describes being in Portugal and Spain in the 1660s, read as if they were drawn from notes taken at the time and Richard refers to journals he kept as ambassador, notes for his diplomatic dispatches.

Ann does not seem ever to have renounced her literary efforts as Mary Evelyn would do, surrendering her intellectual ambitions to social convention. In the 1670s Mary refused a request from her son's tutor for copies of old letters to show his friends at Oxford: 'Women were not born to read authors, and censure the learned, to compare lives and judge of virtues, to give rules of morality, and sacrifice to the muses. We are willing to acknowledge that all time borrowed from family duties is misspent… and if sometimes it happens by accident that 1 of a 1000 aspires a little higher, her fate commonly exposes her to wonder, but adds little of esteem.'[4]

The names of the people who gave Ann receipts indicate a deep immersion in her family – evident in her memoirs, too – and her devoted Royalism. Political links were as important as ancestry. Royalist names recur throughout Ann's receipt book – Dalkeith, Denbigh, Cleveland, Mordaunt, Portland, Middleton, Northampton – although it would be astonishing to find any Parliamentary names, given Ann and Richard's complete commitment to their cause. Mrs Wyndham was Charles II's wet nurse and first mistress; Lady Wilmot was the wife of his boon companion and mother of the poet-earl, Rochester; Lady Browne was the wife of the stalwart English Resident in Paris and mother of Mary Evelyn; Lady Lucas was the writer Margaret Cavendish's sister-in-law. Even in the receipts she received from friends Ann was defining herself as a follower of the king.

Very few receipts come from other collections like those of Henrietta Maria and the countesses of Kent and Arundel. Ann does not seem to have known Katherine Ranelagh or any of the Boyle family, notable gatherers of receipts, though their social circles (just) overlapped. Sir Kenelm Digby was the exception, a kinsman and friend of the Fanshawes as well as a Royalist receipt-collector. It's harder to understand the lack of any receipt from John and Mary Evelyn, but perhaps it was only Richard and John who were friends, despite the interest Ann shared with both Evelyns in receipts and remedies and despite her collecting receipts from Elizabeth Mordaunt, Mary Evelyn's close friend, as well as her mother, Lady Browne.

Another absence is Edward Hyde, Richard's old friend and patron, whom Ann blamed for not supporting Richard's career hopes and who, in turn, blamed Ann for not allowing Richard fully to support Charles. There is nothing from him or his wife, although the wives of both Richard's other companions in exile in the late 1640s and early 1650s, Lady Nicholas and Lady Hatton, feature, and in letters Hyde referred to his wife as being a keen distiller. Interestingly, Lady Barclay or Berkeley, wife of Sir John, and Charles II's doctor, Sir Alexander Fraser, contributed receipts – both were political opponents of Hyde, though loyal servants to the exiled king.

Having said that, one element of a receipt book was that it crossed political boundaries. Every Englishwoman needed one, regardless of her political affiliations. Ann and Brilliana Harley, the doughty Puritan who had defended her home from Royalist forces in 1643, may have been separated by their views on religion and the crown but, as shown by their receipt books, they shared a common world view. This would make conciliation, when at last it came, much easier.

In January 1657 the military rule of the Major-Generals and the Decimation Tax are abandoned as unpopular and unworkable. In March Parliament offers Oliver Cromwell the crown which, after two months' thought, he refuses – although in June he is installed as Lord Protector, a title he had held since 1653, wearing a purple, ermine-lined robe, in a ceremony remarkably similar to a coronation. The Sealed Knot, dormant since the failure of

Penruddock's rising three years earlier, secretly begins to agitate on behalf of the king once again.

Ann shared her persistent hope for better times ahead with her fellow Royalists who seem, by 1657, to have reached a turning point. Was it principle or did Cromwell intuit how unpopular he would be as king when he rejected Parliament's offer of the throne? The Puritan Lucy Hutchinson commented that although he had 'much natural greatness' the idea of Cromwell in a crown 'suited [him] no better… than scarlet on the ape': the whole land, she said, had grown 'weary of him'.[5] The Conway family letters have a reference in March 1656 of plans to go 'a-Maying to Hide Park':[6] a small change in attitude, but a significant one. At Christmas that year, John Evelyn, who had agonized over how to celebrate in previous years, threw caution to the wind: 'I invited some of my neighbours and tenants according to custom, and to preserve hospitality and charity'.[7]

It was perhaps a sign of things to come that when Cromwell's two younger daughters married, both in 1657, Frances wed the son of a Royalist, Lord Rich, nephew of the diarist Mary Rich, in a civil ceremony (the socialite dowager countess of Devonshire gave them an expensive present), while Mary married the Parliamentarian Lord Fauconberg in a church ceremony using the Book of Common Prayer. Similarly, the young duke of Buckingham – who'd been raised with Charles and lived with him in exile through the early 1650s – returned to England the same year to marry the daughter of the Parliamentarian general Lord Fairfax, a turnaround Royalists could hardly believe. The lines between sides, only ever faint at best, were becoming even more confused.

The Sealed Knot, crushed after Penruddock's failed rising three years earlier, was active again. One of its members was rumoured to be Elizabeth Tollemache, later duchess of Lauderdale, chatelaine of Ham House. Women supported the Royalist cause abroad, too: the rich Rotterdam widow Mrs Beynham lent generous amounts of money to impoverished exiles.

Mary Knatchbull, abbess of the Benedictine convent at Ghent, was a regular correspondent of Edward Hyde and Ormonde and acted as a secret 'royal postmistress',[8] forwarding information to them from friends and agents in England. As a woman and a nun her letters were assumed to be unimportant and were therefore less likely to be checked by Cromwell's spymaster, John Thurloe, than those of Hyde and his male associates, but they also valued her counsel and contacts. 'My intelligence is small,' she told Nicholas early in 1658, with appropriate feminine humility, 'but the world knows I am a hearty lover of his Majesty, and therefore sends me good news when any is stirring.'[9]

Charles was still living precariously, roaming the Continent with his shabby band of followers, unable to pay his staunchly loyal domestic servants for months on end. His debts were said to be insupportable and he'd had to pawn his father's most treasured jewel, sent to him by Charles from the scaffold, an onyx engraved with St George and the Dragon, the insignia of the Order of the Garter. Worse, his dignity was being eroded by his poverty. Lacking the structure and resources of a court, he had become casual, unprincely. 'Till the K. shall himself take more majesty on him he will always, and from all these peoples, find every day more and more neglect and disesteem,' observed Nicholas to Hyde, his frustration with his young master bubbling over. 'I wish the K. would set a better value on himself and not use familiarity with persons of so much inferior quality.'[10]

Once again in 1657, after a gap of five years, Richard's name began to reappear in the correspondence of the Royalist exiles centred around Hyde, Nicholas and Ormonde. In July Hyde urged Ormonde to ask Sir John Berkeley, 'who once loved him [Richard] as well as any person living',[11] to recommend him to Charles as secretary to his brother James, duke of York.

For the moment, Richard and Ann were still living quietly in Ware with their children. Gradually, as they recovered their health, their hopes for the future revived. At forty-nine and thirty-two respectively, they were still vigorous, still full of passion for their cause: the return of Charles to the English throne and with it the recovery of their family's fortunes. One day their circumstances would change and when they did Ann and Richard would be ready.

CHAPTER 16

1658
A good Restorative after a long Sickness

Take Coltsfoot, Red Rose Leaves, Burnett, Betony and Comfrey Rootes of each a handful, pike & wash them cleane them & flie the Rootes, boyle them all in a pottle of water to a Quart, then straine it & putt to a pound of Sugar, and boyle it to a Syrrup, drinke it first in the morning, and last at night, 6 spoonfulls at a time.

'This has ben ye severest winter that any man alive had known in England,' wrote John Evelyn in March, having lost two small sons that season. 'The crowes feete were frozen to their prey.'[1]

Through 1658, Hertfordshire relatives, friends, kinsmen and neighbours of Ann and Richard's were becoming more deeply involved with resistance to Cromwell's rule. Two of the original six members of the Sealed Knot had connections with the Fanshawe family: Lord Belayse's first wife had been a relative of the Botelers, and Sir Richard Willys, another Hertfordshire man (he had sold Balls Park to Sir John Harrison in the 1630s), had been Richard's brother Simon's commanding officer in the 1640s and negotiated his release when he was made a prisoner of war in 1646. Simon, 'a gallant gentleman, but more a libertine than any of his family'[2] (Ann's description is confirmed by the portraits of Simon, with his ruddy cheeks, blond curls and well-covered belly), had played no active part in the Royalist struggle after his imprisonment but his loyalty was undimmed. He became an eager conspirator: Alan Brodrick, secretary to the group and one of Hyde's regular informants, described him in February 1657 as being 'a partner with us from the beginning, and will hold out as firmly as any in England'.[3]

As Cromwell's popularity wanes, Royalist hopes for the king's return swell. Charles moves to Antwerp, from where he hopes to launch an armada. Although neither the Spanish pension nor its invading fleet materialize as promised, Charles still hopes that Spanish ships will land him and his small army on the south coast where he will be met by uprisings across the country.

In April 1658, the Royalist activist John Mordaunt was arrested and charged with high treason for planning one such uprising. At thirty-two, he was just a year younger than Ann. His father, the earl of Peterborough, had supported Parliament in 1642, serving in the earl of Essex's army before his death in 1643. His elder brother had abandoned their father to follow the king, going into exile in the late 1640s after a failed rebellion, in which he was supported by his brother John, and then returning to compound in 1649.

John Mordaunt had returned to England by 1652, when he

was briefly imprisoned for challenging someone to a duel. In 1654 he wrote to Edward Hyde, pledging him his loyalty; in 1657 he married the beautiful Elizabeth Carey, who was at once devoutly Puritan and passionately Royalist, and who contributed receipts to Ann's book including oatmeal pudding and cherry brandy; in 1658 he made contact with Richard's patron and friend, the marquess of Ormonde. He promised he could raise several thousand mounted soldiers for the king.

His trial took place at the beginning of June. At first he insisted that he would not plead his case – like Charles I, Mordaunt refused to recognize the authority of the court trying him, forty judges selected by the Protector to hear his case in Parliament's Painted Chamber. Elizabeth managed to smuggle a note into the Tower to him: 'For God's sake, plead, plead, for my sake, and stand disputing it no longer'.[4] He changed his mind and pleaded innocent.

Somehow Elizabeth apparently managed to persuade the chief witness against John, a Colonel Mallory, not to turn up to testify. The next day, partly because Elizabeth had spoken to each of the judges beforehand and partly because one, Colonel Pride, was ill, her husband was cleared by a count of twenty to nineteen, escaping execution 'by one voys [voice] only'. It was, she wrote in her journal, a 'meracolous blesing'.[5] 'Prased be the Lorde for ever, for He hathe preserved the Life of my Deare Husband, from the poure [power] and malis of his enemis, and hathe blesed us with mercis on every side.'[6]

A year earlier, as a bride, she had begged God for support as she embarked on a new life by her activist husband's side. 'Send helpe unto me, for my enymys ar many that so counsel to gether aganst me, that which is derer to me than my Life, my Honer... O lete me not ade to my Hepe [Heap] the gilte of revenge, but geve me grace to forgeve, and then forgeve me my scins, and forgeve me if I resent their ingerys to [injuries too] muche, and forgeve my dulnes in devotion, and my neglect of it, and derect me how to manage my selfe in this bisnes'.[7] When she needed it, she had found that strength and direction.

Although Mordaunt's arrest and trial were intended as a caution against other Royalists supporting Charles's cause, his faith and determination – alongside the fact that Cromwell could not scrape together enough judges to convict him – only encouraged Cromwell's enemies. Later, Hyde would praise the 'vivacity, courage and industry' with which Mordaunt's example 'revived the hearts [of Royalists] which were near broked before Cromwell's death'.[8] Less than six months after his trial Mordaunt, undaunted, was renewing his pledge of allegiance to Charles, seeking to build up the alliance between Royalists and Presbyterians that would bring the king home.

On 3 September 1658, Cromwell dies at Whitehall, following a bout of quartan ague complicated by a kidney infection and, at the last, septicaemia. His son Richard is declared Protector the following day. No one weeps as the Protector's body, adorned with crown and sceptre, is drawn through London to Westminster Abbey by six horses on a velvet bed of state.

John Evelyn rejoiced in his diary: 'Died that arch rebel Oliver Cromwell, cal'd Protector'.[9] Ann and Richard, in the Priory at Ware, rejoiced too. 'This place we accounted happy to us, because in October [a mistake – she means September] we heard the news of Cromwell's death, upon which my husband began to hope that he should get loose of his fetters, in which he had been seven years'.[10] It was the only comment she made in her memoirs on the year 1658.

The news of Cromwell's demise was all the tonic that Ann and Richard needed, though Ann no doubt had also made this sweet herbal cordial as her family was restored to health and energy during their quiet year in Ware. One indication that they were still convalescing was that Ann seems not to have been pregnant at all during this time.

Cromwell was buried at the end of November, at what Evelyn called 'the joyfullest funerall that ever I saw'.[11] Edward Nicholas told Charles, in Antwerp, that the 'rebels endeavour to set up Cromwell's son rather than a republic'.[12] This must have been a hopeful sign, both because there was evidently no general public appetite for a republic and because Richard Cromwell was considered weak and inadequate. Even those who were not active Royalists thought him 'a wretch who durst not reign'.[13]

A satirical receipt book entitled *The Court and Kitchin of Mrs Joan Cromwell*, published in 1664, shows the widespread unpopularity of Cromwell and his family by the time he died. While Henrietta Maria's bestselling receipt book had presented her as a good English housewife, *The Court and Kitchin* made out Elizabeth Cromwell (whom the book derisively dubbed Joan) to be vulgar, stingy and un-English, possessing the vices of a Turkish seraglio and the greed of Lombard money-lenders, selling off the presents she received as the Protector's wife. Her book did not include the valuable skills of the gentle mistress of the house, medical receipts and confectionery-making; instead she served peasant food – barley-broth, hog's liver, marrow-pudding – and brewed her own small ale. She was, the book concluded, 'a hundred times fitter for a Barn than a Palace':[14] just like her husband, was the implication.

Taking advantage of the uncertainty following news of the Protector's death, almost immediately Richard broke his bonds to ride from Ware to London – a journey of less than a day – where he met his old friend Philip, earl of Pembroke. Pembroke's father had been a moderate Parliamentarian and, on succeeding to his title, Pembroke had also served as an MP through the Commonwealth and Protectorate. Their meeting shows that England was no longer as polarized as it once had been: friendships could now cross the old political divide.

Having chafed at the restrictions placed upon him since 1651 during his 'captivitie', Richard 'lamented his case of his bonds to him that was his old and constant friend'.[15] ('Methinkes in the country, for want of good conversation, one's Witt growes mouldy,'[16] as John Aubrey observed of Thomas Hobbes at about this time.) The next morning Pembroke offered him a job and his freedom. 'Mr. Fanshawe, I must send my eldest son into France; if you will not take it ill that I desire your company with him and care of him for one year, I will procure you your bonds within this week.'[17] Overjoyed, Richard agreed and with all haste began to make the preparations for his journey as tutor or bear-leader to seventeen-year-old William, Lord Herbert. His passport was issued on 24 September, just three weeks after Cromwell died. I wonder whether anyone claimed his £4000 bond or whether in the upheaval and confusion of the times it was forgotten.

In Ware, as the winter drew in, Ann gathered her children about her and waited for Richard's letter summoning her to his side.

CHAPTER 17

1659
A Strengthening and Cooling Broth

Take a good bigg Chicken, and the Bones of a Knuckle of Veale, boyle them in a pottle of Water to somewhat lesse then a Quart, putt therein 10 Raisins of the Sunne stoned, 5 Leaves of Bugloss & 2 Leaves of Succorie [chicory], 5 Leaves of Endive, & 2 Sprigs of Time & one Sprigg of Rosemary, & one of sweet Marjoram, together with the bottome of a Manchett [a loaf of best quality bread], and when it is boyled enough straine it and let it settle, then powre out the cleane into a pott, & give the same as often as the sicke Party requires it, & make as often fresh as you need.

1659 began with 'a very dry starveling Spring'.[1] Richard, 'got loose'[2] at last of his bonds, had reached Paris with his young charge, while at home in Ware Ann awaited his instructions.

The sense of optimism that had greeted the Protector's death the previous autumn was gradually being translated into something less abstract among Charles's followers in England and abroad as the spring of 1659 unfolded. Anticipation was becoming momentum; momentum would bring action.

In March, John Mordaunt was given permission by Charles to

begin agitating for another rising, a move that infuriated some members of the old Sealed Knot, jealous of their role as his chosen champions. Instead of hoping for foreign aid Mordaunt's group, the Great Trust and Commission, relied upon an alliance of Englishmen loyal to Charles, uniting devoted Royalists like Mordaunt with Presbyterians including, most notably, Sir George Booth, who had long been known to look favourably on Charles's cause despite his membership of the Commonwealth and Protectorate Parliaments.

On 2 March, Elizabeth Mordaunt promised to receive the sacrament and dedicate £5 in gold to the service of God every year on that day if he preserved the life of Booth 'and the Life [of] all thos that wer ingaged in that bisnes, for the Church and King'.[3] On a more practical level, her family connections at the court of Elizabeth of Bohemia, the Winter Queen and elder sister of Charles I, enabled her to raise money there for the Stuart cause: £20,000 came from Lord Craven, the exiled queen's devoted admirer.

Another prospective convert from the Parliamentary side was General Monck, who the Royalists were courting throughout the spring. He had fought for the king until Charles I's death, turning then to Cromwell who was his friend as well as master. As Commander-in-Chief of the Parliamentary army in 1659, he was perhaps the single most influential man in the country. In March, an agent in London reported to Hyde that 'Monk's little son, being asked by a Lord who he was for, whether for a King, a Protector, or a Free State, he answer'd that he was for ye King and soe was his mother; and ye truth is she hath contributed very much to ye bringing matters to this passe'.[4] Monck would not commit for another few months but the very fact that he was considering converting was cause for confidence.

Amid this atmosphere of renewed Royalist hopes, John Thurloe intensified his surveillance of their correspondence and activity, aided by spies like Sir Richard Willys. 'I would now very willingly informe you of the state of our affaires heere, which are as bad as bad may be,' wrote Ralph Verney to a friend in France, 'but all letters are now opened, & such as speake of newes are stopt, therefore at the present it must be forborne by me'.[5] It is estimated that Thurloe managed to intercept three out of every four Royalist letters sent by open post.[6]

Trust, caution and discretion were thus constant watchwords in Royalist correspondence. Identifying names were used as rarely as possible; different correspondents had their own aliases and codes. In this atmosphere of secrecy, women became increasingly important. The assumption that their letters would contain nothing of interest placed them almost outside suspicion, just as the idea of women in general as gossips and not very bright made them doubly useful as spies, emissaries and mediators. When one of Hyde's London agents, Sir Henry Moore, mishandled his post, Hyde began using Moore's more reliable wife, Mary, instead. Even Sarah Jinner included a method for making invisible ink in her almanac.

In Ghent, Abbess Knatchbull, a Catholic Englishwoman from an aristocratic family who had chosen life in a nunnery in Europe over concealing her faith at home, received news and information from London as well as letters for Charles, Hyde and Ormonde, scattered over the Continent, and forwarded them on with covering letters and analysis. When codes changed, she provided them with the new ciphers and transmitted sensitive information in her own codes; several times, when she thought her network

Although Charles wears armour, not a drop of blood was shed during his triumphant reentry to England as king in 1660. In the background, as the sun rises, a phoenix shakes out its wings and a helpful angel vanquishes discord.

had been infiltrated, she rerouted it. She also guaranteed Charles's loans with her contacts in the Low Countries. None of this was done without an agenda: she hoped her support for Charles would lead to religious toleration for Catholics in England when he was restored to the throne.

Charles, Hyde and Nicholas were in direct contact with Elizabeth as well as John Mordaunt throughout this period; she had access to their codes as well as a private code for correspondence with her husband. In March the king sent her a blank patent for a viscountcy for Mordaunt; in another he beseeched 'your ladyship to transmit the enclosed [note] to your best friend'.[7] Her influence stirred up jealousy among the other Royalist wives: Hyde was told that some were 'much in wrath that my Lady Mordaunt's husband should be more active, and by that in a better esteem than theirs' and hated Elizabeth because they couldn't 'incite their phlegmatic husbands to such generous actions'[8] in Charles's name. We know Ann didn't hate Elizabeth – the receipts in her book attest to a friendship – but it's not hard to imagine she might still have harboured hopes that her adored Richard would be covered in glory like Mordaunt.

In April Richard Cromwell is forced to dissolve the Parliament he had summoned the previous November, after his father's death. Inadequate to the challenges of uniting the divided country, he resigns in May and the Protectorate is effectively over, although nothing as yet replaces it. A political void is waiting to be filled.

'Greate confutions and alterations is dayleye lookte for, and I hope in God itt will produce exselente things for the Kinge,'[9] wrote the marquess of Newcastle from his handsome house in Antwerp to Nicholas, contemplating a return home after nineteen years of exile.

It was at about this time that Richard first made contact with his old friends and comrades, Hyde and Nicholas, and through them with Charles, but it was not the joyful reunion he had, perhaps, imagined. His letters to Hyde don't survive, but Hyde's to him do. The first is dated 10 May and, although Hyde concluded, 'Your master is as kind to you as you can wish... [and] you shall be very happy if it ever be in my power to serve you,'[10] he did not spare his criticism 'that you were to blame in not giving your friends seasonable notice of all your concernments'.[11] What he meant was that if Richard had chosen to remain in England rather than following his king into exile, he should at least have let Charles – and Hyde – know of his continued loyalty. Hyde received another letter from Richard on 15 May, evidently outlining all the difficulties and delays that had kept him from being in touch, and responded two weeks later that he would not 'retract one word of my chiding'[12] but sending Richard a cipher so they could continue to communicate in private. Richard's code-name was Mr Richard Francis.

They would not turn him away or question his loyalty, but Richard's remaining in England, even under the financial obligations and physical restrictions by which he had been bound, and chafing against them, had not been good enough. Though he and Charles had never doubted Richard's affection, his 'omission' – not telling the king 'of your pretence', that his loyalty to Charles was undiluted by his decision to remain in England – had made Charles, Hyde reported, 'the most out of countenance I ever saw him'.[13] He knew now that Richard had written the previous October, as he planned his flight from Ware, but because the letter had taken more than six months to reach him the damage had been done.

Richard replied; Hyde responded on 14 June. 'Your master will make you all the recompense he can for the wrong he has done you, and yet I must say to you again that you were to blame not to help his memory in these catching times'.[14] Richard had been hoping since the 1640s for the post of Secretary of State. Through Hyde, Charles promised him the offices of Latin Secretary and Master of Requests, neither of which was especially lucrative or influential but 'from whence to be Secretary [of State] is a very natural step'.[15]

Richard wrote to summon Ann and little Dick, Katherine and Margaret to his side; the two youngest girls would stay with Ann's sister in Hertfordshire. There was no question of Ann not joining him and he'd found a good school in Paris for the children. They can't have had any idea how long they might need to stay away but, bearing Hyde's scolding in mind, there was surely no thought of leaving Charles's service until he was back on the throne.

In June Ann went to London to get a pass for travel, first contacting her cousin Henry Nevill (a Mrs Nevil contributed a receipt to her book) at the High Court, then sitting in Whitehall. Nevill 'went in to the then masters, and returned to me, saying, "that by a trick my husband had got his liberty, but for me and his children, upon no conditions we should not stir." I made no reply, but thanked my cousin, Henry Nevill, and took my leave'.[16] Sitting in the anteroom after receiving this news, Ann racked her brain for a solution. 'If I were denied a passage then, they would ever after be more severe on all occasions, and it might be very ill for us both. I was ready to go, if I had a pass, the next tide, and might be there before they could suspect I was gone: these thoughts put this invention in my head'.[17]

She went to Wallingford House on Whitehall, where passes were issued, 'in as plain a way and speech as I could devise, leaving my maid at the gate, who was a much finer gentlewoman than myself'.[18] (This is the only personal mention Ann makes of any servant, although one would have been with her almost every waking minute of the day throughout her life, even in their most pinched circumstances.) 'With as ill mein and tone as I could,'[19] Ann told the man she found there that she wanted a pass to join her husband, a merchant, in Paris, for herself, three children, a man and a maid. He charged her a crown, telling her that a malignant would pay £5 for such a pass, and wrote it out in the name of Ann Harrison.

Thanking him, Ann took the pass back to her lodgings, where the children waited, 'and with my pen I made the great H of Harrison, two ff, and the rrs, an n, and the i, an s, and the s, an h, and the o, an a, and the n, a w, so completely, that none could find out the change'.[20] Off they hastened, taking a barge to Gravesend and a coach from there to Dover. In Dover, the guard checked her pass, saying, 'Madam, you may go when you please… [but (*sotto voce*, to his friend)] I little thought they would give a pass to so great a malignant, especially in so troublesome a time as this'.[21] By nine that night Ann and her small family were on a packet-boat; by eight the next morning they had landed at Calais.

Resting for a few days in Calais before beginning the journey to Paris, she heard that a messenger from court had gone to her lodgings in London to find out 'why, and upon what business, I went to France', and from there had sent a post to Dover to stop her leaving the country. The thought of having foiled them and their disappointment at missing her made Ann laugh, 'and so did your father, and as many as knew the deceit'.[22]

Ann hired a wagon-coach, packed up her children, her man and her maid, and set off for Paris: it was like old times, journeying through Europe. At Abbeville, the Governor sent her word that he'd seen Richard in Paris the week before, he was well, and the Governor had promised him he'd look out for Ann as she passed through because of the danger of highway robbery. Ten soldiers escorted her safely past a troop of about fifty mounted men. Ann, questioning her escorts, discovered that they were part of the troop too but, having been paid to guard her, could ensure she passed unmolested. They met Richard in Saint-Denis, a blissful reunion after eight months.

In England, over the summer, the rebellion Mordaunt and Booth had been trying to raise in Charles's name fizzled out after Booth's men were defeated in Cheshire and Booth was arrested; the spymaster Thurloe had known of their plans all along. Mordaunt had travelled to the Low Countries to swear fealty to Charles, who was waiting there with a small army funded by Spain, but his abrasive manner and commitment to a Presbyterian alliance antagonized the king's immediate advisors – a feeling heartily reciprocated. (Mordaunt would describe Alan Brodrick, the secretary of the Sealed Knot, as 'sadly given to drink'[23].) This mutual distrust meant that the separate groups of men rising across the country in Charles's name were as unsynchronized as they were ill-prepared. Using Richard Willys's information, John Thurloe anticipated their every move.

On 6 July, Mordaunt wrote to Charles deploring the sloth and cowardice of the king's party in England despite the universal disposition to his restoration. At the end of the month he summed up their misadventures to Hartgill Baron: 'Thus you see how we miserably jest away kingdoms… dayley and hourely considerable people turn to the king, and the confusion now is so great, that had these gentlemen not done thus horridly, in reason all would have succeeded. I begin to feare foul play, but am so tender of men's honor I will not be positive.'[24]

They were not quite ready to strike. Hyde wrote to tell Richard in August that there was 'so much discourse of plots and of treachery, that I cannot be without apprehension for a little more time', adding a few weeks later that part of the reason for the rising's failure was the treachery of Richard Willys, who had at last been denounced to Charles by the spymaster John Thurloe's disillusioned secretary, Samuel Morland. Hyde called him 'a false brother among our friends who did infinite mischief… [to the plans] upon which you and I have so much depended'.[25] Weeks later he returned to the subject of Willys, warning Richard to tell all their friends of the dangers he posed.

Another reason, with which Richard himself was indirectly connected, was the way certain Royalist leaders had overestimated the support they could contribute in their enthusiasm for the cause. One such culprit was Simon Fanshawe, Richard's brother, whose 'gaiety… too far advanced the number of horse [mounted men]'[26] he could raise in Hertfordshire, the area commanded by the traitor Willys: he'd counted the men in his wishes, not in his command. 'The like overvalue he gave for his own brother [Sir Thomas, not Richard], nephews and kindred,'[27] reported Brodrick to Hyde on

16 July, while a mere month earlier Mordaunt had been assuring Hyde confidently that 'the Fanshawes act together'.[28]

Brodrick sent Hyde a more detailed analysis of the Fanshawe family on 11 July, discussing 'the two Fanshawes, young and old, and their relations with Sir Thomas and his brother [either Simon or Richard]. Every one [of them] is suspected for some reason or other: his wife [that was Richard], mistress, priest, poverty or lack of conscience.'[29] This quote is a condensation of the original letter, in which Brodrick does not directly name Richard, the most prominent member of the Fanshawe family involved in the Royalist cause, but observes with a literary shrug, 'uxorious men are doubted for ther wives'.[30] Richard's seven years away from Hyde and Charles cannot have helped burnish his name when this kind of conversation arose; it seems Ann was blamed but they could not be considered individually. Her influence had made it impossible to rely upon him. One can only imagine Hyde's view of Ann and the children joining Richard in Paris while he contemplated the last stage of their long campaign to restore Charles to his throne.

Sir Thomas Fanshawe, Richard's elder brother, who had earlier been proposed as an alternative to Mordaunt as a possible leader of the Royalists in England, was arrested on 30 July alongside his cousin Thomas Leventhorpe (various Leventhorpes were frequent contributors to Ann's receipt book) and others as being 'implicated in the intended insurrection'.[31] They were released after two weeks, but in September, having subsequently been charged with High Treason, they gave themselves up and were committed to the Tower where they were held until the following February.

The good news for Richard was that he and Hyde were communicating like fond friends once again. Pointedly, Richard told

Hyde about the foreign languages he had been studying since his 'captivite': 'thus idle and frivolous I have been in later years, and perhaps otherwise I had not now been at liberty. *Cautum* as well as *dulce est desipere in loco* [it is prudent as well as pleasant to be playful]'.[32] Hyde responded with a request for some books and told Richard how much he wanted to read his new translation of *Querer por solo querer*. 'God send us into a place where we may spend our time better, and bring us well together'.[33]

For Ann the late summer of 1659 was marked by another tragedy. Her dates are unreliable, but soon after they arrived in Paris all three of the children travelling with her fell ill with smallpox, the disease that had taken Nan from them five years earlier. There was nothing she could do but pray: Sir Kenelm suggested a saffron infusion and Henrietta Maria's book recommended saffron in treacle but neither with much conviction. Saffron was used as a diaphoretic, promoting sweating, especially for children – perhaps an attempt to soothe smallpox's attendant fever. Although Ann neglected Katherine and Margaret to nurse Dick, at twelve her oldest surviving child and only son, 'yet it pleased God they recovered and he died, the grief of which made me miscarry, and caused a sickness of three weeks'.[34] Dick was buried in the Protestant churchyard in Paris, the seventh child of Ann's to die.

It's very hard to read about a mother neglecting – Ann's word – some children to tend another: the implication of preference is shocking by modern standards and a reminder that the relations between seventeeth century children and their parents could be pitiless as well as loving. Today, when almost all our children survive to adulthood and outlive their parents, we can afford to value each child individually and equally. But for Ann, her precious only son, her husband's heir, at twelve almost an adult, would have been a more terrible loss than one of her four girls, the older two then aged seven and six, if only because he had been with her, like Nan the companion of her struggles, for longer.

Keeping your children alive and healthy was a constant struggle. The Verney letters, written in real time, reveal in a way that Ann's retrospective memoirs can't the impact of infantile disease on growing children and their parents' efforts to counter them. Because of rickets caused by malnutrition when he was at nurse (the wet nurse's malnutrition passed on to him: it was called 'ill suck'), Jack Verney grew up with painfully crooked legs; he was also a stutterer, a condition arguably exacerbated by being left behind when his parents went into exile. Edmund, or Mun, wore an iron and leather corset to correct his rickets-induced crookedness and suffered from terrible toothache, which was treated by lancing his gums and pressing cotton soaked in aqua vitae on them. Little Peg, scarred by smallpox, was 'crooked' too: she held her head 'worse than ever, not only down, but very much awry',[35] wrote her concerned father. Dancing lessons didn't help; they tied her head in place to try to force it straight.

Ann's receipt book contains numerous remedies for children's illnesses, from convulsion fits to worms ('with this medicine I cured a child of mine yt had a desperate feaver caused by the wormes,' reads one note), thrush and measles. Two extensive remedies for rickets were crossed out, one including a bath, an ointment and a syrup to be taken internally, indicating they had been tried and failed; another was retained. When a child was ill, Ralph Verney urged his wife to give it 'no physic but such as midwives and old women… doe prescribe; for assure yourself they by experience know better than any phisition how to treat such infants'.[36]

After this second dreadful bout of smallpox, Ann would have used a feather to dab an ointment made from boiled cream on her daughters' scabs to try to prevent them scarring, something Kenelm Digby recommended. I wonder if she had had the disease so that she could nurse her children without fear of infection, either as a child (when it was usually less likely to be fatal), or as an adult, or not at all. She didn't say.

Perhaps she also gave them this Strengthening and Cooling Broth, another recipe from her mother, as they began to recover. Although to modern eyes, as a stock or soup, it is food, to Ann it was a remedy. It is firmly in the medical section of Ann's book, between 'A rare medecene for a Thrush in the mouth for a Child or old Body' and 'An excellent receipt for any weakness in the Back'. The nourishing chicken and veal broth was protein- and mineral-rich and each of the herbs had an important medicinal value as tonics, stimulants and diuretics, cleansing the blood and inproving the functioning of the liver. Endive is high in vitamin K and manganese which promote bone health. Rosemary, apart from stimulating circulation, is also good for a weak heart; both rosemary and thyme ease headaches.

Despite the plethora of medicines for scurvy, her book doesn't always contain the remedies I imagine Ann would have needed. Judging by the number of receipts for plague water, plague was a very real fear; worms, kidney stones and the bloody flux – or dysentery – were all well catered for, as well as burns, ulcers and sore breasts, possibly cancerous ones. There isn't much on smallpox but perhaps that's simply because Ann knew there was no cure and therefore there was no point assuaging her desire to help with palliatives. As Kenelm Digby observed, 'in this Disease the less you meddle, the better it is commonly for the Patient'.[37] But where is the advice for recovering from labour, or what was known as a fallen fundament (a prolapsed womb), surely a problem after more than ten pregnancies? Other books suggest a seventeenth century version of vaginal steaming, sitting over the fumes coming from a hot brick infused with frankincense, cypress and myrtle, or anointing the uterus with a 'stinking rotten addle Egge'.[38]

Throughout the autumn in Paris, as Ann, Katherine and Margaret convalesced, mourning the loss of Dick, regular letters bounced between Charles, Edward Hyde, the Mordaunts and the king's other followers, scattered across northern Europe. Elizabeth Mordaunt worried that 'all those expresses [express letters delivered by messenger rather than by public post]'[39] were running them vastly into debt; a cousin, Hartgill Baron, braved miserable weather and 'many hazards'[40] to deliver letters from Mordaunt to Hyde and James, duke of York.

At the start of September, John Mordaunt reflected to Charles that God must still be angry with them, 'when we reflect upon the sad ruins he makes us authors of to ourselves', but passionately declared, 'had I a thousand lives and fortunes they should all lay at your feet'.[41] At the end of the month, his wife assured 'your Majestie of my willing submission to all the hazzards my deare husband exposes himself to in your Majesties service'. Despite the difficulties, she rejoiced 'that I had interest in a person, that in this degenerate age, retained so strict a duty for your Majestie'.[42] Her support was vital to Mordaunt's cause. He was waiting for her to arrive in Calais, bringing money with her, so that they could set off for a brief visit to England together on Charles's orders. Her funds were essential but even without them, he told Hyde, it would hardly have been worth him going without her. 'I should have carried only a body without a soule. I should not have been capable of businesse'.[43]

From England, in October, Mordaunt wrote to tell Hyde with joy that, 'if I judge truly, the King's restoration is not far off'.[44] Later he told Charles, 'I see not how your affaires can miscarry'.[45] To Elizabeth he was more realistic: 'All stands very faire, and my only feare is the P[resbyterians] prevailing who will tye up the King I know, all they can. The whole consists in dispatch. God in heaven blesse Deare'.[46]

Charles was grateful for their service, writing to Elizabeth Mordaunt in December to tell her 'how much I think myself beholding to you and your husband' and signing himself, 'your very affectionate friend, Charles R.'.[47] Concrete rewards would accrue from his gratitude. Some, like Hyde (later earl of Clarendon and already Lord Chancellor-in-waiting) and Abbess Knatchbull, hoped for rewards once Charles was restored to power; the Mordaunts began to see the privileges of their proximity to Charles almost immediately. There was the viscountcy in March 1659; in November Nicholas Armorer, an agent who brought the news to Charles of the final expulsion of the Rump Parliament (which had been dismissed as unworkable by Cromwell in 1653, reinstated after Richard Cromwell's removal from the Protectorate in May 1659 and dissolved itself that October preparatory to the formation of a new, post-Protectorate regime), was appointed an equerry and wrote to thank his patrons, Hyde and Lady Mordaunt.

From November 1659 letters began flooding to Elizabeth Mordaunt from cousins and contacts wishing her and John well. Even though 'the things I dare write are so different from ye things I would say if I were with you,' her cousin Lady Mary Carey, in slightly hero-worshipping tones, wanted Elizabeth to know she has 'been verie sensible of every change has of late been in your condition. And yet since you have scaped the danger, cannot say I am verye sorrie you have been in some, for in the age we live, tis not easy to sever suffering from the honour of doing one's dutie; And I know you prefere that so much before the lazy quiet most here place their happinesse in, that I must defer my wishes, if I should desire you back upon those termes'.[48] Mary's sister Lady Elizabeth wrote too, as well as Elizabeth's 'cousine' Lady Ormonde, Ann's friend; even her own father told her of 'the honour of being so nearly allyed to you in bloud'.[49]

Richard's name occurred with increasing frequency over these months in letters to and from Hyde, Nicholas and Ormonde. In September Hyde asked him to keep him informed 'of as many particulars concerning persons or things as you can, for in this dispersion of our friends we know little more than the prints [newspapers] inform us';[50] in November he informed him that, 'Your friends in England hold up their heads again, and I hope we may once more meet there'.[51] For the first time in their fifteen years of correspondence there was a possibility of this wish coming true.

In November Richard refused to draft a communiqué from Charles to French ministers updating them on his prospects in England, perhaps feeling that they were overly optimistic; John Mordaunt did it instead, commenting, 'the King's business in England is ripening too fast for these slow councils'.[52] It was perhaps this exchange that prompted Hyde to defend Richard to Mordaunt 'as honest and as discreet a person, as I know, and one of whom the King and my Lord Lieutenant [of Ireland; the marquess of Ormonde] have a singular esteeme'.[53]

In November, Charles visited Henrietta Maria at Colombes, outside Paris, and Ann and Richard went to pay their respects to mother and son. Ann had last seen the young king-in-waiting as a sixteen-year-old boy in Jersey, thirteen years earlier. He told her 'that if it pleased God to restore him to his kingdoms, my husband should partake of his happiness in as great a share as any servants he had. Then he asked me many questions of England, and fell into discourse with my husband privately two hours'.[54] Richard reported to Hyde that he found his master '(without flatterie to him or the companie he hath kept) improved every way far beyond my expectation'.[55]

From Colombes, Charles went to Flanders and Richard followed him, while Ann and the girls went to Calais. Charles's renewed 'singular esteeme' for Richard was reflected in a December memo signed by Hyde and Richard promising him the office of principal Secretary of State (there were two), which George Digby, earl of Bristol and one of Henrietta Maria's long-standing favourites, and thus overwhelmed by Hyde's ascendance, was about to relinquish; the other, in office on and off since 1641, was Sir Edward Nicholas. Richard would be sworn in by the king before the end of May 1660 or when the king next summoned him to attend him, once – and this is the crucial point – he'd procured a gift or loan of £2000 for Charles. Richard put his trust in this promise but the promises of princes can be unreliable: Charles had also offered the post to Sir Henry Bennet, formerly a messenger for Ormonde, a convivial fellow of Charles's age (rather than the generation above) who had been with Charles or his brother James throughout the 1650s and was said also to have been involved with Lucy Walters, Charles's discarded mistress, indication of their shared tastes.

CHAPTER 18

1660
A Water comparable to Gold

Take a gallon of white Wine, 4 Ounces of Gentian, and 24 ounces of Centaury, stamp them together, putt the Wine to them & let them soake together 5 dayes, then distill them in an ordnary Still, & keep the water in a close Vessell, & when you use it take 2 Spoonfulls morning and evening.

This Water preserveth the Body from all manner of Diseases, it putteth away all Imposthumes, it maketh good Coulour, it resisteth Plague, avoideth stuffit Stomachs, it breaketh the Stone in ye reines [kidneys], it reparates & putts away watry humrs [humours] of ye Spleene, it purgeth ye Belly also, it purgeth all Coler and corrupt Blood, it healeth all Wounds in ye Belly, it healeth poysened bitings, & it cleareth ye Sight, to the healing of wounds ye powder of Centaury ought to be drunke with it the weight of 4 or 6 at a time.

In January 1660, Ann, her two elder daughters and her two servants were waiting in Calais for a boat back to England, where she planned to raise money – one last time – with which to return to Richard, who was by now somewhere in the Low

Countries with Charles, the young king-in-waiting, going from Newport to Ghent to Bruges. Ann joined them in Brussels, bringing £150, all she could raise of the £2000 Charles had requested as downpayment for the role Richard hoped for as Secretary of State.

At some point in this early part of 1660, while they were in the Low Countries, Ann is thought to have sat for a portrait by 'Toniars' which she would leave her son in her will. A faded inscription on a painting owned by her great-granddaughter in 1773 read 'My ever loved and deare mother Lady Fanshawe, thirty-five years old, and poor little Mary, by Teniers, 1660.'[1] The portrait shows a woman closely resembling the Ann of her 1643 portrait, with brown eyes and curling dark hair drawn sharply back from her forehead. She looks thirty-five – her age according to the note – and although her face is thinner, that would be right, after the life she had led between the two portraits. On her lap is a plump baby wearing a white cap and blue dress, identified as Mary, then three but living in Hertfordshire – perhaps painted using a model, to show Ann with her youngest child even though they were temporarily apart. The baby is the wrong age, though: she still wears the clothes of an infant rather than the mini-adult costume of a three-year-old.

Both Ann and her baby are heavily bejewelled. Little Mary wears pearl bracelets and a pearl drop brooch and a gold rattle is attached to her gold link belt; Ann's pearl drop earrings are the size of marbles and she wears, along with the pearls at her neck and wrists and in her hair, a large diamond bow brooch. (Samuel Pepys bought his wife three rows of 'very good' pearls in 1665 for £80, while Lucy Hay, countess of Carlisle, pawned hers for £1500 in 1647.) The jewels seem excessive because the Fanshawes can't have had extra money for jewellery, although they'd never lived in poverty as terrible as many of their friends. However, many sitters for portraits borrowed jewels to present themselves to posterity as more prosperous than they were. In the 1630s, when she was painted by Van Dyck, Lady Sussex didn't mind 'another age to thinke me richer than I was' although she did complain about how fat and ugly he had made her: 'thow I bee ill favoured, i think that makes me wors than I am'.[2] Ann had been given rings by friends such as Lady Ormonde and it's not unreasonable to suppose that she and Richard stored some of their wealth in portable jewels.

The attribution to Toniars in Ann's will must be a misspelling of Teniers and therefore one of the dynasty of David Tenierses working between Antwerp and Brussels throughout the seventeenth century. The only one alive in 1660 was David Teniers II who specialized not in portraiture but in peasant scenes inspired by his father-in-law, Jan Brueghel the Elder. Looking at his work, it is clear both that this portrait is not by him and that he was very unlikely to have accepted a commission to paint Ann. The steeple in the background looks like Bruges rather than Antwerp or Brussels, although Ann might have been in any of those places in the early spring of 1660.

Recent research has concluded that the painting is not by David Teniers and is not a portrait of Ann and Mary Fanshawe, despite its long-standing connection to the family and the now illegible label on the reverse.[3] But even if this is not it, there was another, now lost, painted in the Low Countries in 1660 that Ann bequeathed to her son and that must have looked much like this, along with the earlier portraits of her and Richard and their miniatures set in gold.

The Fanshawes were in tune with their times and class as regular commissioners of portraits, an expensive habit slowed down but not halted by the civil wars. The family archive at Valence House in Essex contains an extraordinary collection of portraits going back to the early seventeenth century and so extensive that on their vast family tree almost every name can be accompanied by at least one image. Ann and Richard are there and several of their children alongside Richard's brothers and sisters – including the matriarch, Alice, Lady Bedell, bearing a surprising resemblance to Oliver Cromwell, and the boastful 'libertine', Simon, who'd overestimated his followers during Booth's rising the previous year. Richard's sister-in-law, who died in childbirth in 1627, is shown in the late stages of pregnancy, in exquisite lace and a fashionable beaver hat with a sweeping plume.

A great many members of the seventeenth century family were painted by Peter Lely or his student, Mary Beale. Lely painted companion portraits of Richard and Ann which are now on display at Ardgowan House in Scotland. In 1677 Charles Beale's diary records that his 'Dearest Heart... finished the face and breast of Mrs Fanshawe's picture at the fourth sitting';[4] this was almost certainly Ann, aged fifty-two, in a portrait recently donated to Valence House (see plate section), visibly older and thinner and wearing a large bow-shaped diamond brooch very like the one in the 'Toniars' portrait. Mary Beale charged £5 for a head-and-shoulders portrait and £10 for one of three-quarter length.

I love the portraits of their children (see plate section): Dick, who'd died the year before, thin and grown up in a nineteenth century copy taken from a lost joint portrait with his father and a greyhound by Lely and probably painted in 1658 when he was ten, the year before he died; and portraits of Margaret and Ann, then aged about twelve and ten, both with hair in elaborately ringleted bunches in imitation of Charles's youngest sister, Princess Henriette, painted in the mid-1660s by Theodore Russel with huge eyes and pale, serious expressions. Both are wearing the same oversized pearl drop earrings, a heavy pearl drop necklace and ropes of pearls in their hair, much like the headdress, earrings and necklace of the woman who isn't their mother in the 'Toniars' portrait. Except for the colour of their eyes – Margaret's, like her mother's, are brown; Ann's, like Richard's, are blue-grey – and their dresses, respectively coral and yellow, they are portrayed identically.

In January 1660, Lord Fairfax, a former Parliamentary general, urges General Monck, Commander-in-Chief of the Parliamentary army, to restore the monarchy. Monck marches on London and calls for the Long Parliament of 1648 to be recalled, including the MPs purged before Charles I's trial. It meets in March, votes for its own dissolution and calls for free elections. When, following the elections, the new Convention Parliament assembles it declares, on 8 May, that Charles II had been rightful king of England since 30 January 1649. The scene is set for his Restoration.

While Ann and Richard were in the Low Countries in early 1660, we can rely upon the opening pages of Samuel Pepys's diary for a feel of London's atmosphere at the start of this eventful year. As Hyde put it to Richard in January, 'Indeed the turns in England turn my head, that I know not what to say or think of them'.[5]

In February Pepys noted that, 'Boys do now cry, "Kiss my Parliament" instead of "Kiss my arse," so great and general a contempt is the Rump come to among all men, good and bad.'[6] Mixed in with his observations on the state of the government were more private, everyday entries of the kind seldom included in a memoir like Ann's: he began to wear buckles on his shoes in January, a new style for him; he dined on ordinary days on poached eggs, bread and cheese, leftover roast meat or even just posset (although for friends his wife would prepare a fine dinner of up to ten dishes); he practised his lute and viol and consulted his mother when he had a canker sore (she sent her maid, Besse, to Cheapside to buy herbs to make a water for it). By March, he reported, Londoners were openly drinking the king's health. 'For all I see, [Charles's return] is the wishes of all and all do believe that it will be so.'[7]

Elizabeth Mordaunt, back in England in March, also noted the changes. When she'd been there in September, she told Hyde, 'most persons [were] afraid to see me and I more afraid to see them our estate and all our things seised and we overjoyed to be out of our own country… now I return welcomed by all'.[8] A mere six months later their property and goods had been returned and the warrants issued for their arrest rescinded.

On May Day, Pepys heard that in Deal the people had 'set up 2 or 3 maypooles and have hung their flags upon top of them, and do resolve to be very merry today, it being a very pleasant day. I wished myself in Hide parke'.[9] In London, to a backdrop of bell ringing and bonfires, people drank the king's health on their knees in the streets and the City declared it would only have a government of King, Lords and Commons. Eight days later Charles's Restoration was officially declared without a single condition attached to Parliament's invitation for Charles to return.

So many Royalists, eager to declare their loyalty to their king, flocked to his side in Holland, that Katherine Philips could make a joke about it:

> Hasten (great prince) unto thy British Isle,
> Or all thy subjects will become exiles.[10]

Pepys was one of them, joining his patron, Lord Sandwich, in The Hague, where he marvelled at the 'gallantry of the town. Everybody of fashion speak French or Latin, or both. The women, many of them very pretty and in good habitt, fashionable, and black [beauty] spots.'[11] How I would love to know if Ann was included in this description. She was in The Hague at the beginning of May, with her fashionable court dress and her fluently French- and Latin-speaking husband, thrilled at the kindness of her reception by the glamorous Queen of Bohemia, Charles I's sister Elizabeth. 'Here the King and all the Royal Family were entertained at a very great supper by the States [the Dutch States General]; and now business of state took up much time'.[12]

Part of this business of state was Charles appointing officials in preparation for taking up the reins of government. In Breda in April he swore Richard in as Master of Requests, one of six, with a life annuity of £100. Again, he promised him the post of Secretary of State, this time witnessed by Ormonde and Hyde, 'yet that false man [Hyde] made the King break his word for his own accommodation,' remembered Ann furiously. Instead Hyde would place an undistinguished Presbyterian, Sir William Morice, 'that never saw the King's face'[13] (according to Ann), in the position over Richard. Hyde needed to reward the Presbyterian Parliamentarians who had welcomed his master back, even if it was at the expense of Richard's long looked-for prize. Pleasing everyone was a difficult business, as he would learn.

Richard can't have been disappointed by the favour Charles showed him on his return home, providing Ann and her children with a handsome space on the frigate *Speedwell*, while inviting Richard to travel with him on his own ship. The *Speedwell* was laden down with gifts from the States General for Charles's followers: 'a tierce of claret, a hogshead of Rhenish wine, six dozen of fowls, a dozen gammons of bacon, a great basket of bread, and six sheep, two dozen of neats' [cows'] tongues, and a great box of sweetmeats'.[14] Ann and Richard had only rarely gone hungry in Charles's name, but Hyde and Nicholas – and Charles himself – had been desperately short of money mere months earlier: this new feasting must have felt as bizarre as it was welcome.

The royal flotilla set sail in the afternoon of 23 May to the accompaniment of shouts of goodwill from the shore and joyful volleys of shot. Its mood was celebratory: the wind was so favourable 'that the ships' wherries went from ship to ship to visit their friends all night long,' wrote Ann.

> But who can sufficiently express the joy and gallantry of that voyage, to see so many great ships, the best in the world, to hear the trumpets and all other music, to see near a hundred brave ships sail before the wind with vast cloths

> and streamers, the neatness and cleanness of the ships, the strength and jollity of the mariners, the gallantry of the commanders, the vast plenty of all sorts of provisions; but above all, the glorious majesties of the King and his two brothers, were so beyond man's expectation and expression! The sea was calm, the moon shone at full, and the sun suffered not a cloud to hinder his prospect of the best sight, by whose light, and the merciful bounty of God, he was set safely on shore at Dover in Kent.[15]

As they sailed, Pepys recorded Charles telling his companions, Richard among them, of his escape from Worcester in 1651: how far they had come since that unhappy time.

It took Pepys to put the scene in perspective. He disembarked on a barge with one of Charles's footmen 'with a dog that the King loved (which shit in the boat, which made us laugh and me think that a King and all that belong to him are but just as others are)'.[16] Charles may have regained his father's throne, but, for many, the divine mystique of royalty had been irreparably tarnished over the intervening years.

People lined the route all the way from Dover to Whitehall so that it seemed like one long street from harbour to palace. Ann and her family stayed a night in Dover and then went on to London in a coach belonging to Sir Arnold Braemes, the developer of Dover's seafront, where they stayed in a house in the Savoy area. The next day, in the Strand with her friend Katherine Fanshawe, née Ferrers, the unlikely 'highwaywoman' married to Richard's nephew, they watched the king and his brothers enter the city with all pomp and splendour. (Katherine, aged twenty-six and shown in a portrait with a delicate face and smiling eyes, must have very quickly developed a fatal illness or had an accident, for she was buried in Ware two weeks after this day of celebration.)

The day after that Ann went 'with other ladies of the family' to Whitehall to welcome and congratulate the king, 'who received me with great grace, and promised me future favours to my husband and self. His Majesty gave my husband his picture, set with small diamonds, when he was a child: it is a great rarity, because there never was but one'.[17] Portraits were often copied to be given away as presents; Lady Sussex paid Van Dyck £50 for her portrait and another £8 for a copy.

Richard began work as Master of Requests, acting as judicial intermediary between the king and petitioners for his favour, but, apparently with Hyde's approval, his old companion in exile Sir Edward Nicholas (the other Secretary of State since 1654, and in the early 1640s for Charles I too) initially 'engrossed all the petitions'[18] which Ann thought should have come through Richard's office and for which Richard, rather than Nicholas, should have collected the fees. This injustice was especially vexing, noted Ann, because Hyde, whose wife was a daughter of a former Master of Requests, would have known better. It was an ominous start to Richard's post-Restoration career.

The Fanshawes took a house in Portugal Row, Lincoln's Inn Fields, near where they had lodged in harder times thirteen years earlier while Ann was petitioning for Richard to compound. If this was a time of advantage, alongside all the stresses that brought, it was also a time of great expense, with rich new clothes and immaculately liveried servants required for grand court occasions and their London house to furnish. But they now had an income, too, and at last in 1661 Ann recorded that she and Richard were able to pay off the debts they had run up over the past eighteen years. The life of wealth and influence in royal service to which they had looked forward for so long was now within their grasp.

They sent for their five-year-old daughter Nan from Kent, where she had been staying with her aunt and uncle, Joan and Philip Warwick. Their youngest, Mary, died in Hertfordshire in August, aged four, before she could rejoin them. Now there were just three Fanshawe children of the eleven Ann had borne: Katherine, eight, Margaret, seven, and Nan, five. Every child had been born in a different place and only two of her eight dead children (Mary and the first Henry) were buried in the same churchyard, Ann's childhood church in Hertford near her father's house.

Ann was pregnant in the summer of 1660 for the first time since 1656 and her long illness. 'In the latter end of the summer I miscarried, when I was near half gone with child, of three sons, two hours one after the other,' she wrote. The miscarriage she blamed on overwork. 'I think it was with the hurry of business I then was in, and perpetual company that resorted to us of all qualities, some for kindness and some for their own advantage'.[19] Later, it would be Ann's turn to haunt court in hopes of a friend or a favour.

She would have had resort, once again, to her trusty receipt book: to the 'red powder good for miscarrying' and the various cordials and drinks that revived spirits and strength and on which she had so often relied in the past. This precious 'Water comparable to Gold' contains fortifying gentian, helpful in relieving chronic exhaustion, and centaury, which purifies the blood; both herbs are very bitter and are still used as tonics for increasing resistance to disease, reducing fever and inflammation and improving appetite and digestion. Princes or patrons might let you down, but a receipt book could be relied upon.

WINTER

Cold as the Feete of Rocks so Winter ſtands. | Admit ſhe coue'rd in warme habitt goe,
With Maſked face and Muff vpon her hands. | Though black without her ſkin is white as ſnowe

4

‘We should ourselves be sorry to think that posterity should judge us by a patchwork of our letters, preserved by chance, independent of their context, written perhaps in a fit of despondency or irritation, divorced, above all, from the myriad little strands which colour and compose our peculiar existence, and which in their multiplicity, their variety and their triviality, are vivid to ourselves alone, uncommunicable even to those nearest to us’.

VITA SACKVILLE-WEST, INTRODUCTION TO
The Diary of Lady Ann Clifford, 1923

‘I want this journal to live. I suppose I must always have wanted this, or I would not have tended it, treasured it so carefully… I would like to think of other people, years and years hence, reading it with interest, sympathy, perhaps some admiration?’

JEAN LUCEY PRATT, JOURNAL ENTRY, 28 JUNE 1948

EPILOGUE

'A Complete Little Globe of Human Life'

I wish I could write that, with their king's return and Richard finally in proper service to him, Ann, Richard and their children settled into the life for which they had been waiting and hoping for nearly twenty years. But high politics, as they would learn, can be as capricious a mistress as exile or retreat.

At last they were able to pay off their debts and begin a settled existence in London. Richard, 'very well known and very beloved'[1] by Charles, seemed in a prime position to capitalize on his loyal service to the charismatic young king. His brother Thomas was granted letters patent returning the hereditary office of King's Remembrancer to him and his family; Richard, his brother and his nephew (also Thomas) were all elected MPs in 1661. Edward Hyde was already Lord Chancellor but he swiftly became Lord Hyde and then, in 1661, earl of Clarendon; Richard's patron Ormonde became a duke as well as a Privy Councillor and Lord High Steward. As Charles's Vice-Chamberlain, George Carteret, the Fanshawes' affable host in Jersey in 1647, organized the coronation in April 1661 in which Richard rode at Charles's left hand.

For all these portents of success, though, perhaps ageing Edward Nicholas's fate was more instructive: pushed out of office after decades of service in the worst of conditions and replaced as Secretary of State in 1662 by Charles's favourite, the amiable rake Henry Bennet, he could not afford to accept the peerage he was offered as consolation. He was not alone in feeling betrayed and disillusioned. As Andrew Marvell wrote,

> To see them that suffered for father and son,
> And helped to bring the latter to this throne,
> That with lives and estates did loyally serve,
> And yet for all this nothing can deserve;
> The King looks not on 'em, preferments denied 'em,
> The Roundheads insult and the courtiers deride 'em.

Instead of relying upon the devoted band of loyalists like Nicholas, Hyde and Richard, who had served him in exile through thick and thin, but who (as former servants of his father) could not help treating him as a naughty child, once on his throne Charles tended to prefer men closer to him in age whose roguish charm masked their unscrupulousness and ambition. These men, including Henry Bennet, who rose to become earl of Arlington through his procurement of mistresses for the king, and the dissipated poet-earl, Rochester, would come to define the Restoration era.

But Ann blamed Hyde, her political nemesis. 'Now,' she wrote, 'it was the business of the Chancellor to put your father as far from the King as he could, because his [Hyde's] ignorance in state affairs was daily discovered by your father, who showed it to the King; but at that time the King was so content that he [Hyde] should almost and alone manage his affairs, that he might have more time for his pleasure'.[2] By August 1661 (according to Ann), Hyde had masterminded Richard's exit: he informed Richard that the king had chosen him to go to Portugal, bearing the king's portrait, to negotiate his marriage with Catherine of Braganza, although the fact that Richard was perhaps the only gentleman of sufficient rank and experience at court who spoke fluent Spanish and passable Portuguese was surely another element in his appointment.

Charles's letter to the Infanta Catherine described his messenger as 'a trusty and well-beloved gentleman of my household... who has served me for many years faithfully and honourably'.[3] It was an honour – Ann admitted it – but she was sure 'the design from that time forth was to fix'[4] Richard there, away from the English court where he might undermine Hyde's weakening sway. She remained at home in London while Richard went off on his mission to Portugal. A last daughter, Elizabeth (their third Betty), was born in February 1662.

Even before Catherine arrived to marry Charles the following May, Richard was attempting to extract himself from his role as Portuguese envoy and place himself – and Ann – back at Whitehall. Catherine wrote to her betrothed weeks after Richard got to Lisbon requesting that he be given 'some considerable office in my household [and]... his wife, Donna Anna, the office to be that woman of my bedchamber, unto whom it belongs also to be Lady of the Jewels'.[5] This would be the plum position in the new queen's household although she had not, at that point, yet met Donna Anna.

But the Infanta's request fell on deaf ears. Instead Richard was appointed Ambassador to Portugal, another 'honour', whence he, Ann and their three elder daughters set off in August. In her memoirs Ann delighted in the honours accorded them, the exotic presents they received and the favour and confidences of the Portuguese royal family. They returned to England the following year. Ann, 'to add to my content... met with my little girl Betty, whom I had left at nurse',[6] while Richard was sworn in as Privy Councillor.

In January 1664, they packed up again for his new posting in Madrid where, once again, Ann revelled in the luxury of the Spanish court, recalling extravagant compliments paid to her and visits to extraordinary palaces and gardens. Lovingly she described the magnificent brocade outfit in which Richard was first received by the king in Madrid, laced with nine silver and gold laces 'every one as broad as my hand', his scarlet stockings, shoe-strings and garters, his Flanders lace-edged linen, his black beaver hat, his curiously wrought gold chain from which hung a miniature of the king, and his twenty footmen in their dark green livery, 'with a frost upon green lace'.[7] She delighted in the plays, bull fights and elaborate entertainments of water-works and fireworks, in being transported in their official coach of crimson velvet laced with gold and silver, and being given lavish presents including cases of amber and orange-flower water, barrels of olives and, most beautiful of all, a chest a yard and a half long covered with green silk and silver lace and filled with sweetmeats wrapped in gilt paper.

But notwithstanding all, she wrote, 'your father and myself both wished ourselves in a retired country life in England, as more agreeable to both our inclinations'.[8] In August 1665, their final child, a second Richard, was born (another boy had been born two years earlier but lived for only a few hours). Ann was forty and, counting miscarriages, he was her twentieth baby: one born on average every year for her entire adulthood, pausing only during severe illness (and not always then) – and of those babies only five made it to adulthood themselves, her son Richard and four daughters, Katherine, Margaret, Ann and Elizabeth.

Richard negotiated a treaty between England and Spain which, almost before the ink was dry, was rendered irrelevant by war with the Dutch; Charles refused to sign it, appointing the charming earl of Sandwich, Samuel Pepys's patron and previously a supporter of Cromwell, ambassador in Richard's place. As Ann put it, Sandwich, who understood nothing 'but a vicious life', was 'shuffled into your father's employment to reap the benefit of his five years' negotiation of the peace between England, Spain and Portugal'.[9] He delivered the papers of revocation to Richard in May 1666.

Aged fifty-eight, Richard died of a fever within the month. A lesser man might have cursed the fate that had led him to the Iberian peninsula and the political wilderness but one senses that he would have met his maker with dignity rather than resentment. He would be remembered as a man of reserved grace, a gifted poet and translator whose sense of honour and discretion defined his many years of service to Charles II. The fact that he was also a devoted husband and father only burnishes his memory but he would have considered that a purely private matter.

Devastated, Ann turned to writing for solace, composing a prayer that would sustain her as she learned to live without her beloved husband.

> O all powerful good God, look down from Heaven on the most distressed wretch upon earth… Have pity on me, O Lord, and speak peace to my disquieted soul, now sinking under this great weight, which, without thy support, cannot

> sustain itself... Lord, pardon me; O God, forgive whatsoever is amiss in me; break not a bruised reed... [but] enable me to fulfil thy will cheerfully in this world, humbling beseeching thee that, when this mortal life is ended, I may be joined with the soul of my dear husband, and all thy servants departed this life in thy faith and fear, in everlasting praises of thy Holy Name. Amen.[10]

Mariana, the Spanish queen regent, offered Ann a generous pension if she and her children would convert to Catholicism and stay in Madrid. Ann was tempted – the unhappy queen had become a friend – but instead she decided to struggle home. Defeated by Richard's loss, forced to sell their silver and presents from the queen to pay off their Spanish debts and fund their journey, she found herself no longer rising to the call of adventure but pitifully worn out, setting off for home 'with my son but twelve months old in my arms, four daughters, the eldest but thirteen years of age, with the [embalmed] body of my dear husband daily in my sight for near six months together, and a distressed family [a household of more than thirty], all to be by me in honour and honesty provided for, and to add to my afflictions, neither persons sent to conduct me, nor pass, nor ship, nor money to carry me one thousand miles, but some few letters from the chief ministers, bidding, "God help me!" as they do to beggars'.[11] Her cri de coeur sounds as immediate as if she was uttering it as she wrote, although in fact she was remembering it from a distance of a decade.

On her return she was forced to petition for the money Richard was owed by the crown (ambassadors by custom not claiming their expenses until their return), over £5000 to be reimbursed and £2000 in arrears of salary. Lord Arlington – the Henry Bennet who had replaced Edward Nicholas (and by extension nudged out Richard himself) as Secretary of State – offered to help her and received Spanish amber, gloves and chocolate as well as a copy of a large Titian worth £100 in return. Despite his support and that of William Coventry, the most talented statesman of this younger generation, to whom she also gave presents, it took more than two years for her to be repaid and she had to write off a loss of £2000, equivalent to Richard's salary during those six years of service. A Spanish proverb saved among Richard's papers reads, '*A muertos y a idos no hay mas amigos*': the dead and the absent have no friends.[12]

As she had during the years of war and exile, Ann was forced to challenge the expected role of a woman, relinquishing passive obedience to take on the role of claimant and agent once again. With stability restored to England alongside the monarchy the reins of power had been taken back by men, and women were relegated once more to private and domestic roles. This is not to say women couldn't play prominent roles in society – but that when they did, those roles were explicitly associated with their sexual availability: I'm thinking of Charles's gallery of mistresses, from the orange girl and actress Nell Gwyn to the duchess of Cleveland, Barbara Villiers, notorious for her profligacy. Intellectual women like Robert Boyle's sister and collaborator Katherine Ranelagh or the receipt book-writing Talbot sisters, the countesses of Kent and Arundel, simply faded from public consciousness. After 1666, without Richard or the Royalist cause to justify it, Ann's old appetite for business had faded alongside the willingness of others to admire or even endure a woman forced by circumstance to act in an 'unwomanly' way. She would become known as a difficult woman, marked by her dogged pursuit of what was due to her and to Richard's memory.

Even before Richard had died we can catch a glimpse of Ann's stubborn refusal to play the game, in the argument Pepys reported between her and her former friend, Elizabeth Carteret. Lady Carteret was the young wife of the Governor of Jersey in 1647 whom Ann met and became close friends with – she oversaw her goddaughter, little Nan, while she was at nurse in Jersey, while Richard and Ann went on to France. A slightly later Carteret receipt book contains a receipt for ice cream very similar to the one in Ann's book, indicating a source shared between intimates.

But by 1662 Samuel Pepys, who worked with Elizabeth's husband, recorded that Ann had 'fallen out with her [Elizabeth], only for speaking in behalf of the French; which my lady wonders at, they having been formerly like sisters.'[13] A disagreement over the king's foreign policy – in which, as ambassador, Richard was intimately concerned – led to the severing of a bosom friendship. Ann would not back down in defence of her husband, even if it meant losing a friend; the fact that the Carterets were flourishing in Charles's service at court can't have helped ease her sense of grievance. Once again, Ann is shown as taking her husband's work, by extension her life, too personally.

Her treatment after Richard's death was a humiliation too far, after (as Ann wrote with excusable exaggeration) 'near thirty years' suffering by land and sea, and the hazard of our lives over and over, with the many services of your father, and the expense of all the monies we could procure, and seven years' imprisonment [she means in England in the 1650s], with the death and beggary of many eminent persons of our family, who when they first entered the King's service, had great and clear [of debt] estates'.[14] Confirmation of the family's descent came in the 1660s when Richard's nephew, Lord Fanshawe, who inherited Ware Park, sold it to a London brewer (one can almost hear Ann's outrage) for £26,000. Memories of those once great and clear estates and of her beloved husband were now all she had left.

Back in England, still only in her early forties and with a one-year-old son and four older daughters to raise alone, Ann shaped her life to her newly narrowed circumstances, spending her 'time in lament and dear remembrances of my past happiness and fortune',[15] those years of struggle, exile and adventure that had turned out to be the happiest of her life. She lived in Hertingfordbury, a village near her father at Balls, until he died in 1669. 'None ever had a kinder and better father than me,'[16] she wrote. Still owed £6000 by The Crown, he left Balls to his son and £3000 as part of a manor in Norfolk to Ann and her younger sister Margaret. For a while in the early 1670s Ann returned to London, renting rooms in Lincoln's Inn Fields, and in 1674 she moved into her last house, Little Grove, East Barnet, halfway between London and Ware and within easy reach of both. The house had belonged to the Bourchiers, a family connection of the Fanshawes, Brownes and Evelyns. Even though she had lost her currency at court, her wider family remained a valuable safety net.

She did not find life as a respectable widow in reduced circumstances satisfactory. That heady dream of being Catherine of Braganza's influential Lady of the Jewels had disappeared in a puff of smoke and the perfunctory attentions she received from the king and queen on her return from Spain did not console her.

Richard's elder sisters, Alice and Joan, whom she had loved dearly, died in the late 1660s; her role within the family, as godmother to the children of various Fanshawes, her sister Margaret and her younger half-brother, she considered noteworthy but it did not make up for what she had lost. All she could think about were the 'many miscarriages and errors' that had led to her fall 'from that happy estate I had been in'. Ultimately, she resolved not to shut herself away but, for her children's sake, 'suffer, as long as it pleased God, the storms and flows of fortune'.[17]

Managing the resources that remained to her became a distraction. 'I had, about this time [the late 1660s], some trouble with keeping the lordships of Tring and Hitching [*sic*], which your father held of the Queen-Mother [Henrietta Maria]; but I not being able to make a considerable advantage of them, gave them up again,' she told her son, 'and then I sold a lease of the Manor of Burstalgarth, which was granted for thirty-one years to your father from the King.'[18] These properties were royal grants, bequests to Richard in happier times that made up part of Ann's income after his death, the income from which she was naturally keen to maximize.

Perhaps she permitted herself a small smile at Hyde's fall from grace. By the mid-1660s, he had begun lecturing the king on his faults and refused to ingratiate himself with his extravagant, excessive mistress, Barbara Villiers (niece of his and Ann's old friend Lady Morton). The gout-ridden Lord Chancellor's inability to listen to criticism combined with England's humiliating defeat at Dutch hands in 1667 (a war he had never recommended) led to his impeachment and a second period of exile in France from which he would never return. Those who acted against him included

Arlington and William Coventry – the two officials favoured by the king to whom Ann noted she 'made presents'[19] on her arrival home from Spain in November 1666.

Hyde died in Rouen in 1675, the year before Ann began the memoir she addressed to her youngest child, Richard, who had been eleven months old when his father died. Writing one's life story was in vogue in the 1670s: in 1672, Mary Rich, at forty-seven an exact contemporary of Ann's, noted spending 'all the rest of this whole day, as I did the t'other day, in recording my own fore-past life'.[20]

Ann's manuscript was at once a description of Richard, an account of their life and happiness together (on every page she remembered 'the joys I was blessed with in him'[21]) and a defence of their actions during the civil wars, when they had sacrificed so much for the king whom she now knew to be thankless and ungrateful. When she wrote about their happy months at Tankersley before Nan died in 1653, she added a note that encapsulated her melancholy mood: 'my Lord Strafford says now, that what we planted is the best fruit in the North'.[22]

At the start of her memoir Ann listed 'with all reverence' numerous members of her family and Richard's. Most were now dead, she concluded, 'but their memories will remain as long as their names, for honest, worthy, virtuous men and women, who served God in their generations in their several capacities, and without vanity none exceeded them in their loyalty [to the crown] which cost them dear'. The Fanshawe family's annual income before the wars, she added, had been nearly £80,000, which they lost in serving the Stuarts, 'and this I have often seen a list of and know it to be true'.[23]

Ann's writing was, in part, an effort to stem the decline wrought in the family fortunes by the civil wars. Places of memory were important, whether in funerary monuments or as part of the design of a house or garden, but for Ann, lacking such space, writing was her way of guarding and commemorating her husband's and their forbears' memories. This is part of the reason her receipt book and her memoirs took on such importance for her: they were her bequests to her children, manuals for their lives when she would no longer be there to guide them.

Counting the pages Ann devoted to different sections of her memoirs offers an interesting assessment of the importance she placed on the successive phases of her life. In my copy of her memoirs, just four pages cover the ten years after Richard died while fifteen at the start detail her and Richard's ancestors and respective childhoods (his in slightly more detail than hers). Thirty-one pages deal with the civil wars and their aftermath, eighteen years of her life from 1642 to 1660, but seventy-six are devoted to the six years that followed, before Richard's death, when they lived 'in as great splendour as the most ambitious can desire'[24] as England's representatives at the Spanish and Portuguese courts. These were her glory years, though for us as readers they are little more than lists of magnificent things she'd seen or honours done to her or Richard.

Ann made her will in 1679, a few months before her death. It reveals a distressed gentlewoman seeking to preserve the remaining accoutrements of her gentility for her children. Little Grove and all its contents were to be sold; her main income, the lease of a manor in Essex, she left to Richard, then fourteen years old, on condition that when he had a job (serving the crown, was the implication) and could afford it he would surrender it to his sister Katherine. Richard was also to receive the portraits of his parents by Lely and 'Toniars' and their miniatures, as well as Ann's seals and gold coins and Richard's sticks, guns and swords. Among the papers and manuscripts young Dick was left were the memoirs Ann had written for him three years earlier as well as his father's remembrances, which do not survive.

To Katherine, Anne and Elizabeth she left legacies from her father Sir John of £600 each but she did not mention their sister, Margaret, because she was married when Ann wrote her will and would have already received a dowry. It is a long way from the £10,000 she so confidently expected when she married in 1644. Katherine, perhaps as the eldest, was to receive 'the Work written by herself, by her said daughter Katherine, or by her sisters',[25] indicating both that all five of them had helped copy out the receipts over the years and that the receipt book, 'the Work', was considered valuable enough to merit this prominence in her will: aside from money, it was her significant bequest to her daughters just as the original receipts had been her mother's bequest to her. In other families, books like these might be copied out for each child, but that doesn't seem to have happened here.

Young Richard died in 1695, having lost first his hearing and then his speech in a fever; he would have been about thirty. His father's baronetcy, granted by Charles II in 1650, making Mr Fanshawe Sir Richard, and Ann Lady Fanshawe, died with him. His sisters, Margaret and Ann, who were married, and Katherine, who was not, were his co-heirs. Elizabeth was not mentioned, although her sister Ann included her in her 1679 will; perhaps this exclusion was because of her longstanding affair with Lord

Somers before and after her marriage to a lawyer, Christopher Blount, in 1684.[26] All but Elizabeth were mentioned in their aunt Margaret's husband's 1704 will.

It was through Ann's great-granddaughter, Charlotte Colman, that her memoirs were first copied in 1766 and read outside the family (Lady Eleanor Butler, one of the Ladies of Llangollen, transcribed a copy in 1785 for a generous cousin, Sarah Tighe), ultimately leading to their publication in 1829 and several times thereafter.

The first indirect mention of Ann in print after her death is unconnected to her memoirs or the receipt book. It dates to a salacious, early eighteenth century *roman à clef* by Delarivier Manley, *The New Atalantis*, a satire of the Restoration court in which Ann appeared briefly as the courtesan Thaïs's unnamed mother, wife of the Spanish ambassador at the Roman court, described as 'more impertinent than charming'. Mrs Manley implied an affair with the king who, 'diffusive like the sun, took all Women into his Embraces, at least for once', and after which Charles, too kind to reject her fully, had to pretend business in order to avoid her invading his 'Ear and Closet'. Sent off to Spain, partly to get rid of her, she rather than her husband was said to make policy: 'the Lady's Spirit of Government, and Caesar's favour, had lodged the Power in her'.[27]

None of this reads as a realistic portrait, but the peculiar spite of it is magnified by the fact that Mrs Manley had been friends with the younger Misses Fanshawe, Ann and Elizabeth, in the 1690s, both of whom were married by then (they would have been in their thirties) but neither especially well. They had introduced the ambitious young writer to their neighbour Charles II's one-time mistress, Barbara Villiers, duchess of Cleveland – the name Cleveland appears several times in the receipt book – who acted as her patron when she embarked on her career. That acquaintanceship lends the final accusation made by Mrs Manley some credence. Not only did the fictional ambassador's wife dominate her husband but she was profligate with what he left her, saving nothing for her children, 'through Negligence and Excess, [so] that they could never hope to marry any of their own Rank'. Despite what she called their 'extravagant education', Mrs Manley reported that the ambassador's daughters turned out libertines.

When I first read this, I took it at face value. Despite the fact that nothing in Ann's writing indicates any deviation from her devotion to Richard and her children or any tolerance of infidelity or interest in the court as an arena for debauchery, and that Mrs Manley was a deliberately salacious satirist writing decades after Ann's death and had never known her, my initial response was to wonder what truth there was to this rumour: was it possible that Ann had some kind of affair with the young king or that she was a neglectful mother breeding dissolute daughters? I felt as though my note cards had been thrown up into the air like a pack of cards in a magic trick.

But a far more plausible explanation, if we choose to rely on Ann's account of herself rather than Mrs Manley's fictional and much later one, is that, having persisted in making herself prominent at court by demanding the money due to her after Richard's death, Ann had somehow laid herself open to accusations of promiscuity as well as meddling. It is to the period after Richard's death when Ann was forced to thrust herself into the masculine world of the Restoration court that Mrs Manley's malicious critique belongs. Being a political woman, braving comment and ridicule to pursue what was owed her, made slander like this inevitable, even by other women, particularly when the times and mores had returned, after their years of crisis and upheaval, to an order recognized as normal in which only women who were immoral occupied the public stage.

The Vita Sackville-West quote that opens this epilogue comes from her book on her seventeenth century ancestor, Anne Clifford, she of the curious self-portrait triptych showing herself surrounded by books, described in Chapter 11. Anne Clifford, like Ann Fanshawe, was what today is called a 'life-writer', and, as with Ann's writings, it can be very hard to tease apart the real person from the self they're constructing in their memoirs and diaries. (Irresistibly they remind me of the identities we create online.)

Then, too, there's the other impulse, encapsulated by Jean Lucey Pratt's justification for her journal, that of wanting later generations to have a sense of what life was like not just generally in the time in which you lived but specifically: what it felt like to inhabit your body, with your feelings, your hopes, your dreams and disappointments – to seek to reconstruct, however inadequately, our own 'peculiar existence', the vivid and various tiny strands that make up our consciousness and which even we only ever imperfectly comprehend.

Some years after *The New Atalantis* had been published and faded away again, Ann's memoirs began to be circulated in manuscript. Horace Walpole conceded they were 'not unentertaining' in 1792 although a correspondent of the *Gentleman's Magazine*, five years earlier, thought they were 'too private… ever to be given to the public'.[28]

When they were published in 1829, between Lucy Hutchinson's Puritan biography of her husband (1808), Brilliana Harley's loving letters to her son (1854) and the sparkling letters of Dorothy Osborne (1888), the reviewer in the *Gentleman's Magazine* praised Ann for 'the beauty of her character… [her] devotedness… [the] heroic sacrifices which she made for him [Richard] and her children', concluding (in case his emphasis had not been clear enough), 'and the moral importance of this work is that it is an excellent lesson for wives'.[29]

J.H. Shorthouse, author of the 1902 Cavalier romance *John Inglesant*, had obviously read Aubrey's *Brief Lives* and Delarivier Manley, for his Lady Fentham, a mixture of the fictional ambassador's wife and Dr Kettle's wild Mistress Fenshawe, was a friend of Lady Isabella Thynne whose affair Shorthouse's virtuous hero prevents.

When the memoirs were released in a third edition in 1907, the *Times Literary Supplement* asked the young Virginia Woolf to review them. She was 'flurried' at the prospect, she told a friend, because the memoirs contained 'only a thread of her story, and some nameless descendant has tied a volume of dry little [foot-] notes to her tail',[30] but despite these caveats her review was characteristically insightful.

> The memoirs of Lady Fanshawe are probably the memoirs of many other ladies of her time who did not go to the trouble of writing them down. Such were the stories that were current

> in halls and manor houses all over England in the luxurious Restoration days... The atmosphere is singularly clear; you see what happens now and what comes next, the clothes Sir Richard wore, the wondrous fruits that dropped from trees, the commodities of the land, the detail and solidity of things as in a child's story of adventure. It is a method full of charm; a method, it seems, that marks another age.

Woolf commented approvingly on the multitude of footnotes that gave Ann and her thread of a story some context but, taken altogether, she found the book limited. 'The curiosity of such speculations is great; some one with a fiery imagination might fuse the text and its notes into such a whole as should constitute a complete little globe of human life; meanwhile the book remains curious, delightful so far as Lady Fanshawe is concerned, elaborate and admirable so far as we can absorb her editor.'[31]

In recent years, as very early examples of their genres, Ann's memoirs and receipt book have, usually separately, attracted attention from students of life-writing, gender, seventeenth century diplomacy and the history of receipt books. 'In Fanshawe's case it is clearly the civil wars that liberates her from the acquiescence and passivity required by the gender ideology to which she is profoundly attached,' writes one. 'It is therefore the war which gives her story a plot.'[32] (I can't help feeling the historian is a little disappointed by how attached Ann was to her gender ideology.)

Woolf's image of Ann is the one that has resonated most with me. I think what she is implying with her idea of a 'complete little globe of human life' is that inside each of us, if anyone were to look, there is the subject of the kind of stream of consciousness novels Woolf would later write: an individual universe beating in every soul. (A snow-globe, a globe artichoke with its fractal layers of leaves, a tiny world.) Almost dismissed as a mere woman of her times, telling the story of her life that many others could have told – neither a great writer nor occupying an especially important or pivotal place in history (the privileges of class, which permitted her to record her life in the first place, aside) but ordinary, like you or me – has somehow made Ann powerfully real to me despite what necessarily remains elusive.

There's something about Ann that crystallizes the sense I often have of people in the past being at once far away and very close. I picture myself working alternately with a microscope and a pair of binoculars, stalking Ann through tangled thickets of tangential sources and the grasslands of letters and recipes, always trying to remember, if I am lucky enough to get close, that even the dead must be allowed to keep some secrets. The great social historian Emmanuel Le Roy Ladurie described it so much more poetically: to observe people from the past, he said, is to be both parachutist and truffle-hunter. Vladimir Nabokov talked about the 'delicate meeting place between imagination and knowledge, a point arrived at by diminishing large things and enlarging small ones'.[33]

She lived through times I can't imagine (that old quip about Royalists being 'wrong but wromantic' is as close as I can get to her politics) but, just as she did, and just as my mother and grandmother did, I have a bashed-up folder containing recipes I've collected over the years like the chocolate biscuit cake everyone in my mother's family including me has had at their wedding. It's no more than a trick of timing that mine are still paper – in ten years' time no doubt even the most technologically unsophisticated of us will save our recipes digitally – but regardless of its form my butter-spattered folder is a link to Ann Fanshawe and her receipt book, a reminder that centuries may pass and fashion and politics and habits may change, but we are all still the same under the skin.

When I scraped a knee or burned a finger at my grandparents' house as a child, my grandmother always gave me a special ointment called pommade divine to rub onto the sore spot. Pommade divine was a magical ointment that could cure anything. It came in a brown glass jar that looked as if it had been new when my mother was young and it smelled of nutmeg, cloves and cinnamon – very seventeenth century medicaments.

It turns out the original pommade divine was first manufactured in Ann Fanshawe's lifetime in France (Louis XIV's sister-in-law recommended it), which explains not only the ingredients but also the idiosyncratic spelling of the word pomade and the French pronunciation, enduring to the present day. Gang rationed it out very sparingly, because it was almost impossible to get hold of. After she died my mother gave me one of the precious jars she'd been hoarding and now it's my turn to ration it out – very sparingly – for my own children's grazes. When I use it, I think of Ann Fanshawe and her lovingly made salves and ointments, handed down to her by her mother, which must have held the same talismanic properties for her as my jar of pommade divine.

Like all of us, Ann was lucky in some ways and less so in others, trying to make the best of the circumstances that confronted her. The great joy of her life, shining out in her memoirs, was her happy marriage; her great achievement, holding together her family as society fell apart during the civil wars, using the means available to her to nourish and nurture her husband and children. Her courage and sense of adventure, the relish with which she faced the challenges of her times, are as infectious as they are inspiring.

Her writing, in the receipt book as well as her memoirs, I see as her consolation and her declaration of identity, her statement of selfhood: I write, therefore I am; I write my life because I want others to know I lived a life that may not have been ideal but was nonetheless mine. She both describes her world to us and epitomizes its urge to communicate the self that finds a mirror in our own times. The fact that her descendants preserved her works and they have survived more than four hundred years to speak to us today as vividly as they would have spoken to her own children is nothing short of triumphant.

Characters

(Asterisks mark contributors to Ann's receipt book.)

The Harrison family

Ann Fanshawe, née Harrison (1625–80), was the daughter of **Margaret*** (confusingly, née Fanshawe), who died in 1640, and **Sir John Harrison** (c.1590–1669) of Balls Park, Hertfordshire. Ann's older brother **William** was killed in 1644; her younger sister **Margaret***, her companion for much of the 1640s, married **Sir Edmund Turnor** in the early 1650s. Aged fifty-six Sir John married for the second time to **Mary Shadbolt** and had a son, **Richard**, who inherited Balls from him.

The Fanshawe family

Richard Fanshawe (1608–66) was the youngest son of **Sir Henry Fanshawe** (1569–1616) of Ware Park and his wife, **Elizabeth Smyth** (1577–1631). His eldest brother Thomas inherited Ware from Sir Henry, as well as the hereditary position of King's Remembrancer, and became first **Viscount Fanshawe;** Thomas's first wife died in childbirth and he married for the second time **Elizabeth Cokaine*** in about 1630. Richard described their 'mutual love... [as] ever beyond that of brothers'.[1] Another brother, **Simon** (1604–78), was a keen, if inept, Royalist; the heiress **Katherine Ferrers** (1634–60), who would marry his brother Thomas's son, was his stepdaughter.

Richard's elder sisters were hugely important to Ann: **Alice, Lady Bedell*** (a widow when Ann knew her; her husband Sir Capel had died in 1643), born in the early 1600s, whose daughter married into the **Leventhorpe*** family and who lived at Hamerton in Huntingdonshire; **Mary***, married to Sir William Newce; and **Joan*** (baptized in 1607), married first to Sir William Boteler (d. 1644, fighting for the king) and then in 1647 to **Sir Philip Warwick*** (1609–83) of Frogpool, Kent.

Ann and Richard's children

Their first son, **Harrison**, was born and died within two weeks in 1645. Their first daughter, Ann, or **Nan**, was born on Jersey in 1646 and died of smallpox at Tankersley in Yorkshire in 1654. Their next two sons, **Henry** and **Richard**, or Dick, died at two and eleven, respectively, at nurse and of smallpox. Their second daughter, a first **Elizabeth**, was born and died in Madrid in the summer of 1650. Another **Elizabeth**, their third daughter, was born in 1651 and died in 1655 of a fever. **Katherine**, the daughter to whom Ann left her receipt book and their eldest child to survive them, was born in London in 1652; she was their seventh child. Her younger sister **Margaret***, who also lived to adulthood, was born the following year. Their second **Ann**, who also survived, was born in 1655. **Mary** was born in 1656 and died in 1660. **Henry** was born and died in 1657, when Ann was herself seriously ill. A third **Elizabeth***, or Betty, was born in 1662 and survived to adulthood. A second **Richard** was born in 1663 but lived only a few hours; a third was born in 1665 and survived to adulthood – it is he to whom Ann addressed her memoirs. There were also several miscarriages, taking the number of children carried by Ann to twenty. When Ann died she had four daughters, Katherine, Margaret, Ann and Elizabeth, and one son, Richard, living.

Extended family, friends and godparents

Confusingly, there were three Thomas Fanshawes: Richard's brother, later Lord Fanshawe, who lived at Ware; his son, who married Katherine Ferrers, and who Pepys described as witty but rascally; and lastly **Sir Thomas Fanshawe of Jenkins** (1628–1705), a cousin and friend, whose wife was **Margaret Heath*** (d.1674). **Sir John Evelyn** (1620–1706), the memoirist, was another cousin (a little more distant) and friend, with similar Royalist views and literary and scientific inclinations, married to **Mary Browne.** Their prosperity was directly linked to the wars: the Evelyn fortunes derived from gunpowder production. **Sir Kenelm Digby*** (1603–65) was yet another friend and kinsman with wide-ranging intellectual interests. He was also a Catholic and a close friend of Henrietta Maria.

Joseph Avery was one of Richard's secretaries (I assume), who travelled with the family in the late 1640s and early 1650s, acting as godfather to the Fanshawes' second daughter. As scribe, his hand is the first in Ann's receipt book. **Anne Younge** and **Margaret Ayloffe*** were both cousins and godparents. **Lady Rockingham** was another godmother with Royalist connections – her father was the earl of Strafford who was executed by bill of attainder in 1641 and her brother rented Tankersley, in Yorkshire, to the Fanshawes in 1653.

The **earl of Pembroke** (1621–69) hired Richard as tutor or bear-leader to his son **William, Lord Herbert** (1641–74), on his tour round Europe in 1658, freeing him from seven years of house arrest in England.

Court

Charles I was as old as his century and thus in his forties when the civil wars broke out and forty-nine when he died. His queen, **Henrietta Maria**, born in 1609, was the daughter of Marie de Medici, powerful if misguided Queen Regent of France. She died near Paris of an accidental opium overdose in 1669.

Their children: **Charles**, Prince of Wales, later Charles II (1630–85), married **Catherine of Braganza**, the Portuguese Infanta (1638–1705), in 1662, in a marriage arranged by Richard. **James**, duke of York, later James II (1633–1701), was deposed as king of England in 1688 and replaced on the throne by his daughter Mary and her husband and first cousin William III of Orange. Mary was the daughter of James's first wife, Ann (d.1671), daughter of Edward Hyde (this was a source of humiliation rather than pride for Hyde who fell open to unfair accusations of overmightiness). Charles and James's elder sister was Mary, who married William II of Orange, and provided a European base for her exiled brothers in the Netherlands through the 1650s; her son was William III, who became the William of William and Mary.

Prince Rupert (1619–82) was the nephew of Charles I, the son of his sister Elizabeth, a dashing soldier in the civil wars. He was accompanied on the battlefield by his large white hunting poodle, Boye, whom Parliamentary propagandists liked to portray as a witch's familiar, and who was killed at Marston Moor in 1644.

Powerful women at court included the uber-glamorous and uber-ambitious **Lucy Hay**, née Percy, countess of Carlisle

(1599–1660), Lady of the Bedchamber to Henrietta Maria whose first court lover was the duke of Buckingham (somehow he found time out from his other relationships) and then had affairs successively with the earl of Strafford (executed in 1641) and one of his Parliamentary opponents, John Pym. Later on, she was said to have had an affair with her cousin, **Lord Holland** (1590–1649, executed for treason), for whose army she pawned her pearls for £1500. (Two of Holland's children were the unhappily married beauty **Lady Isabella Thynne**, b. 1623, and her younger sister **Diana**, d. 1658, the letter-writer Dorothy Osborne's best friend.) Lucy Hay is meant to be the model for Alexandre Dumas's villainess, Milady de Winter in *The Three Musketeers*.

As a prominent Catholic and Lady of the Bedchamber to Henrietta Maria, **Elizabeth Savage, Countess Rivers** (1581–1650) – who advised Ann to make it her business to know her husband's business – was the focus of sustained popular attacks through the 1640s. **Catherine Howard, Lady d'Aubigny** (c.1620), was married for the first time to Lord George Stuart, a cousin of the king, in deepest secrecy. After he was killed at Edgehill in 1642, aged just twenty-four, she married the temperamental Viscount Newburgh. She was intimately involved in Charles's struggle to regain his throne until her death at The Hague in 1650, one of the few women respected by Edward Hyde.

From the Villiers family, connections of the divine/depraved duke of Buckingham, James I's lover and Charles I's great friend, come **Anne Villiers, countess of Morton*** (c.1610–54), his niece, godmother and governess to the youngest princess, **Henriette**, who bravely spirited the little girl out of England in 1646 to reunite her with her mother in France and was, apparently, secretly beloved by Edward Hyde; and **Susan Villiers, countess of Denbigh*** (1583–1652), another niece and Lady of the Bedchamber, whose elder son broke her heart by fighting for Parliament. **Barbara Villiers** (1640–1709), later mistress of Charles II and successively Lady Castlemaine and then duchess of Cleveland, was another connection. She was famously extravagant: when Charles II gave her Nonsuch Palace, she had it pulled down and sold the building materials to pay her gambling debts. Pepys got an erotic thrill from seeing her linen fluttering on the washing line in the Privy Gardens at Whitehall.

Various courtiers: **Endymion Porter** (1587–1649), a Gentleman of the Bedchamber to Charles I and a diplomat as well as a man of letters and a collector of art, whose letters to his wife, Olive (another Villiers connection), and other friends are among the most delightful of the seventeenth century; **Christian Bruce, dowager countess of Devonshire** (d.1675), who wrote to her nephew about the new fashions at court. She was an ardent Royalist but, through connections with Cromwell, maintained a career as a society hostess through the Protectorate.

Richard's colleagues, fellow Royalists in Charles II's service

The brilliant **Sir Edward Hyde**, later earl of Clarendon (1609–74), and his wife Frances Aylesbury, was the leader and encourager of the exiled Royalists throughout the 1650s, aided by his friend **Sir Edward Nicholas** (1595–1669), on-and-off Secretary of State, not that that title meant much living in penury in The Hague with his wife Jane*. Richard's particular friend and patron was the **marquess of Ormonde** (1610–88), the Anglo-Irish statesman and soldier; his wife **Elizabeth**, née Preston, and sister **Eleanor Muskerry**, with whom the Fanshawes stayed in Ireland in 1650, were particular friends of Ann's. **Lord Capel** (b. 1608) sat on the Prince of Wales's council with Richard and Hyde in the 1640s; exactly the same age as Richard, they were also connected through Alice Bedell, Richard's sister, as Hertfordshire neighbours and kinsmen. In about 1640 he and his family were handsomely painted by Cornelius Johnson (it's in the National Portrait Gallery), who painted Ann around the time she was married. He was executed for treason in 1649.

Christopher, Lord Hatton (1605–70) – his alias for secret correspondence was Simon Smith – was another cousin of Richard's who came from near Ware; his wife was **Elizabeth Montagu***. **Sir Alexander Fraser*** (1610–81) was Charles's doctor, described by Hyde as 'good at his business, otherwise the maddest fool alive'.[2] He was said to have performed trepanning on Prince Rupert.

Sir John Berkeley (1602–78), famous for his exaggerated accounts of his own adventures, was a soldier rather than a courtier, who helped Charles I on his ill-fated escape from Hampton Court in the autumn of 1647. He spent most of the 1650s in Europe with James, duke of York, whose guardian he was. Along with Sir George Carteret he was involved in the foundation of New Jersey in the 1660s. His wife, **Christian Riccard, Lady Berkeley***, contributed to Ann's book. Berkeley was a kinsman of Henrietta Maria's adoring favourite, **Lord Jermyn** (1605–84), later earl of St Albans, who was despised by Hyde's group serving Charles II. **Sir Robert Long** (1600–73), secretary to the Prince of Wales's council in the 1640s, was effectively Henrietta Maria's voice on the council. Hyde would later suggest that he used his office improperly to line his own pockets; Ann's memoirs make clear her loathing of him. **Lord George Digby** (1612–77), later earl of Bristol, was another of Henrietta Maria's charming but unwise counsellors whose personal ambition, vanity and contemptuous atttitude to the truth would serve her (and her husband) very badly. Hyde described him as 'the only man I ever knew of such incomparable parts that was none the wiser for any experience or misfortune that befell him'.[3]

Lady Abbess Mary Knatchbull of the Benedictine convent in Ghent was an important contact, correspondent and sorting house for European exiles in the 1650s; she hoped her support would move Charles towards official toleration for English Catholics. **Sir Richard Willys** (1614–90), one of the founder members of the Sealed Knot, would betray his colleagues throughout the 1650s. **Alan or Allen Brodrick** (1623–80) was the heavy-drinking secretary of the Sealed Knot. **Lord John Mordaunt** (1626–75) and his wife **Elizabeth**, née Carey*, threw themselves into the Royalist cause in the late 1650s; their devotion to returning Charles to his throne served as an important inspiration for their friends. **Sir George Booth** (1622–84), who led an abortive Royalist rising in 1659, and **General Monck** (1608–70) were former Parliamentarians whose conversion to the Royalist cause in 1659 and 1660 and support for Charles II would prove decisive.

Convivial **Sir Henry Bennet**, later earl of Arlington (1618–85), was one of Charles II's best friends both in exile in the 1650s and after his return through the 1660s. His closeness to Charles's mistress, Barbara Villiers, Lady Castlemaine, benefited his career immeasurably. As Charles II's Commissioner to the Navy and Secretary to the Admiralty, **Sir William Coventry** (1628–86) made a vast fortune. Samuel Pepys, who served under him, thought consistently well of him (as compared to the other 'knaves' with whom he worked).

Acquaintances from abroad

Sir George Carteret (1610–80) was Governor of Jersey in the mid-1640s when the Fanshawes met him and his wife **Elizabeth** (née Carteret – they were cousins), initially a close friend of Ann's. He rose to become Treasurer of the Navy under Charles II.

Sir Richard Browne (1605–83) was ambassador to the court of France from 1641 to 1660 and as such, he and his wife, **Lady Browne***, met every English person who came to Paris in that time. Their daughter Mary married Sir John Evelyn. Other friends from Paris were the poet **Edmund Waller** (1606–87) and his second wife **Mary Bracey**, to whose daughter Ann acted as godmother in 1651 alongside Mary Evelyn.

Parliamentarians

Oliver Cromwell (1599–1658) was the ultimate Parliamentarian, an austere Puritan, creator of the New Model Army and patriotic statesman so noble he turned down the crown, with a fervent belief that God was guiding his victories. **General Lord Thomas Fairfax** (1612–71) was a talented military commander who, perhaps influenced by his outspoken wife, **Anne de Vere**, became disenchanted with Cromwell during Charles I's trial. Because of this, he was one of the few Parliamentarians to escape retribution after the Restoration. Although **Sir Henry Vane** the younger (1613–62) also refused to take part in Charles's execution, his radicalism during the civil wars meant that he was tried for treason in 1662 and executed. Deeply principled, he was a consistent champion of religious toleration. **John Thurloe** (1616–68) was Cromwell's highly effective spymaster, from his positions as Secretary of State from 1652 and Postmaster General from 1655. He was arrested but not tried in 1660 and served Hyde as an informal advisor during the 1660s. **Edward Montagu, first earl of Sandwich** (1625–72), served Cromwell as an officer in the army initially and then the navy. Despite his importance in the Cromwell administration he was one of the first Parliamentarians to declare for Charles II, a clever tactical decision for which he would be well rewarded. He replaced Richard as Spanish ambassador in 1666.

Contemporary sources

The account-keeper **Margaret Spencer** (1597–1613) was the youngest daughter of the first Lord Spencer, who lived at Althorp. **Lord Henry Spencer, first earl of Sunderland** (1620–43), was his grandson and Margaret's nephew, though he was born after her death. His beautiful, witty wife **Lady Dorothy,** or **Doll, Sidney** (1617–84), from Penshurst in Kent, had rejected the poet Edmund Waller (who eulogized her as Saccharissa) to marry Henry.

Sir Edmund Verney (d. 1642) was the patriarch of the Verney family, who (thankfully for historians) kept all their papers for centuries preserved at their Buckinghamshire house, Claydon House. His son **Sir Ralph** (1613–96) initially supported Parliament but fled England for France as a Royalist in 1644, under the alias Ralph Smith, with his wife, **Mary Verney** (d. 1650). Other Verney letter-writers include Ralph's sisters Cary and Betty; Ralph's friend Roger Burgoyne, aka Mr Good; and his children Mun, Jack and Peg.

Sir John Oglander (1585–1655) kept detailed household accounts and notes on his estate which became a diary. He lived on the Isle of Wight and was an ardent Royalist. **Thomas Kynvett** (1596–1658) was a Norfolk gentleman whose letters to his wife when he was away from home (including a stint in prison as a Royalist in the early 1640s) are full of affection and charming period detail. The antiquarian **John Aubrey** (1626–97)'s idiosyncratic *Brief Lives* illuminates his contemporaries and their era. The naval administrator **Samuel Pepys** (1633–1703) and his wife Elizabeth apparently both kept diaries, though only his survived.

Poets, philosophers, divines and artists

Cornelius Johnson (1593–1661), to use the Anglicized version of his name, was a Dutch artist born in London and moving between England and the Low Countries. He was popular at court in the 1630s, painting Ann as a young woman around the time of her wedding and a pair of portraits of the Fanshawes on display at Argowan House in Scotland. High-living **William Dobson** (1611–46) succeeded Van Dyck as Charles I's court painter, working from a studio in St John's College, Oxford. After Oxford fell to the Parliamentary forces, he returned to London where he died in poverty, released from Debtors' Prison just to die. The Dutch painter **Peter Lely** (1618–80) was appointed court painter to Charles II in 1660 and painted ten court beauties (some of whom were royal mistresses) to hang in Windsor Castle – they are now at Hampton Court. **Mary Beale** (1633–99) learned how to paint by watching Peter Lely; she was an astute businesswoman and published writer as well as an artist.

The poet **Thomas May** (1595–1650) and his friend Richard

Fanshawe agreed to disagree over politics – May's admiration for the ancients made him a convinced republican. Another poet and friend of Richard's, **John Denham** (1615–69), worked as a Royalist encipherer and agent. Aubrey described Denham memorably: tall and long-legged, with a 'stalking' gait, 'his Eie was a kind of light goose-gray, not big; but it had a strange Piercingness, not as to shining and glory, but… when he conversed with you he look'd into your very thoughts'[4] – a useful skill for a spy. As Poet Laureate **Sir William Davenant** (1606–68) wrote the last masque performed at the Stuart court, *Salmacida Spolia*, and enjoyed a successful career as a poet and playwright after the Restoration; he liked to claim he was William Shakespeare's natural son, not just his godson. Dashingly handsome **Richard Lovelace** (1617–57) was the archetypical Cavalier, soldier and poet, reportedly adored by women. The metaphysical poet **Andrew Marvell** (1621–78) combined poetry with politics, sitting as an MP intermittently between 1659 and his death. He was tutor to Lord Fairfax's daughter, Mary, in the early 1650s, when he wrote 'To His Coy Mistress'; she later married the second duke of Buckingham.

Lady Hester Pulter (1596–1678) and **Katherine Philips** (1632–64) were both Royalist poets, but Philips was celebrated during her lifetime as 'the Matchless Orinda' while Pulter's manuscript of verse has only recently been rediscovered among her family papers. Philips circulated her poems privately, among a select group of friends; her major public success was a translation of Corneille's *La mort de Pompée*, performed and published to acclaim in 1663.

Izaak Walton (1594–1683) began life as an ironmonger but, through his literary and spiritual interests, became friends with John Donne, Charles Cotton and other luminaries of the early seventeeth century intellectual scene. He retired in 1644, after the Battle of Marston Moor, and spent the rest of his life writing biographies of friends and writing and adding to his masterwork, *The Compleat Angler*. **Henry Lawes** (1595–1662) was a musician and composer, one of the Gentlemen of the Chapel Royal until Parliament banned church music. He returned to the Chapel Royal at the Restoration, composing an anthem for Charles II's coronation. **Jeremy Taylor** (1613–67) was a cleric and theologian known as the 'Shakespeare of Divines' for his literary style. He was imprisoned several times for his Royalist beliefs and associations during the 1650s.

The political philosopher **Thomas Hobbes** (1588–1679), whose *Leviathan* established the theory of the social contract, was in 1647–8 maths tutor to Charles, Prince of Wales. Charles was also a student of **William Harvey** (1578–1657), the doctor who first described the circulation of the blood and how embryos develop in the womb.

Radical republican **Nicholas Culpeper** (1615–54) was a botanist, herbalist, astrologer and doctor, the first person to translate medical books into English and sell them cheaply in a deliberate effort to democratize what had previously been arcane, elite knowledge.

Female writers

Brilliana, Lady Harley (1598–1643), bravely defended her house, Brampton Bryan, in Herefordshire, against Royalist siege for three months in 1643, only to die of a cold soon afterwards. Her letters to her son Ned, studying at Oxford, are wonderfully revealing of seventeenth century life as well as the early events of the civil wars. She also kept a receipt book that has survived as part of the Egerton papers in the British Library. **Dorothy Osborne** (1627–95) wrote to **William Temple** (1628–99) for the final two years of their seven-year secret courtship; once they married, very few of her letters survive.

The young playwrights **Ladies Jane and Elizabeth Cavendish** (respectively 1621–69 and 1626–64) were granddaughters of Bess of Hardwick. Elizabeth married John Egerton and became, as **countess of Bridgewater**, a writer of religious meditations, especially prayers for her children. She died delivering her tenth child. Jane married Charles Cheyne and lived in Chelsea; her only surviving piece of poetry after her marriage is an elegy for Elizabeth, but historians have speculated that she continued to write throughout her life. Their stepmother, **Margaret, née Lucas, countess of Newcastle** (1623–73), a self-conscious eccentric, wrote and published her own life to a very mixed reception (Mary Evelyn deeply disapproved but John found her rather fascinating).

Elizabeth Grey, countess of Kent (1582–1651), and **Alethea Howard, countess of Arundel** (1585–1654), were both born Talbot, also granddaughters of Bess of Hardwick but through their mother. Both wrote receipt books which were published posthumously in the 1650s. Along with her husband, Alethea was a great traveller, patron and collector of art and important early seventeenth century taste-maker.

Another accomplished set of siblings were the children of Richard Boyle, the self-made first earl of Cork known as the Great Earl. **Robert Boyle** (1627–91) is today considered the father of experimental science and modern chemistry; **Katherine, Lady Ranelagh** (1615–91), was a respected intellectual in her own right as well as collaborator with her brother, with whom she lived for the last twenty-three years of their lives; **Mary Rich, countess of Warwick** (1625–78), wrote her autobiography along with spiritual meditations and a diary covering eleven years; **Lettice Goring** (1610–57), married to a Royalist soldier notorious for his dissolute ways, also contributed to a family receipt book.

Anne Sadleir (1585–1671) was another autobiographical writer whose meditations reveal her passionate Royalism and unhappy marriage. **Isabella Twysden** (1605–57) kept a journal while her Royalist husband, Sir Roger, was in prison in the 1640s. **Lady Elizabeth Delaval** (c.1648–1717)'s youthful diaries, dating from when she was about fourteen and had just become a Maid of Honour to Catherine of Braganza, chronicle her upbringing with particular reference to her efforts to control her passions (including overindulging in cherries) and live a more virtuous life. Like Ann, **Lucy Hutchinson** (1620–81) wrote a life of her husband, a Parliamentarian colonel, which was just as much a portrait of herself; she was a rare female Latin scholar, the first person to translate Lucretius's *De rerum natura* into English, as well as a poet.

Jane Anger was the first woman to publish a defence of women in English, *Jane Anger Her Protection for Women*, in 1589. Nearly a century later **Sarah Jinner** is a candidate for first woman to earn a living with her pen, with her successful series of almanacs for women in the 1650s and 1660s. Nothing is known about her except her books, which are remarkable for their medicinal frankness, their political outspokenness and their spirited assertion of women's rights to speak and think freely. **Jane Sharp** was the first female midwife to publish a book on her craft, *The Midwives Book*, in 1671. As with Anger and Jinner, no biographical facts are known about Sharp except what she revealed in her writing.

Acknowledgements

So many people have helped me with this book: it's been a network of favours and generosity worthy of Ann and her friends and family.

First, the Wellcome Collection, which houses the manuscript of Ann's receipt book. Huge thanks to Tim Morley, Helen Wakely, Phoebe Harkins, Gillian Scothern and Emily Philippou for their time, knowledge and enthusiasm. Louisa Lane Fox and Dr Elizabeth Williamson kindly allowed me to look at their work on Brilliana Harley's receipt book. Through Mayasuni Habsburg I met the extraordinary herbalist Marcos Patchett, who illuminated the plants used in Ann's receipts as well as the ideas behind much of seventeenth century medicine. Emmeline Stevenson put me in touch with Veronica Bunbury, née Fanshawe, for an interesting conversation about the Fanshawe family, past and present. Andrew Edmonds advised me about finding rare Hollar prints. Lucinda Chetwode and Ludovic Shaw Stewart kindly sent me images of the Fanshawe portraits on display at Ardgowan House, which belong to Archie Stirling. Venetia Morrison introduced me to Ham House, where Sarah McGrady and Victoria Bradley were enormously helpful about still-rooms, while Dr Kate Harris at Longleat was informative about lutes. I am very grateful to Marjo Meijer and Carla van de Puttelaar for their correspondence.

As ever, I did much of my research at the British Library with the aid of its ever-helpful staff; thanks are also due to the staff of the Bodleian Library as well as Leeanne Westwood, curator at Valence House, and Clare Sexton, borough archivist there.

Starting with Margaret Stead and leading on to James Nightingale, and alongside Susannah Hamilton, Karen Duffy and Will Atkinson, it has been fantastic being back at Atlantic. Thank you, Tamsin Shelton, for your thorough and excellent copy-editing (any remaining mistakes are entirely mine), Alex Bell for the index and for the beautiful layout, Lindsay Nash. Grateful thanks, too, to my agent, the wonderful Clare Alexander.

Finally, although this book is dedicated to my sisters (and has the spirit of my grandmother running through it), I want to thank Justin, Xan and Otto, too, with all my heart.

Bibliography

BL MS

BL Add MS 15858, 12184: Sir Richard Browne's correspondence

BL Add MS 27466: Sir John Evelyn's receipt book

BL Add MS 41161: Lady Fanshawe's original memoirs

BL Egerton MS 2214: Brilliana, Lady Harley's receipt book

BL Sloane MS 1367: Lady Ranelagh's receipt book

BL Add MS 27351–6: papers of the countess of Warwick, Mary Rich

BL Add MS 62092: Margaret Spencer's account book 1610–13

Wellcome Library

(these are all digitized)

Lady Frances Catchmay's Booke of Medicens c. 1625

Mary Doggett's receipt book, 1682

Lady Fanshawe's receipt book

Lady Ranelagh's receipt book (another version)

Primary Sources

(all published in London except where stated; many are available on the Early English Books Online website)

Anger, J., *Jane Anger Her Protection for Women*, 1589

Bagshawe, H., *A Sermon Preacht in Madrid, July 4 1666 occasioned by the Sad and much Lamented Death of his late Excellency Sir Richard Fanshawe*, 1667

Bankes, G., *The Story of Corfe Castle*, 1853

Barwick, P., *The Life of the Reverend Dr John Barwick*, 1724

Bennit, F.W., 'The Diary of Isabella, Wife of Sir Roger Twysden, Baronet, of Royden Hall, East Peckham, 1641–1651', *Archaeologia Cantiana*, LI, 1939

Benson, P.J. and V. Kirkham, eds., *Strong Voices, Weak History: Early Women Writers & Canons in England, France and Italy*, Ann Arbor, MI, 2005 (contains Bentley, T., *Monument of Matrons*)

Blundell, W., *A Cavalier's Notebook. Being Notes, Anecdotes and Observations* (ed. Rev. T. Ellison Gibson), 1880

Bowerbank, S. and S. Mendelson, eds., *Paper Bodies: A Margaret Cavendish Reader*, Ontario 2000 (contains Cavendish, M., 'A True Relation of my Birth, Breeding and Life', 1656)

Braithwaite, R., *The English Gentlewoman Drawn Out to the Full Body*, 1631

Brennan, M., N. Kinnamon and M. Hannay, eds., *The Correspondence of Dorothy Percy Sidney, Countess of Leicester*, Farnham 2010

Bromley, G., ed., *A Collection of Original Royal Letters*, 1787

Brown, S., ed., *Women's Writing in Stuart England: The Mothers' Legacies of Dorothy Leigh, Elizabeth Joscelin and Elizabeth Richardson*, Stroud 1999

Bunworth, R., *The Doctresse*, 1656

Burnet, G., *History of His Own Time* (ed. T. Stackhouse), Guernsey 1991

The Card of Courtship or, the Language of Love, 1653

Carte, T., *A Collection of Original Letters… found among the Duke of Ormonde's Papers*, 1739

Cerasano, S.P. and M. Wynne-Davies, *Renaissance Drama by Women: Texts and Documents*, 1996 (contains Brackley, Lady E. and Cavendish, Lady J., *The Concealed Fancies*, c.1645)

Chambers, D.D.C. and D. Galbraith, eds., *The Letter Books of John Evelyn*, Toronto 2014

Chauncy, H., *The Historical Antiquities of Hertfordshire*, Dorking 1975 (reproduction)

Calendar of the Clarendon State Papers, Oxford 1767

The Calendar of the Clarendon State Papers Preserved in the Bodleian Library, Oxford 1970

Clarendon, Earl of, *The History of the Rebellion* (ed. P. Seaward), Oxford 2009

— *The Life of Edward, Earl of Clarendon... by Himself*, Oxford 1760

Culpeper, N., *A Directory for Midwives*, 1652

— *Galen's Art of Physick*

— *Complete Herbal*, Ware 1995 (Wordsworth edition)

Davenant, Sir W., *Salmacida Spolia*, 1639

Davies, R., ed., *The Life of Marmaduke Rawdon of York*, 1843

Defoe, D., *Memoirs of a Cavalier*, Stroud 2006

De morbis foemineis, the woman's counsellour: or, The feminine physitian, 1659

Digby, Sir K., *Choice and Experimental Receipts in Physick and Chirurgery*, 1688

Evelyn, J., *Memoirs of J.E. Esq. FRS* (ed. W. Bray), 1819

— *A Character of England as it was lately presented in a Letter to a Nobleman of France*, 1659

— *The Diary of John Evelyn* (ed. E.S. de Beer), Oxford 1955

Evelyn, M., *Mundus muliebris: Or, The Ladies Dressing-Room unlock'd and her Toilette spread*, 1690

— 'The Letterbooks of Mary Evelyn' (ed. F. Harris), *English Manuscript Studies 1100–1700*, 7, 1998

Fanshawe, A., *Memoirs* (ed. N.H. Nicolas), 1830

— *Memoirs* (ed. B. Marshall), 1905

— *Memoirs* (ed. H.C. Fanshawe), 1907

— *Memoirs* (ed. J. Loftis), 1979

Fanshawe, Sir R., *Poems* (ed. Peter Davidson), Oxford 1999

— *Il Pastor Fido*, 1648

— *Camoes's The Lusiads* (ed. G. Bullough), 1963

— *Correspondence* (Historical Manuscripts Commission, The Manuscripts of J.M. Heathcote, Esq.), 1899

Fea, A., *The Flight of the King*, 1897

'The Gallant She-Souldier', 1655

Gouge, W., *Of Domesticall Duties*, 1622

Greene, D.C., ed., *The Meditations of Lady Elizabeth Delavel*, *Surtees Society*, CXC, Gravesend 1978

Grey, E., Countess of Kent, *A Choice Manuall of Rare and Select Secrets in Physick*, 1653

Griffin, J., ed., *Selected Poems of Abraham Cowley, Edmund Waller and John Oldham*, 1998

Harley, Lady B., *Letters* (ed. T.T. Lewis), *Camden Society*, 58, 1854

Harrington, J., *The Commonwealth of Oceana* (eds. S. Mukherjee and S. Ramaswarmy), New Delhi 1998

Harvey, Dr G., *The Family Physician and the House Apothecary*, 1676

Hensley, J., ed., *Collected Poems of Anne Bradstreet*, Cambridge, MA, 1967

Herbert, G., *Verse and Prose* (ed. W. Cope), 2002

Herbert, Sir T., *Travels in Persia, 1627–1629* (ed. Sir W. Foster), 1929

Herrick, R., *Hesperides*, 1647

Hobbes, T., *Leviathan*, 1651

Hollar, W., *Ornatus muliebris Anglicanus: The Severall habits of Englishwomen*, 1640

— *Theatrum mulierum*, 1643

— *The Four Seasons*, The Costume Society Extra Series No. 6 (intro J.L. Nevison), Kings Lynn 1979

Howard, A., Countess of Arundel, *Natura Extenterata*, 1655

Hudson, R., *The Grand Quarrel: From the Civil War Memoirs of Mrs Lucy Hutchinson; Mrs Alice Thornton; Ann, Lady Fanshawe; Anne, Lady Halkett; & the Letters of Brilliana, Lady Harley*, 1993

Hunter, L., ed., *The Letters of Dorothy Moore 1612–1644*, Aldershot 2004

Jinner, S., *Almanack*, 1658, 1659, 1660

Luke, Sir S., *Letterbook 1644–5* (ed. H.G. Tibbutt), 1963 no.664

A.M., *A Rich Closet of Physical Secrets*, 1652 (printed by Gertrude Dawson)

MacKay, C., ed., *The Cavalier Songs and Ballads of England from 1642 to 1684*, 1863

Manley, D., *The New Atalantis* (ed. R. Ballaster), 1991

— *The New Atalantis*, 7th edition, 1741

Markham, G., *The English Housewife*, 1668

Marvell, A., 'An Horatian Ode upon Cromwell's return from Ireland'

Mercurius diutinus, December 1646–January 1647

Mildmay, Lady G., *The Diary of Lady Mildmay*, CD Rom at BL

Moderate Intelligencer, or The Loyal London Mercury, 1645–49

Montpensier, Mlle de, *Memoirs* (trans. P.J. Yarrow, ed. W. Brooks), 2010

Mordaunt, E., *The Private Diarie of Elizabeth Viscountess Mordaunt*, Duncairn 1856

Mordaunt, J., *Letter Book 1658–1660* (ed. M. Coate), 1945

Morgan, F., *A Woman of No Character: An Autobiography of Mrs Manley*, London 1986

Nicholson, M.H., ed., *The Conway Letters*, Oxford 1992

Oglander, Sir J., *A Royalist's Notebook*, 1936

Ollard, R., ed., *Clarendon's Four Portraits: George Digby; John Berkeley; Henry Jermyn; Henry Bennet*, 1989

Osborne, D., *Letters to Sir William Temple 1652–1654* (ed. K. Parker), Aldershot 2002

The Queen's Closet Open'd, 1655

Pennington, R., *A Descriptive Catalogue of the Etched Work of Wenceslaus Hollar*, Cambridge 1982

Pepys, S., *Diary* (ed. R. Latham and W. Matthews), 1970–76

Philips, K. *Collected Works of Katherine Philips, the Matchless Orinda. Vol. I: Poems* (ed. P. Thomas), Stump Cross 1990

— *Printed Letters* (ed. P. Loscocco), Aldershot 2007

Pilkington, C., *To Play the Man: The Story of Lady Derby and the Siege of Lathom House, 1645–1651*, Preston 1991

Plat, H., *Delightes for Ladies*, 1630

Powell, A., ed., *John Aubrey's Brief Lives*, 1949

Read, A., *Most Excellent and Approved Medicines*, 1651

A Rich Closet of Physical Secrets, 1652

Sackville-West, V., ed., *The Diary of the Lady Anne Clifford*, 1923

Scofield, B., *The Knyvett Letters*, 1949

Sharp, J., *The Midwives' Book*, 1985 (facs. 1671)

Spalding, R., *The Improbable Puritan: A Life of Bulstrode Whitelock*, 1975

Suckling, J., 'Ballad upon a Wedding', 27 January 1641

Townsend, D., *Life and Letters of Mr Endymion Porter, Sometime Gentleman of the Bedchamber to Charles I*, 1897

Travitsky, B., ed., *The Early Modern Englishwoman, Series I, Part 2, Vol. 8: Mother's Advice Books*, Aldershot 2001 (contains E. Clinton, *The Countess of Lincoln's Nurserie*; E. Grymeston, *Miscelanea, Meditations, Memoratives*, 1610; E. Jocelin, *The Mother's Legacie*, 1622; D. Leigh, *The Mother's Blessing*, 1621)

Verney, M.M., *Memoirs of the Verney Family*, 1971 (1892)

Vernon, J., *The Compleat Schollar, Or, a Relation of the Life, and Latter-End Especially, of Caleb Vernon*, 1666

Walker, E., *The Holy Life of Mrs Elizabeth Walker*, 1690

Walker, R.M. and W.H. Liddell, *The Papers of Sir Richard Fanshawe, Bart.*, 1999

Walton, I., *The Life of Sir Henry Wotton and Reliquiae Wottoniae*, 1651

— *The Compleat Angler* (ed. J. Bevan), Oxford 1983

Warner, G.F., ed., *The Nicholas Papers: Correspondence of Sir Edward Nicholas, Secretary of State*, 1886–1920

Warwick, P., *Memoires of the Reign of King Charles I*, 1702

Woolley, H., *The Accomplisht Ladys Delight: In Preserving, Physick, Beautifying and Cookery*, 1675

Secondary Sources

(all published in London except where stated)

For further reading Diane Purkiss's *The English Civil War* is an excellent, broad-brush introduction to the times and I can't recommend highly enough C.V. Wedgwood's classic books about the period.

Abate, C.S., *Privacy, Domesticity and Women in Early Modern England*, Aldershot 2003

Adair, J., *By the Sword Divided: Eyewitness Accounts of the English Civil War*, Bridgend 1998

Akkerman, N., and B. Houben, eds., *The Politics of Female Households*, Leiden 2014

Anderson, P., *Friendship's Shadows: Women's Friendship and the Politics of Betrayal in England, 1640–1705*, Edinburgh 2012

Aylmer, G.E., *The King's Servants: The Civil Service of Charles I 1625–1640*, 1974 (1961)

Balleine, G.R., *All for the King: The Life Story of Sir George Carteret (1690–1680)*, St Helier 1976

Bassnett, M., '"All the Ceremonyes and Civilityes": The Authorship of Diplomacy in the Memoirs of Ann, Lady Fanshawe', *The Seventeenth Century*, 26, no.1, Spring 2011

— 'Restoring the Royal Household: Royalist Politics and the Commonwealth Recipe Book', *Early English Studies*, 2, 2009, www.uta.edu/english/ees/fulltext/bassnett2.html

Beckett, R.B., *Lely*, 1951

Bennett, M., *The Civil Wars Experienced: Britain and Ireland 1638–1661*, 2000

Betcherman, L., *Court Lady and Country Wife. Royal Privilege and Civil War: Two Noble Sisters in the Seventeenth Century*, Ontario 2005

Botonaki, E., *Seventeenth Century English Women's Autobiographical Writings*, Lewiston, NY, 2004

Brett, A.C.A., *Charles II and His Court*, 1910

Brotton, J., *The Sale of the Late King's Goods*, 2006

Brownley, M.W., 'The Women in Clarendon's Life and Works', *The Eighteenth Century*, 22, no.2, 1981

Burke, V.E. and J. Gibson, eds., *Early Modern Women's Manuscript Writing*, Aldershot 2004

Butter, J., *Precarious Life: The Powers of Mourning and Violence*, 2004

Campbell, C., ed., *Peter Lely: A Lyrical Vision*, 2012

Carlton, C., *Going to the Wars: The Experience of the British Civil Wars, 1638–1651*, 1992

Cavallo, S. and L. Walker, *Widowhood in Medieval and Early Modern Europe*, Harlow 1999

Chalmers, H., *Royalist Women Writers*, Oxford 2004

Charlton, K., *Women, Religion and Education in Early Modern England*, 1999

Chedgzoy, K., *Women's Writing in the British Atlantic World*, Cambridge 2007

Chernaik, W., *The Poetry of Limitation: A Study of Edmund Waller*, New Haven, CT, 1968

Clark, A., *Working Life of Women in the Seventeenth Century*, 1982 (1919)

Connerton, P., *How Societies Remember*, Cambridge 1989

Coward, B., *The Stuart Age, 1603–1714*, 1980

Crawford, P., *Blood, Bodies and Families in Early Modern England*, Harlow 2004

Crawford, P., and L. Gowing, eds., *Women's Worlds in Seventeenth Century England: A Sourcebook*, 2000

Cressy, D., *Birth, Marriage and Death: Ritual, Religion and the Life Cycle in Tudor and Stuart England*, Oxford 1997

— *England on Edge: Crisis and Revolution, 1640–1642*, Oxford 2006

Croft, R.B., *A Short Note on the Fanshawe Vaults in the Ware Parish Church*, Ware 1908

Darley, G., *John Evelyn: Living for Ingenuity*, New Haven, CT, 2006

Davidson, P., 'Green Thoughts. Marvell's Gardens: Clues to Two Curious Puzzles', *Times Literary Supplement*, 5044, 3 December 1999

Davies, G.A., 'Sir Richard Fanshawe, Hispanist Cavalier', *University of Leeds Review*, 20, 1977

Daybell, J., *Women and Politics in Early Modern England 1450–1700*, Aldershot 2004

Delany, P., *British Autobiography in the Seventeenth Century*, 1969

Demers, P., *Women's Writing in English: Early Modern England*, Toronto 2005

DiMeo, M., 'Katherine Jones, Lady Ranelagh (1615–91): Science and Medicine in a Seventeenth-Century Englishwoman's Writing', University of Warwick Thesis, 2009

DiMeo, M., and S. Pennell, *Reading & Writing Recipe Books, 1550–1800*, Manchester 2013

Donagan, B., *War in England 1642–1649*, Oxford 2008

Dowd, M., *Women's Work in Early Modern English Literature and Culture*, Basingstoke 2009

Emsley, J., *Elements of Murder: A History of Poison*, Oxford 2005

Fairchilds, C., *Women in Early Modern Europe 1500–1700*, Harlow 2007

Fanshawe, H.C., *The History of the Fanshawe Family*, 1927

Fell Smith, C., *Mary Rich, Countess of Warwick, 1625–1678: Her Family and Friends*, 2001

Ferguson, M., *Dido's Daughters: Literacy, Gender and Empire in Early Modern England and France*, Chicago, IL, 2003

Fildes, V., *Wet Nursing: A History from Antiquity to the Present*, Oxford 1988

— ed., *Women as Mothers in Pre-Industrial England*, 1980

Fissel, M., *Vernacular Bodies: The Politics of Reproduction in Early Modern England*, Oxford 2004

Fraser, A., *The Weaker Vessel: Women's Lot in Seventeenth Century England*, 1999 (1984)

— *King Charles II*, 1980 (1979)

Gallagher, C., 'Embracing the Absolute', *Genders*, 1, Spring 1988

Gaskill, M., *Witchfinders: A Seventeenth Century English Tragedy*, 2005

Gentiles, I., J. Morrill and B. Worden, eds., *Soldiers, Writers and Statesmen of the English Revolution*, Cambridge 1998

Gillespie, K., *Domesticity and Dissent in the Seventeenth Century*, Cambridge 2004

Gittings, C., *Death, Burial and the Individual in Early Modern England*, 1984

Godfrey, E., *Home Life Under the Stuarts 1603–1649*, 1903

Goodman, E., *The Cultivated Woman: Portraiture in Seventeenth Century France*, Tubingen 2008

Gowing, L., *Domestic Dangers: Women, Words and Sex in Early Modern London*, Oxford 2008

— *Common Bodies: Women, Touch and Power in Seventeenth Century England*, New Haven, CT, 2003

Graham, E., *Her Own Life: Autobiographical Writings by Seventeenth Century English Women*, 1989

Greene, G., *Lord Rochester's Monkey*, 1974

Griffey, E., *Henrietta Maria: Piety, Politics and Patronage*, Aldershot 2008

Groote, J. de, *Royalist Identities*, Basingstoke 2004

— 'Space, Patronage, Procedure: The Court of Oxford 1642–1646', *English Historical Review*, 474, November 1968

Grundy, I., and S. Wiseman, eds., *Women, Writing, History 1640–1740*, 1989

Hamling, T. and C. Richardson, *Everyday Objects: Medieval and Early Modern Material Culture and Its Meanings*, Aldershot 2010

Hardacre, P., *The Royalists During the Puritan Revolution*, The Hague 1956

Havens, E., *Commonplace Books: A History of Manuscripts and Printed Books from Antiquity to the Twentieth Century*, New Haven, CT, 2001

Healy, M., *Fictions of Disease in Early Modern England: Bodies, Plagues and Politics*, Basingstoke 2001

Herbert, A.E., *Female Alliances: Gender, Identity and Friendship in Early Modern Britain*, New Haven, CT, 2014

Herrup, C., *A House in Gross Disorder: Sex, Law and the Second Earl of Castlehaven*, Oxford 1999

Hickman, K., *Daughters of Britannia*, 2000

Hill, C., *The World Turned Upside Down*, Harmondsworth 1975

Hobby, E., *Virtue of Necessity: English Women's Writing 1646–1688*, 1988

Hollander, A., *Sex and Suits: The Evolution of Modern Dress*, New York, NY, 1994

Hole, C., *The English Housewife in the Seventeenth Century*, 1953

Holstun, J. ed., *Pamphlet Wars: Prose in the English Revolution*, 1992

Houlebrooke, R., *The English Family 1450–1700*, Harlow 1984

Hubbard, E., *City Women: Money, Sex and the Social Order in Early Modern London*, Oxford 2002

Hufton, O., 'Reflections on the Role of Women in the Early Modern Court', *The Court Historian*, 5, 1, May 2000

Hughes, A., *Gender and the English Revolution*, Abingdon 2012

— ed., *Seventeenth-century England: A Changing Culture*, 1980

Hunter, L., and S. Hutton, eds., *Women, Science and Medicine 1500–1700: Mothers and Sisters of the Royal Society*, Stroud 1997

Huxley, G., *Endymion Porter: The Life of a Courtier*, 1959

Iyengar, S., *Shakespeare's Medical Language: A Dictionary*, 2011

Johnson, S., parody of receipt books in *The Rambler*, 51

Jones, A.R. and P. Stallybrass, *Renaissance Clothing and the Materials of Memory*, Cambridge 2000

Knoppers, L., *Politicizing Domesticity from Henrietta Maria to Milton's Eve*, Cambridge 2011

— 'Opening the Queen's Closet: Henrietta Maria, Elizabeth Cromwell, and the Politics of Cookery', *Renaissance Quarterly*, 60.2, 2007

Kwint, M., C. Breward and J. Aynsley, eds., *Material Memories*, New York, NY, 1999 (Marta Ajmar, 'Toys for Girls')

Lewalski, B., *Writing Women in Jacobean England*, Cambridge, MA, 1993

Liddy, B., *Women's War Drama in the Seventeenth Century*, Amherst, NY, 2008

Loraux, N., *Mothers in Mourning*, Ithaca, NY, 1998

Loxley, J., *Royalism and Poetry in the English Civil Wars*, Basingstoke 1997

MacKay, J., *Catherine of Braganza*, 1937

Manning, B., *1649: The Crisis of the English Revolution*, 1992

McElligott, J., and D.L. Smith eds., *Royalists and Royalism During the English Civil Wars*, Cambridge 2007

McManus, C. ed., *Women and Culture at the Court of the Stuart Queens*, Basingstoke 2003

Millar, O., *The Age of Charles I: Painting in England 1620–1649*, 1972

— *Sir Peter Lely, 1618–1680*, 1978

Nagy, D., *Popular Medicine in the Seventeenth Century*, Bowling Green, OH, 1988

Newton, H., *The Sick Child in Early Modern England 1580–1720*, Oxford 2012

Nicolson, A., *Gentry: Stories of the English*, 2011

Nicholas, D., *Mr Secretary Nicholas (1593–1669): His Life and Letters*, 1959

O'Day, R., *Women's Agency in Early Modern Britain and the American Colonies*, Harlow 2007

Olney, J., ed., *Autobiography: Essays Theoretical and Critical*, Princeton, NJ, 1980

O'Malley, S., *'Custome is an Idiot': Jacobean Pamphlet Literature on Women*, Chicago, IL, 2004

Oman, C., *Mary of Modena*, 1962

Otten, C.F., ed., *English Women's Voices 1540–1700*, Miami, FL, 1992

Pacheco, A., *Early Women Writers: 1600–1720*, 1998

Patterson, A., *Censorship and Interpretation: The Conditions of Writing and Reading in Early Modern England*, Madison, WI, 1984

Pelling, M., *Medical Conflicts in Early Modern London: Patronage, Physicians and Irregular Practitioners, 1550–1640*, Oxford 2003

Phillippy, P., *Painting Women: Cosmetics, Canvases and Early Modern Culture*, Baltimore, MD, 2006

— *Women, Death and Literature in Post-Reformation England*, Cambridge 2002

Picard, L., *Restoration London*, 1997

Plowden, A., *Women All on Fire: The Women of the English Civil War*, Stroud 2004

Pollack, L., *With Faith and Physic: The Life of a Tudor Gentlewoman*, 1993

Porter, R., ed., *Rewriting the Self: Histories from the Renaissance to the Present*, 1997

Potter, L., *Secret Rites and Secret Writing: Royalist Literature 1641–1660*, Cambridge 1989

Prior, M., ed., *Women in English Society 1500–1800*, 1985

Pugh, S., *Herrick, Fanshawe and the Politics of Intertextuality*, Farnham 2010

Purkiss, D., *The English Civil War: A People's History*, 2006

— *Literature, Gender and Politics during the English Civil War*, Cambridge 2005

— 'Desire and Deformities: Fantasies of Witchcraft in the English Civil War', *Journal of Medieval and Early Modern Studies*, 27, 1997

Raylor, T., *Cavaliers, Clubs, and Literary Culture*, Cambridge 1989

Reynolds, M., *The Learned Lady in England 1650–1760*, Boston 1920

Rickman, J., *Love, Lust, License in Early Modern England: Illicit Sex and the Nobility*, Aldershot 2008

Root-Bernstein, R. and M., *Honey, Mud, Maggots, and Other Medical Marvels*, 1999

Rose, M., *Gender and Heroism in Early Modern English Literature*, Chicago, IL, 2002

Ross, S., 'Tears, Bezoars and Blazing Comets: Gender and Politics in Hester Pulter's Civil War Lyrics', *Literature Compass*, 2, The Seventeenth Century, 2005

Sambrook P.A. and P. Brears, *The Country House Kitchen, 1650–1900*, Stroud 2010

Scott, E., *The King in Exile: The Wanderings of Charles II from June 1646 to July 1654*, 1904

— *The Travels of the King: Charles II in Germany and Flanders 1654–1660*, 1907

Seelig, S., *Autobiography and Gender in Early Modern Literature*, Cambridge 2006

Sell, J.A., *Rhetoric and Wonder in English Travel Writing 1560–1613*, Aldershot 2006

Sharpe, K. and S. Zwicker, eds., *Reading Society and Politics in Early Modern England*, Cambridge 2003

Shepard, A., S. Hindle and J. Walter, eds., *Remaking English Society: Social Relations and Social Change in Early Modern England*, Woodbridge 2003

Shifrin, S., ed., *Women as Sites of Culture*, Aldershot 2002

Slater, M., *Family Life in the Seventeenth Century: The Verneys of Claydon House*, 1984

Sloan, A.W., *English Medicine in the Seventeenth Century*, 1996

Smith, G., *The Cavaliers in Exile, 1640–1660*, Basingstoke 2003

— *Royalist Agents, Conspirators and Spies*, Farnham 2011

Snook, E., *Women, Beauty and Power in Early Modern England*, Basingstoke 2011

— *Women, Reading and the Cultural Politics of Early Modern England*, Aldershot 2005

— 'The Greatness in Good Clothes: Fashioning Subjectivity in Mary Wroth's *Urania* and Margaret Spencer's Account Book', *The Seventeenth Century*, XXII, 2, 2007

Spencer, C., *Prince Rupert: The Last Cavalier*, London 2007

Spiller, E., *Seventeenth-century English Recipe Books*, Aldershot 2008

Spufford, M., *Small Books and Pleasant Histories: Popular Fiction and Its Readership in Seventeenth Century England*, 1981

Spurling, H., *Elinor Fettiplace's Receipt Book*, 1987

Stauffer, *English Biography before 1700*, Cambridge, MA, 1930

Stoyle, M, 'The Road to Farnon Field: Explaining the Massacre of the Royalist Women at Naseby', *English Historical Review*, 133, 2008

Theophano, J., *Eat My Words: Reading Women's Lives Through the Cookbooks They Wrote*, New York, NY, 2002

Toynbee, M., and P. Young, *Strangers in Oxford: A Side Light on the First Civil War 1642–1646*, Chichester 1973

Traub, V., M.L. Kaplan and D. Callaghan, eds., *Feminist Readings of Early Modern Culture*, Cambridge 1996

Trill, S., K. Chedgzoy and M. Osborne, eds., *Lay By Your Needles, Ladies, Take up the Pen: English Women's Writing 1500–1700*, 1997

Tynacke, N., ed., *The English Revolution c. 1590–1720: Politics, Religion and Communities*, Manchester 2013

Underdown, D., *Royalist Conspiracy in England 1649–1660*, New Haven, CT, 1960

Urban, M., *Seventeenth Century Mothers' Advice Books*, Basingstoke 2006

Vickery, A., *Behind Closed Doors*, 2009

Vincent, S., *Dressing the Elite: Clothes in Early Modern England*, Oxford 2003

Walker, C., 'Prayer, Patronage and Political Conspiracy: English Nuns and the Restoration', *History Journal*, 43, 2000

Wall, W., *Staging Domesticity: Household Work and English Identity in Early Modern Drama*, Cambridge 2002

Wedgwood, C.V., *The King's Peace, 1637–1641*, 1964 (1955)

— *The King's War 1641–1647*, 1966

Wilcher, R., *The Writing of Royalism 1628–1660*, Cambridge 2001

Wilcox, H., ed., *Women and Literature in Britain 1500–1700*, Cambridge 1996

Wiseman, S., *Conspiracy and Virtue: Women, Writing and Politics in Seventeenth Century England*, Oxford 2006

Whyman, S., *Sociability and Power in Late Stuart England: The Cultural World of the Verneys 1660–1720*, Oxford 1999

Woolf, V., *The Flight of the Mind: The Letters of Virginia Woolf Volume I: 1888–1912*, 1975

Worden, B., *The English Civil Wars*, 2009

Notes

Abbreviations

AF: Ann Fanshawe's *Memoirs*, 1905 edition reprinted by the Dodo Press

Cal. CSP: Calendar of Clarendon State Papers

CSP Dom.: Calendar of State Papers Domestic

CSPV: Calendar of State Papers, Venetian

EEBO: Early English Books Online

HMC: Historical Manuscripts Commission

RF: Richard Fanshawe's correspondence, Historical Manuscripts Commission (HMC): *The Manuscripts of J.M. Heathcote, Esq.*

Introduction

1 'the same chocelaty' Ann Fanshawe's receipt book, Wellcome Collection online

2 'in tents, like' AF 13

3 'rich and important' Knoppers, *Politicizing Domesticity* 113

4 'he loved hospitality' AF 3

5 'ye passion… stockings' Mary Doggett at the Wellcome Collection, online

6 'rare cordials for' Cavendish sisters, *Fancies*, in Cerasano, *Renaissance Drama by Women* 143

7 'to make… Neophite courtier' Davenant, *Salmacida Spolia* EEBO

8 'this scribbling age' Hudson, *The Grand Quarrel* ix

9 'that masse of' Sawday in Porter, *Rewriting the Self* 44

10 'Now as… one Sapho' Lovelace, 'On Sanazar's being honoured'

11 'Why [should] women' Jinner, *Almanack* 1658 EEBO

12 'I hope my' Cavendish in Bowerbank, *Paper Bodies* 63

13 On Katherine Philips – Elaine Hobby in Pacheco, *Early Women Writers* 8
14 Paraphrasing Rose, *Gender and Heroism* 59
15 'Like them, she' Fairchilds, *Women in Early Modern Europe* 6
16 'a powerful expression' Spiller, *Seventeenth-century English Recipe Books* x

Chapter 1: 1643

1 'a man… no clothes' AF 13
2 'The scene… our lives' ibid.
3 'We lived in' AF 12
4 'learned as well… hoyting girl' ibid.
5 'as an… tender mother' AF 10–11
6 'queer tin vessels' Nagy, *Popular Medicine in the Seventeenth Century* 5 describing the Verney still-room at Claydon
7 'silver thimbell… of pistolls' Snook, *Women, Beauty and Power* 76
8 'end in a' Coward, *The Stuart Age* 123
9 'No neutrality is' Hardacre, *The Royalists in the Puritan Revolution* 2
10 'I had all' Donagan in McElligot, *Royalists and Royalism* 82
11 'concerning the public' AF 13
12 'If there could… drawing room' Wedgwood, *The King's War* 121
13 'I do not… my conscience' Verney, *Memoirs* II 126 (Verney)
14 'I praye have' Verney II 94
15 'you ded… lawful king' Verney II 100
16 'The parlement has' Verney II 71
17 'at the value' Nicholas, *Mr Secretary Nicholas* 168
18 'We have no' Fraser, *Charles II* 30
19 'they could never' Adair op.cit. 74
20 'We had the' AF 13
21 'that modest, courageous' Warwick, *Memoires* 263
22 'I know you' Betcherman, *Court Lady* 255
23 'dear brother William' AF 13
24 'He was a' AF 11
25 'through the streets' de Groot, *Royalist Identities* 6
26 'She is not' Adair op.cit. 180

27 'maidenly indulgences' Prior, *Women in English Society* 191
28 'Many an houer' Greene, *Meditations* 109
29 'in exquisite and' Cerasano op.cit. 164
30 'Hid Park and' Verney III 435
31 'studying a little' Evelyn, *Diary* I 29
32 'the young women' Carlton, *Going to the Wars* 296
33 'Little gettings… a day' Trill, etc., *Lay By Your Needles* 137
34 'yet it is' Sharp, *The Midwives Book* 256
35 'longing after hurtful' Sharp op.cit. 257
36 'the disease of' Healy, *Fictions of Disease* 8

Chapter 2: 1644

1 'out of God's' Symmons, 'A Militarie Sermon' 1 EEBO
2 'The complete… ancient valour' Symmons op. cit. 16
3 'likely to prove' AF *Memoirs*, 1830 edition 340
4 'Being the king's' AF 15
5 'strong and… nature soever' AF 2
6 'Glory be… in him' AF 3
7 '£5000 besydes' Osborne, *Letters* 77
8 'Alasse, how can' Trill, etc. op. cit. 190
9 'at the ordinary' Osborne, *Letters* 149
10 'had better married' Osborne, *Letters* 144
11 'the talk of' Osborne, *Letters* 159
12 'I have… spoiled it' Osborne, *Letters* 148
13 'go a little' quoted in Vincent, *Dressing the Elite* 92
14 'Weare your clothes' Snook op.cit. 91
15 'Mens apparel is' quoted in Jones and Stallybrass, *Renaissance Clothing* 4
16 'Loveliness is impressed' Thomas Hoby, quoted in Snook op. cit. 152
17 'A faire woman' Grymeston in Travitsky, *The Early Modern Englishwoman*
18 'How much against' Davies 'Sir Richard Fanshawe, Hispanist Cavalier' 110
19 'past the time' Osborne, *Letters* 149
20 'Hat in… it end' Davies op. cit. 113–14

21 'whether 'tis his' *Fancies* in Cerasano I, iv
22 'condemned to look' *Fancies* in Cerasano II, iii
23 'have you read' *Fancies* in Cerasano II, iii
24 'in private know' *Fancies* in Cerasano I, i
25 'If these times' Slater, *Family Life in the Seventeenth Century* 81
26 'I think my' quoted in Hole, *The English Housewife* 9
27 'expectation... merchant adventurers' AF 14
28 'an excellent green' Harley receipt book BL Egerton MS 2214
29 'sewing into the' Dudley Carleton quoted in Cressy, *Birth, Marriage and Death* 370
30 'him a Puritan' AF 15
31 'but my dear' AF 14
32 'none... be properly' Cressy op. cit. 290
33 'embodied in sexual' Gowing, *Common Bodies* 207
34 'Iff Ever our' Osborne, *Letters* 31
35 'so picquant, and' quoted in Prior op. cit. 184
36 'to go in' Oglander, *Royalist's Notebook* 131
37 'wet her own' quoted in Charlton, *Women, Religion and Education* 47
38 'have their owne' Gouge, 'Domesticall Duties' in Trill, etc. op. cit. 122
39 'I know I' Thomas Kynvett to Katherine in 1642 quoted in Charlton op. cit. 46
40 'the saver of' Sir Roger Twysden quoted in Charlton op. cit. 45
41 'pray put on' Henry Oxinden to his wife Kate, quoted in Nicholson, *Gentry* 163
42 'would often complain' Cavendish in Bowerbank op.cit. 49
43 'Once more and' RF 223
44 'dull, careless and' Cressy op. cit. 43
45 'a most worthy' AF 108
46 'God With Us' Purkiss, *The English Civil War* 358
47 'The land is' Spalding, *The Improbable Puritan* 101
48 'Let horror and' Spencer, *Rupert* 112
49 'Of my uninterrupted' CSPV 1643–7 162
50 'Into the furnace' CSPV 1643–7 163

Chapter 3: 1645

1 'if it sinks' Culpeper, *Midwives* 71 EEBO
2 'denying so much' Toynbee, *Strangers in Oxford* 5
3 15.7 in every 1000; Fairchilds op. cit. 81
4 'Lay no more' quoted in Prior op. cit. 196
5 'Sweet Christ bring' Crawford and Gowing, *Women's Worlds* 20
6 'grant my child' Mordaunt, *Diarie* 15
7 'hysterick water' Harley receipt book BL Egerton MS 2214
8 'into this great' Anne Bathurst quoted in Prior op. cit. 197
9 'wrapped up… of filthiness' quoted in Cressy op. cit. 19
10 'made miserable by' Purkiss op. cit. 5
11 'Only the… very poor' AF 15
12 'It cost me' AF 16
13 'good employment… to themselves' AF 16
14 'the Times are' Patterson, *Censorship and Interpretation* 209
15 'the troopers steal' Nicholas op. cit. 211
16 'inexpressible joy… racked me' AF 17
17 'with many thanks' AF 17
18 'I know… what happened' AF 17–18
19 'a perfect… thought of' AF 18
20 'adventurous women' Barwick, *Life* 60
21 'all on fire' Hughes, *Gender and the English Revolution* 37
22 'pleasure in nothing' Clarendon, *History* 168
23 'a woman of' Hughes op. cit. 36
24 'be more… I think' Osborne, *Letters* 142
25 'with a theorbo' Toynbee op. cit. 32
26 'and all so' Osborne, *Letters* 142
27 'I remember one' Toynbee op. cit. 32
28 'He turned… or family' AF 18–19
29 See Rose, *Gender and Heroism*
30 Lady Grace Mildmay; Elizabeth Delavel
31 'she loved government' AF 56
32 'the consequence will' AF 16
33 'Now, my sense' RF 226
34 'canting… foul' RF 224

35 'take great care' RF 239
36 'that I was' RF 225
37 'one of... man's Court' AF 19
38 'And all places' Warwick op. cit. 288
39 For more on this incident see Stoyle, 'The Road to Farnon Field'
40 See Gaskill, *Witchfinders*
41 About 85,000 died in combat and about 127,000 civilians died as an indirect result of the wars
42 See Carlton op. cit. 260
43 'Ready to Use Both' Purkiss, *Literature, Gender and Politics* 44
44 'This march of' Luke, *Letterbook* 204, 20 March 1645
45 See Hughes op. cit. 142
46 'the king could' CSPV 1642–3 237
47 'For sirs forbear' quoted in Hughes op. cit. 66

Chapter 4: 1646

1 'house and... his own' AF 20
2 'That night following' AF 20
3 'bed was... our last' AF 21
4 'that my... kindness possible' ibid.
5 'keep it from' Harley receipt book BL Egerton MS 2214
6 Birth statistics: Houlbrooke, *The English Family* 133, 136
7 'one or... tender heart' Trill, etc. op. cit. 123–4
8 'troublesome...motherly office' ibid.
9 'like a slatterne... baby' Verney II 294
10 'a merry... thriving childe' Culpeper, *Midwives* 115–16 EEBO
11 'with out gossips' Bennit, 'The Diary of Isabella' 121
12 'begot some... day' Clarendon, *History* 279
13 'sharp replies between' Clarendon, *History* 282
14 'Here in... done this' Huxley, *Endymion Porter* 292
15 'hope that it' Smith, *Cavaliers* 22
16 'I pray send' Nicholas op. cit.217
17 'man and mayde' Verney II 174
18 'to prevent sequestration' Verney II 180
19 'Certainly it would' Verney II 239

20 'women were... privileges' Dr Denton to RV, Verney II 240
21 'like sisters' Pepys, *Diary* III 126
22 'This was the' AF 22
23 'All provisions are' Verney II 253
24 'infenett dear' Verney II 246
25 'my dear heart' Slater op. cit. 67
26 'when one... this place' Verney II 258
27 'whose wife... us free' AF 22
28 'In daily fears' AF 22

CHAPTER 5: 1647

1 'upon thorns' AF 22
2 'no news from' Smith, *Cavaliers* 23
3 'tribute for... of it' *Il Pastor Fido* 1647 Dedication EEBO
4 'this was a' AF 23
5 'pleased to' ibid.
6 'both as... and sufferings' AF 23
7 'by the... the Parliament' ibid.
8 'full of soup' Balleine, *All for the King* 30
9 'if we must' AF 23–4
10 'by the networks' Vincent op. cit. 69
11 'I write not' Townshend, *Porter* 233–4
12 'Those innocent recreations' Nicholson, *Conway Letters* 27

CHAPTER 6: 1648

1 'spoiling [it] for' AF 24
2 'she must... this day' AF 24
3 'I conceive' Oglander op. cit. 121
4 'for news, it' Carte, *A Collection* I 175
5 'which if... of it' AF 24
6 'on his master's' AF 25
7 'till they might' Clarendon, *History* 309
8 'of his... good company' AF 25
9 'The troubles and' Nicholas quoted in Carte op. cit. I, 198
10 'trim in all' Verney II 235

11 'fasyonable mofe' Verney I 256
12 'for making cleane' Verney II 235
13 'well curled in' Verney II 233
14 'cal'd Noahs-Arke' Verney II 100
15 'who promised her' AF 25
16 'much excellent discourse' ibid.
17 'He was such' BL 97
18 'extraordinary stories... gentleman' AF 25
19 'the truth is' Evelyn, *Diary* I 257
20 'that the stills' Nicholas op. cit. 290 Breda, 1658
21 'a memory that' DiMeo, 'Katherine Jones, Lady Ranelagh (1615–91): Science and Medicine in a Seventeenth-Century Englishwoman's Writing' (online)
22 'Paris chemistry' Hunter, ed., *Letters of Dorothy Moore* xxx
23 'watch dial to' DiMeo, 'Katherine Jones...'
24 '*spirit* of... orange pudden' DiMeo, 'Katherine Jones...'
25 'great Chymist' BL 139
26 'a good... and Chirurgery' Hunter and Hutton, *Women, Science and Medicine* 111
27 See DiMeo, 'Katherine Jones...'

Chapter 7: 1649

1 'in the... very hush' Adair op. cit. 233
2 'that execrable... martyrdom' Evelyn, *Diary* II 546
3 'very majestick and' Wilcher, *The Writing of Royalism* 288
4 'that glorious sun' AF 23
5 'rebell Army at' Evelyn, *Diary* II 546
6 'You never heard' Hughes op. cit. 1
7 'the women generally' Verney II 402
8 'burthen of... a KING' Wilcher op. cit. 293
9 '*Vive le roi*' Fraser, *Charles II* 81
10 'the dragon hath' Carlton op. cit. 236
11 'a very good' AF 7
12 'up to the' AF 25
13 'Though nothing was' AF 27

14 'Had the good fortune… I repent it not' AF 26
15 'neither unpleasant nor' Ailesbury HMC 156
16 'If this madness' Smith, *Cavaliers* 59
17 'Not only… and livings' Graham, *Her Own Life* 91 'A True Relation'
18 'found the Countenances' BL 163
19 'to procure a' quoted in Smith, *Cavaliers* 99
20 'quilted in his' AF 14
21 'very cheerfully towards' AF 26
22 'swarming all over' Underdown, *Royalist Conspiracy* quoting Clement Walker
23 'still much expected' Carte op. cit. I 259
24 'very hazardous voyage' AF 26
25 'So soon as' ibid.
26 'so much to' ibid.
27 'all betrayed to' Carte op. cit. II 417
28 'what earthly… of pounds' AF 26
29 'lamentable shrieks… Red Abbey' AF 27
30 'all other… he owed' ibid.
31 'through thousands… could remove' ibid.
32 'the most… the town' AF 28
33 'every person concerned' AF 29
34 'that went… fell off' ibid.
35 'disorder… gone suddenly' ibid.
36 'in the… of them' BL xxv

Chapter 8: 1650

1 'mutual jealousies' Carte op. cit. I 373
2 'noble harbour… with grass' AF 30
3 'all on the' ibid.
4 'you are all' AF 31
5 'with prosperous… well-manned' ibid.
6 'we believed… ever saw' ibid.
7 'knocked and… never master' AF 32
8 'snatched me… that voyage' ibid.
9 Remedies: Oglander op. cit. 218

10 'very well, and' AF 32
11 'the highest... ever saw' AF 32–3
12 'poore Dick Fanshaw' Cal. CSP III 14
13 'That thou... a trayne' Bath MS II 89
14 'not fitt.. may be' Brownley in *The Eighteenth Century* 161
15 'deere little Rogue' Bath MS II 80
16 'the most uncomfortable' Bath MS II 89
17 'Never in my' Smith, *Cavaliers* 94 21 June 1650
18 'thou must not' Bath MS II 91
19 'Be as merry' Bath MS II 88
20 'must die... own country' Cal. CSP III 28
21 'being weary of' Nicholas op. cit. 236
22 'had I not' quoted in Hardacre op. cit. 67
23 'the finest... and sorted' AF 82–3
24 'the quite... in France' Verney I 13
25 'soculate' Bath MS II 88
26 'impudence of that' AF 34
27 'The Spaniards will' Cal. CSP II 70
28 'good words and' RF 4
29 'folly and atheism' Fraser, *Charles II* 87
30 'and of any' RF 4
31 'there was not' Montpensier, *Memoirs* 39
32 'to hear him' RF 4
33 'never travellers saw' Bath MS II 84
34 'as much... not imagine' Bath MS II 85
35 'sat up and' AF 36
36 'Every night, we' ibid.
37 Evelyn says he dined with the Fanshawes in Paris on 24 September 1650 (Evelyn *Memoirs* III 8) but Ann says they didn't arrive in Paris until November
38 'My Lady Herbert' Evelyn, *Diary* I 248
39 'the spectacle was' Evelyn, *Diary* I 250
40 'a very monstrous' Evelyn, *Diary* I 248
41 'down out of... of himself' Evelyn, *Diary* III 40
42 'pretty Patient' Evelyn, *Letterbooks*, 150

43 'In this book' BL Add MS 78419
44 'all we could' AF 37
45 'coach, horses, wagons' Bath MS II 84
46 'that pore riding' Townshend op. cit. 230
47 'much to the' AF 37
48 'in all so' Underdown op. cit. 23
49 'He shall deny' CSP Dom. 1650 437
50 'here I... father's interest' AF 37
51 'God knows how' AF 38

Chapter 9: 1651

1 'cousin Fanshawe... the King' *The Nicholas Papers* I 213
2 'to arm... did me' AF 38
3 'with great expressions' AF 38
4 'more certain measures' Carte op. cit. I 401
5 'them openly that' *The Nicholas Papers* I 208
6 'which has put' ibid. I 208 21 December 1650, Nicholas to Lord Hatton
7 '& receive testimonies' Carte op. cit. I 439 6 April 1651
8 'I shall then' *The Nicholas Papers* I 233 19 April 1651
9 'that I... no good' RF 6 14 April 1651
10 'in that time' AF 38–9
11 'animosities amongst... daily fears' AF 38
12 'all had... the town' AF 39
13 'my cousin Evelyn's' AF 38
14 'seek for reliefe' Cavendish in Bowerbank op.cit. 51
15 'take the... from him' Cavendish in Bowerbank op.cit. 54
16 'which made the' AF 39
17 'dearest life... love' RF 223
18 'my dear... sudden return' RF 226
19 'so fine a' RF 234
20 'wondrous sad and' Adair op. cit. 159
21 'Dear, let me' Carlton op. cit. 299
22 'you cannot imagine' Carlton op. cit. 300
23 'Oh my... the world' Carlton op. cit. 300–01
24 'in a very' AF 39

25 'we are... great person' Carte op. cit. II 14–15 letter dated 5 May 1651
26 'Mr F... his father' *The Nicholas Papers* I 254
27 'in the dark' Carte op. cit. II 32 from Stirling dated 21 June 1651
28 'peacefully in... Deptford again' Smith, *Cavaliers* 108
29 'dead or... fatal news' AF 39
30 'which saved the' AF 41
31 'with impatience... God's disposal' AF 39
32 'all the... her own' AF 40
33 'in a little' ibid.
34 'who is... Charles Stuart CSP Dom. 1651 426
35 'in at... my heels' AF 40
36 'soe confused in' *The Nicholas Papers* I 276
37 'in doleful condition' ibid.
38 'of ye... rejoiced us' Evelyn, *Diary* I 257
39 'much better looking' Montpensier op. cit. 39
40 'I wish he' Cal. CSP III 34
41 'the cold... death's door' AF 40
42 'how I... any terms' ibid.
43 'who gave... the scorbutic' AF 40–1
44 'during the time' AF 9
45 'He there met' AF 41

Chapter 10: 1652

1 'he fell very' ibid.
2 'parcell of papers' Nicholson op. cit. 19
3 'all the Doctor' AF 41
4 Charles I health: Warwick op. cit. 64
5 'the means to' BH 14
6 Paynell in Healy, *Fictions of Disease* 25
7 'are comforted by' Gowing, *Domestic Dangers* 6
8 'if I may' Verney III 51
9 'the Lady who' Evelyn, *Diary* III 49 in December 1651
10 'of many considerable' Evelyn, *Diary* III 58
11 'of haile... were fancies' Evelyn, *Diary* III 71
12 'negligently under... deepe thickett' Evelyn, *Diary* III 69

13 'wanting to… to death' Evelyn, *Diary* III 74
14 'a very great' AF 24
15 'on Thursday… cousin Ayloffe' AF *Memoirs* 1830 edition 216
16 'not had a' November 1652, Smith, *Cavaliers* 94

Chapter 11: 1653

1 'very pleasant and' AF 42
2 'most pleasant and' Chauncy, *Hertfordshire* I 521
3 'full of all' AF *Memoirs* 1830 editon 287
4 'physic herbs… greatly delight' AF 6
5 'God I am' Nicholas op. cit. 277 2 July 1655
6 'I never… think of' Scofield op. cit. 134
7 'the nightingales doe' Scofield op. cit. 140
8 'aguish distemper… their goodness' AF 57
9 Kim Hall, 'Culinary Spaces, Colonial Spaces' in Traub, etc., *Feminist Readings* 169
10 'harmless country life' AF 42
11 'captivitie' Davidson, *Sir Richard Fanshawe's Poems* II 581
12 'settle to a' Fane, 'My Happy Life to a Friend'
13 'with ominous… further events' Underdown op. cit. 56
14 'of a harmless' Loxley, *Royalism and Poetry* 234
15 'to pray… my friends' Ross, 'Tears, Bezoars and Blazing Comets'
16 'Here let us' 'A Retir'd Friendship, to Ardelia'
17 'upon you all' ibid. 163
18 'he loved hospitality' AF 3
19 'Our Stationers Shops' Knoppers op. cit. 107
20 'good household.. the nation' Bassnett, 'Restoring the Royal Household'
21 'Yours to… chief joy' *The Card of Courtship* EEBO
22 'In writing of' Walton op. cit. 59
23 'You will find' Purkiss, *Civil War* 54
24 'achates, onyxes, and' Evelyn, *Diary* I 291
25 'seal's are.. now goe' Osborne, *Letters* 66
26 'wayting for a' Trill, etc. op. cit. 192
27 'very empty… to part' HMC Ailesbury 158

28 'All I can' HMC Ailesbury 159
29 'observed how the' Evelyn, *Diary* I 274
30 ''Tis strange to' Osborne, *Letters* 181
31 'observ'd it at' Evelyn, *Diary* I 269
32 'with great content' AF 42

Chapter 12: 1654

1 'Falls, Blows, Anger' Culpeper, *Midwives* 81
2 sitting on a pillow – this was how Jack Verney went to London, and thence to France, aged eight in 1648. Verney II 310
3 'You cannot... old coats' Vincent op. cit. 59
4 'neat and cleanly' Cavendish in Bowerbank op.cit. 42
5 'Good sweet hart' Sharpe and Zwicker, *Reading Society and Politics* 105
6 'for you... good housewifery' Sharpe and Zwicker, *Reading Society and Politics* 106
7 'carrying letters' etc: Reynolds, *The Learned Lady* 43
8 'in virtue, good' Charlton op. cit. 130
9 'their present... of them' Vernon, *Complete Schollar* 5
10 'O my little' quoted in Houlbrooke op. cit. 135
11 'No man can' Taylor, *The Marriage Ring; or the Mysteriousness and Duties of Marriage* EEBO
12 'ever observed... that' Luke op. cit. 20
13 'of a... forsing waye' Verney II 5
14 'in the morning' Verney III 78
15 'the dear companion' AF 42
16 'We both... her age' ibid.
17 'immediately interred... the living' Gittings, *Death, Burial and the Individual* 48
18 'with plain linen' AF Introduction (no page number)
19 ''twas not the' Slater op.cit. 141
20 'till now I' Slater op.cit. 111
21 'discrete' Verney II 1, Lady Suffolk to Ralph Verney on the death of his mother
22 Lord, I... be enough' Phillippy, *Women, Death and Literature* 159
23 'the joy... the grave' Evelyn, *Diary* III pp 206-210

24 'dead formless… do kiss' Otten, *English Women's Voices* 231
25 Countess of Warwick: Prior, *Women in English Society* 197
26 'Unfit thoughts… secretly repine' Newton, *The Sick Child* 150
27 'let me… heathenish' Prior op. cit. 198
28 'let none wonder' Phillippy op. cit. 155
29 'I do not' Phillippy op. cit. 141
30 'like Lilly leaves' Ross, 'Tears, Bezoars and Blazing Comets'
31 'a newly defined' Rose op. cit. 115

Chapter 13: 1655

1 'to keep in' AF 42
2 'where my husband' ibid.
3 Melancholy Water: Harley receipt book BL MS Egerton 2214
4 'a little merry' Nicholson op. cit. 66
5 'there is no' Nicolson, *The Mighty Dead* 233
6 'impossible undertakings' Underdown op. cit. 89
7 'I confess… them here' Verney III 219
8 'the status competitions' Hall in Traub, etc. op. cit. 171
9 'the natures… publick practise' *De morbis foemineis* EEBO
10 'like a purse' Otten op. cit. 178
11 'We must now' Wilcher op. cit. 328
12 'to adore… come, Sir' Evelyn, *Letters* II 99
13 'Lord, though knowest' Hunt in Burke and Gibson, *Early Modern Women's Manuscript Writing* 213

Chapter 14: 1656

1 'upon New… as ever' AF 42
2 'air would recover' AF 43
3 'all my comfort' AF 102
4 Marriage study cited in Otten op. cit. 130–1
5 'she was… much doubt' Cressy op. cit. 242
6 'thus had… status quo' Hughes op. cit. 68
7 'institutional powerlessness' Abate, *Privacy, Domesticity and Women* 2
8 'as hot as' *The Queen's Closet Open'd* 121 EEBO

9 'weary of the' AF 43
10 'confus'd... to prison' Evelyn, *Diary* I 302
11 'during Oliver's reign' Hudson op. cit. 213
12 'and such a' Nicholas op. cit. 284
13 'so heavily burdened' Underdown op. cit. 177
14 'a very ill' AF 43
15 'I was... like water' ibid
16 'Recipe for Good' Oglander op. cit. 222

CHAPTER 15: 1657

1 'New Disease' Verney III 387
2 'still very... think of' HMC Ailesbury 160–1
3 'You may read' AF 41
4 'Women were not' Mary Evelyn, *Letterbooks* 202
5 'much natural... of him' Hudson op. cit. 213
6 'a-Maying to' Nicholson op. cit. 134
7 'I invited some' Evelyn, *Diary* I 303
8 'royal postmistress' Smith, *Agents* 214
9 'My intelligence is' Nicholas op. cit. 287
10 'Till the K.' *The Nicholas Papers* IV 13
11 'who once loved' Cal. CSP III 336–7

CHAPTER 16: 1658

1 'This has ben' Evelyn, *Diary* III 211
2 'a gallant gentleman' AF 7
3 'a partner with' Underdown op. cit. 189
4 'For God's sake' Fell Smith *Mary Rich, Countess of Warwick* 223
5 'by one... blesing' Mordaunt, *Diarie* 16
6 'Prased be the' Mordaunt, *Diarie* 17
7 'Send helpe unto' ibid. 12–13 15 June 1657
8 'vivacity, courage... Cromwell's death' Mordaunt, *Letters* xxi
9 'Died that arch' Evelyn, *Diary* I 314
10 'This place we' AF 43
11 'the joyfullest' Darley op. cit. 155

12 'rebels endeavour' Fraser, *Charles II* 160
13 'a wretch who' Lucy Hutchinson in Hudson op. cit. 222
14 'a hundred times' Knoppers, 'Opening the Queen's Closet: Henrietta Maria, Elizabeth Cromwell, and the Politics of Cookery'
15 'lamented his case' AF 43
16 'Methinkes in the' BL 152
17 'Mr. Fanshawe' AF 43

Chapter 17: 1659

1 'a very dry' Nicholson op. cit. 156
2 'got loose' AF 44
3 'and the Life' Mordaunt, *Diarie* 35
4 'Monk's little son' *The Nicholas Papers* IV 203
5 'I would now' Verney III 446
6 Thurloe's efficiency: Walker, 'Prayer, Patronage and Political Conspiracy'
7 'your ladyship to' Mordaunt, *Letters* 101
8 'much in… generous actions' Brownley, 'The Women in Clarendon's Life and Works' 160
9 'Greate confutions' *The Nicholas Papers* IV 125
10 'your master is' RF 7
11 'that you were' ibid.
12 'retract one word' ibid.
13 'omission… saw him' ibid.
14 'Your master will' RF 9
15 'from whence to' ibid.
16 'went in to' AF 44
17 'If I were' ibid.
18 'in as plain' ibid.
19 'with as ill' ibid.
20 'and with my' AF 45
21 'Madam, you may' ibid.
22 'why, and… the deceit' ibid.
23 'sadly given to' Fraser, *Charles II* 163
24 'Thus you see' Mordaunt, *Letters* 32

25 'so much... much depended' RF 12–13
26 'gaiety... to far' Underdown op. cit. 250
27 'The like overvalue' Cal. CSP IV 281
28 'the Fanshawes act' Mordaunt, *Letters* 22
29 'the two Fanshawes' Cal. CSP IV 270
30 'uxorious men are' Brodrick to Hyde, 11 July 1659, held by the Bodleian in the Clarendon State Papers
31 'implicated in the' CSP Dom. 1659 56
32 'thus idle and' Davidson op.cit. 663–4
33 'God send us' RF 11
34 'yet it pleased' AF 46
35 'crooked... much awry' Slater op. cit. 126
36 'no physic but' Nagy op. cit. 77
37 'in this Disease' Digby, *Choice and Experimented Receipts*, 1675 30 EEBO
38 'stinking rotten addle' *The Womans Counsellour* 72 EEBO
39 'all those expresses' Mordaunt, *Letters* 79
40 'many hazards' Mordaunt, *Letters* 40
41 'when we... your feet' Cal. CSP III 548
42 'your Majestie... your Majestie' Mordaunt, *Letters* 51
43 'I should have' Mordaunt, *Letters* 57
44 'if I judge' Mordaunt, *Letters* 69
45 'I see not' Mordaunt, *Letters* 77
46 'All stands very' Mordaunt, *Letters* 81
47 'how much... Charles R.' Mordaunt, *Letters* 144
48 'the things... those terms' Mordaunt, *Letters* 100
49 'the honour of' ibid.
50 'of as many' RF 13
51 'Yours friends in' RF 15
52 'The King's business' Mordaunt, *Letters* 132
53 'as honest and' Mordaunt, *Letters* 143
54 'that if it' AF 46
55 '(without flatterie to' Fanshawe, *The History of the Fanshawe Family* 162

Chapter 18:1660

1 'My ever loved' AF *Memoirs* 1830 edition 442
2 'another age… I am' Verney I 258
3 My thanks to the art historian Carla van der Puttelaar who, with Kate Anderson of the Scottish National Portrait Gallery, conducted this research. Their article on the painting is forthcoming.
4 'Dearest Heart… finished' Crawford and Gowing op. cit. 95
5 'Indeed the turns' RF 15
6 'Boys do now' Pepys op. cit. I 45
7 'For all I' Pepys op. cit. I 92
8 'most persons [were]' Mordaunt, *Letters* xviii
9 'set up 2' Pepys op. cit. I 121
10 'Hasten (great prince)' Philips, *Poems* 70
11 'gallantry of the' Pepys op. cit. I 139
12 'Here the King' AF 46
13 'yet that… King's face' AF 46–7
14 'a tierce of' AF 47
15 'that the ships'' ibid.
16 'with a dog' Pepys op. cit. I 158
17 'who received me' AF 48
18 'engrossed all the' ibid.
19 'In the… own advantage' ibid.

Epilogue

1 'very well known' Clarendon, *Life* II 180
2 'Now it was' AF 49
3 'a trusty and' RF 17
4 'the design from' AF 49
5 'some considerable office' RF 23
6 'to add to' AF 63
7 'every one… green lace' AF 77
8 'your father and myself' AF 68
9 'but a… and Portugal' AF 95
10 'O all powerful' AF 102

11 'with my son' AF 107
12 *'A muertos y'* AF *Memoirs* 1830 edition 204
13 'fallen out with' Pepys op. cit. III 126
14 'near thirty years' AF 106
15 'time in lament' AF 107
16 'None ever had' AF 11
17 'many miscarriages… of fortune' AF 108
18 'I had, about' AF 109
19 'made presents' AF 106
20 'all the rest' Fell Smith op.cit. 159
21 'the joys I' AF 3
22 'my Lord Strafford' AF 42
23 'with all… be true' AF 9
24 'in as great' AF 87
25 'the Work written' AF Introduction (no page number)
26 She is identified in the key to Manley's *New Atalantis*, see Ballaster edition 304
27 'more impertinent… in her' Manley, *New Atalantis* IV 65–6
28 'not unentertaining… the public' AF *Memoirs* 1907 edition 221
29 'the beauty of' AF *Memoirs* 1907 edition 222
30 'flurried… her tail' Woolf, *Letters* 301 20 June 1907
31 'The memoirs… her editor' *Times Literary Supplement* 26 July 1907
32 'In Fanshawe's case' Rose op. cit. 67
33 'delicate meeting' Nabokov, *Speak, Memory: An Autobiography Revisited*, 1969, 131

Characters

1 'mutual love' AF *Memoirs* 1907 edition 301
2 'good at his' Evelyn, *Letters* II 193
3 'the only man' Ollard, ed., *Clarendon's Four Portraits* 62
4 'his Eie was' BL 91

Index

Index

A NOTE ABOUT THE AUTHOR

Lucy Moore is an author and broadcaster whose work includes the bestselling *Maharanis: The Lives and Times of Three Generations of Indian Princesses*. She has written for the *Sunday Times*, *Observer*, *Vogue* and *Harpers Bazaar*, and has presented series for the BBC and Sky.

How to order each Herbe or Flower before it is distilled

First a soft Fire maketh sweete water and sweetnes to continue long.

2dly. Coales still the best Water.

3. Wash nothing that you will still: but wipe it with a cleane Cloth.

4 All Hearbs Flowers and Seedes must be gathered when the Dew is of them.

5. That which You will Still must lye at the least sixe houres before you still it.

6. All Spices corrupt your Water, except Ambar Gris; Civett & Muske

7. Scumm your water well.

8. Keepe your Still very cleane.

9. Wash your Still but not often; then dry it with a dry Cloth.

10. A Glasse Still is best.

11. Borrage must be distilled the hearbe with the Roote chopped together.

12. Hysope the Leaues stripped from the Stalkes, when it beares blew Flowers.

13. Camomile in the midst of May the hearbe and Flower being chopt together.

14. Dill × the Hearbes in the beginning of May.

15. Fumitory the whole Substance chopped in the End of May.

16. Mint either red or other; the Hearbe stalke & Leaues chopped in the middle of May.

17. Roses cutting away the white Endes of the Flowers.

18. Rosemary the Flowers Budds and Leaues stripped from ye Stalk in May in the Flowering.